INSIDE IRISH AID

About the Author

Ronan Murphy was Director General, Irish Aid, in the Department of Foreign Affairs from 1991 to 1995 and again from 2004 to 2008. He has served as Ambassador to Austria, Senior Advisor to the UN High Commissioner for Human Rights in Geneva, and Ambassador to the Russian Federation. He is currently Chief Operating Officer at the Mary Robinson Foundation for Climate Change. He lives in Greystones, County Wicklow.

INSIDE IRISH AID

The Impulse to Help

Ronan Murphy

Foreword by
Mary Robinson

The Liffey Press

Published by
The Liffey Press Ltd
Raheny Shopping Centre
Second Floor, Raheny
Dublin 5, Ireland
www.theliffeypress.com

© 2012 Ronan Murphy

ISBN 978-1-908308-15-3

Printed in the UK by the MPG Books Group

CONTENTS

ACKNOWLEDGEMENTS

People from all walks of life with a connection to development aid responded enthusiastically to my approaches for assistance with this book. I have to thank three Presidents who gave me substantial interviews: Michael D. Higgins, Mary McAleese and Mary Robinson. I thank Mary Robinson in particular, not only for sharing memories of Somalia and Rwanda, but for providing a generous foreword to the book.

I was very fortunate to be able to record a long interview with Garret FitzGerald some months before he died. Garret FitzGerald can truly be described as the father of Irish Aid. Bertie Ahern, who was a strong supporter of reaching the 0.7 per cent goal during the good times, also shared his memories with me.

David Cooney, Secretary General of the Department of Foreign Affairs and Brendan Rogers, Director General, Irish Aid, gave me invaluable help. They both read the book but made it clear that the content was for me to decide. Colleagues from the Department of Foreign Affairs gave me not only lots of information but also encouragement. A first draft was read by two former colleagues, Frank Sheridan and Gerry Gervin, and I am grateful to them for pertinent comments which I took on board.

After that it would be invidious to single out individuals since so many contributed – from former Ministers and Ministers of State to NGOs to partners in the field so I will simply list their names alphabetically: Vincent Akulumuka, David Andrews, Gary Ansbro, Tom Arnold, Ruth and Anne Barrington, David Barry, George

Bermingham, Zubeni Bira, Patrick Bitature, Pat Bourne, Alison Boyle, Nicola Brennan, Joan Burton, Dr. Johnson Byabashaija, Sean Calleary, William Carlos, Kevin Carroll, Dr and Mrs Ian Clarke, Anne Cleary, Frank Cogan, Declan Connolly, Jerome Connolly, Joan Corkery, Vicky Cremin, Pat Curran, Paul Dempsey, Donal Denham, Christopher Dillon, David Donoghue, Noel Dorr, Etain Doyle, Joyce Duffy, Aidan Eames, Noel Fahey, Mark Farahan, Kevin Farrell, Fintan Farrelly, Paddy Fay, Fergus Finlay, Hugh FitzPatrick, Anthony Fiume, Lorcan Fullam, Frank Flood, Phil Furlong, Paul Gadenya, Dermot Gallagher, Eamon Geraghty, Catherine Giltrap, Monica Gorman, Mike Greally, Martin Greene, John Grindle, Brian Hanratty, Joe Haughton, Aine Hearns, Margaret Hennessy, Liz Higgins, Sean Hoy, Bill Jackson, Barbara Jones, Michael Jones, Ray Jordan, Koto Kajemba, Kevin Kelly, Joan Kelly, Helen Keogh, Aggrey David Kibenga, Justin Kilcullen, Simon Kimono, Tom Kitt, Helen Labanya, Anne Leahy, Sizya Lugeya, Maura Lynch, Liberaty Macha, Eamon Maher, Rosemary McCreery, Bob McDonagh, Donal McDonald, Jean McManus, Chris Matthews, Brigid Mayes, Benny Maxwell, Prof. Yunus Mgaya, Ed Miliano, John Moffatt, Kevin Moore, John Morahan, Mussa Mrassi, Keith Mukakonizi, Juvenal Mukumuza, Cuthbert Muleko, Dan Mulhall, Jennifer Muwuliza, Andrew Mwenda, Gordon Mwesigye, John Neary, Ben Ngereza, Bill Nolan, Andrew Nugent, Declan O'Brien, Philip O'Brien, Brian O Ceallaigh, Pat O'Connor, Liz O'Donnell, Mary Oduka, Michael O'Hea, Jim O'Keeffe, Michael O'Kennedy, Denis O'Leary, Diarmuid O'Leary, Eddie O'Loughlin, Godrey Omodiya, Professor Francis Omaswa, Grainne O'Neill, Helen O'Neill, Vinnie O'Neill, Col. John O'Reilly, Eamon O Tuathail, Nora Owen, Professor Jim Phelan, Fionnuala Quinlan, Manette Ramilli, Rodney Rice, Liam Rigney, Bride Rosney, Donald Rukare, Mike Scott, John Shiels, Helen Smith, Mary Sutton, Maureen Sweeney, Hugh Swift, Tony Taaffe, Dermot Waldron, Fr. Joe Whelan, Mary Whelan, Dr. Kenneth Whitaker, Hans Zomer.

I availed of the services of the National Library, the National Archive and UCD's Development Studies Library where Sally Corcoran was especially helpful.

Finally, I would like to thank David Givens of The Liffey Press for having faith in the book and seeing it through to publication.

FOREWORD

Mary Robinson

This is an account of Irish Aid compiled by an insider. Not a disinterested insider, but someone with a quiet passion for what Irish Aid has sought to achieve over the years, who wanted that story to be better known. Ronan Murphy served as Director General of Irish Aid from 1991–1995, and again from 2004–2008, during which time the budget grew dramatically. In between those two terms he took a voluntary break from the Irish Foreign service, and worked in the office of the High Commissioner for Human Rights from 1999–2001 as my senior adviser.

From the beginning Murphy was determined to forgo the jargon of the aid experts, and to write in clean concise language which would convey the complexity of the donor country role in development without recourse to obscure acronyms. He was writing for an audience he wants to engage and to inspire, because of his own strong belief in the morality and political appropriateness of countries with greater capacity and resources reaching out to the poorest countries to support their path to sustainable development.

In his reflections on why Irish people have been traditionally generous and engaged in supporting developing countries Murphy rightly refers to the importance of empathy: 'The fact that the Irish can empathise with people living in the developing world is an important factor, as is the absence of colonial baggage. The ability to see things from the point of view of the poor – maybe because we come for the most part from modest backgrounds ourselves and have learned through our history what it is to be on the receiving end – made us more suitable partners than donors from rich countries who often talk down to the recipient countries.'

Part of empathy, as he mentions, is a capacity to listen. Another element – which I feel might have been brought out - is the ability to share the humour of a situation and laugh together, even if the reality on the ground is quite bleak. I have often heard that shared laughter in a group with local people before I actually met the Irish priest or nun or development worker whose accent and comic emphasis I could make out.

The quality of the individuals who met in the early 1970s to establish what would become known as the Agency for Personal Services Overseas (APSO) – Professor George Dawson, Justice Kings-mill Moore, Tom Barrington, Willie Jenkinson and Bill Jackson – showed the calibre of individual leadership which was interested at the time in development issues. This was matched shortly afterwards by the quality of leadership in government shown by Garret FitzGerald as Minister for Foreign Affairs in building Ireland's official development aid programme. Murphy rightly credits Garret FitzGerald with both the vision to see that Ireland needed an official aid programme and the intelligence to accept the proposal of the informal group to establish a working group, chaired by George Dawson, to get APSO off the ground. It is fascinating to read of the influence the Danish model had on the shaping of Irish development aid, how the priority countries at the time were selected, and the arguments over whether Irish aid should be a separate agency or not. The conclusions, by coincidence, of the first and second Lomé Conventions during separate Irish EU Presidencies clearly influenced the outlook on development of both Garret FitzGerald and his successor as Minister for Foreign Affairs, Michael O'Kennedy.

Murphy recognises the significant influence of Irish NGOs on development aid in the 1970s and 1980s, notably Concern, under the leadership of Aengus and Jack Finucane; Trocaire, under Bishop Eamonn Casey and Brian McKeown; and later GOAL, under John O'Shea. But he also acknowledges the role of Christian Aid from an early stage and of Gorta with its emphasis on tackling hunger.

Meanwhile, the semi-state bodies had organised themselves as DEVCO, under the leadership of Brendan O'Regan, and the academic community came together as HEDCO, Higher Education for Development Co-operation. What Murphy traces clearly is the vitality of organisations in a small country, with a strong empathy for development issues, once the government had created the enabling environment.

Murphy's account of the Ethiopian famine and how it gripped all these actors is compelling, including the part played by Bob Geldof and Live Aid. He also describes travelling with me to Rwanda in 1994, when I was the first Head of State to visit, and the subsequent visits. His account brings back painful memories which stay just below the surface of consciousness when you have witnessed the aftermath of some of the worst horrors perpetrated by mankind.

The account of Murphy's two periods leading Irish Aid is informative, because he is a dispassionate observer of political and institutional weaknesses but quick to give praise for generosity or courage from any quarter.

I had not been aware that Murphy already knew of the political desire to decentralise most of the staff of Irish Aid to Limerick before he agreed to come back from his post as Ambassador in Vienna to once more become Director General of Irish Aid in 2004. His understated reaction is typical of him: 'I thought hard about it but in the end I decided to go ahead, my main motivation being that I valued the development world very much.' Despite his strong reservations, he oversaw the move to Limerick loyally and as efficiently as circumstances allowed.

There are poignant human stories recounted, not least in the terrible aftermath of the Asian Tsunami. Even in that account, Murphy can be dispassionate and describe how it proved to be a catalyst in improving our approach to humanitarian crises.

I was aware of Murphy's quiet pride in the process leading up to the launch of the White Paper of 2006, and his satisfaction in the fact that the White Paper initiatives were implemented.

It was clear that Murphy was particularly affected by issues of food security on numerous visits to African countries. He says with typical modesty, 'Peter Power, the last Minister of State I worked for, took on the hunger agenda and made it a central theme of his time in office.' I am sure that Peter, if asked – because he, too, is modest for someone who has served in politics – would be the first to credit Murphy's leadership of the Irish Aid Team for the fact that Ireland has achieved a global reputation – together with our NGOs – for leadership on tackling hunger and malnutrition. The thoughtful advice offered at the end of this account is well worth reading, and should continue to inform Irish, European and global development policy.

In conclusion, let me leave you with another quote from the book, which I found particularly striking. *'While foreign policy can be described as the protection of Ireland's interests abroad, aid and development seem to me to have more to do with the promotion of Ireland's values.'*

I strongly recommend this book to the ordinary reader as well as to those involved in development work, and particularly to young people in Ireland who must carry the torch.

1.

INTRODUCTION

The aim of this book is to tell the story of Irish Aid, the development aid programme through which the Irish Government helps poor countries to escape from poverty. Begun in 1973, Irish Aid has grown from very modest beginnings and a diffuse range of projects to a coherent, professional aid programme which is highly regarded internationally.

It is surprising how little is known about Irish Aid outside of the circle of people working or interested in development aid. When people think of the assistance Ireland gives to the developing world they are likely to think of Concern or Trocaire, or one of the numerous other private Irish aid organisations, the Non-Governmental Organisations (NGOs) as they are called. But the funding provided by the Government through Irish Aid is greater than that of all the NGOs put together. In 2008, Irish Aid's budget was €920 million.

Numerous efforts have been made to get the message out about the work of Irish Aid. There is an Annual Report and many publications both in hard copy and on the highly informative Irish Aid website. A White Paper on Irish Aid was published in 2006 and a summary of its main points was circulated to every household in the country. An Information and Volunteering Office in O'Connell Street in Dublin hosts information events for schoolchildren and the general public.

Yet if you ask the man or woman in the street who gives what, they are unlikely to know much about Irish Aid.

In contrast, people do know that Ireland has had a long engagement with the developing world. Stories have been brought back by missionaries and returned aid workers, by young people who spend time in Africa or Asia during their transition year and, increasingly, through travellers' direct experience of the developing world. And, although many people may not know much about the detail of what the Government does, surveys indicate that there is widespread support for the Government to continue funding assistance to developing countries.

As Director General of Irish Aid from 1991-95, and again from 2004-08, I was fortunate to see the aid programme grow to a stage where Ireland became the sixth largest donor per head of population in the world. It has always been clear to me that more needed to be done to get the message across about Irish Aid's work and some of the measures outlined above date from my time with the programme. Public awareness of the aid programme is essential, especially now that the size of the Government's funding has become so large.

This is the main reason why I have written this book. It seeks to explain how Ireland's aid programme developed since it began in the 1970s, how it operates and why it works the way it does. Since the focus is on the Government's programme, it is not primarily about the many Irish organisations that help in the developing world, though Irish Aid works closely with them and they feature in the story too.

How does Irish Aid differ from what, say, Concern or Trocaire do? The answer is that Irish Aid is money voted by the Government for the developing world and spent through a range of channels – directly managed projects and programmes in selected countries, disaster relief, EU programmes, NGOs, United Nations organisations such as UNICEF and UNAIDS – the whole gamut of situations which require assistance, both emergency and long term. This type of assistance is called 'official' because it is carried out by Governments.

Funding is overseen by a Division of the Department of Foreign Affairs called Development Cooperation Division. 'Irish Aid' is the name given to that Division, though it is not a semi-state body or an independent operation.

In its almost 40 years of existence, Irish Aid has undergone many changes. This is most evident in the size of the budget, which has expanded to the stage where it is larger than that of several Government Departments.

Having been around for this long, it is legitimate to ask how successful it has been. Which projects worked and which did not? How can we be sure that the money is reaching its targets and changing the lives of poor people? How can corruption and weak governance be combated? And there is an even bigger question: why has there not been greater progress out of poverty and under-development, especially in Africa? Does the aid which Ireland and other donors provide really produce long-term results?

A major source for the book – apart from my own memories and records – are the interviews I conducted with over 80 colleagues and former colleagues in Irish Aid and people who had contact of one kind or another with the programme. All those I approached, from President Michael D. Higgins, former Presidents Mary McAleese and Mary Robinson, former Taoisigh Garret Fitz-Gerald and Bertie Ahern, Ministers and Ministers of State to recipients of Irish Aid in the field, were generous with their time and shared perspectives based on their experience with Irish Aid. I would like to thank all concerned for their assistance.

A theme of the many colleagues from the Department of Foreign Affairs that I interviewed was that their time working for Irish Aid was the most rewarding in their careers. Almost without exception they reported that their experience with Irish Aid was interesting – 'a job worth doing'. Many felt that it changed their perspectives on life. That was certainly my experience.

This book is dedicated to all of those who worked hard for Irish Aid over the years and to the Irish people who have shown solidarity in countless ways with the poorest people on the planet.

A Word about Words

Development aid is one of those issues that is beset by jargon. Sometimes it seems like a special language aimed at keeping the non-expert out. I would often despair when reading consultancy reports that were barely understandable. I have kept the language in this book as jargon-free as possible, though some technical language is unavoidable since aid is a complex issue.

Most books on aid start with a series of acronyms and abbreviations. Instead of that, I list below some of the terms commonly used in regard to Ireland's aid programme:

- **Aid:** The very word 'aid' is controversial as it is regarded as not politically correct anymore. Most often the word used today is 'development' or 'development cooperation', the thinking being that this is a less patronising term than 'aid'. There is something to be said for this argument but, at the end of the day, funding transferred from rich countries to poor ones *is* aid and I have used the term interchangeably with development in this book.

- **ODA**: Official Development Assistance is the proper title given to the aid which *governments* give to poorer countries. I say 'proper' because more and more the initials ODA are taken to mean Overseas Development Assistance. Whichever version is used, it invariably refers only to what *governments* give. It does not cover donations the public make to their favourite charities, which in Ireland's case are substantial.

- **Irish Aid:** The title given to the Government's aid programme. This can also be confusing, as the name has been changed several times over the years. Back in the 1990s Irish Aid was the title used, then it was changed to Ireland Aid and later to Devel-

opment Cooperation Ireland. Finally (I hope!) it was changed
back to Irish Aid when the Government published its White
Paper in 2006.

- **Bilateral and multilateral**: The assistance which is given directly to a country by a Government is called bilateral aid. If a
Government chooses to channel its money through some of the
big organisations like UNICEF, the World Bank or the World
Food Programme, this is known as multilateral aid. Like most
donors, Ireland uses both channels to give aid.

- **Emergency/Long term**: Most media coverage of aid concerns
the help given after emergencies such as a famine or a natural
disaster. This is the high profile side of aid. But emergency assistance represents only a small part of development aid. By far
the greater part of aid money is spent on long-term programmes aimed at tackling the root causes of poverty.

- **NGOs**: NGOs, or Non-Governmental Organisations, to give
them their full name, are charitable organisations, the largest
and best known of the Irish ones helping developing countries
being Concern, Trocaire and GOAL. There are hundreds of development NGOs active in Ireland, ranging from long-
established fundraising or awareness-raising organisations to
small, even one-person, initiatives.

- **Sustainability**: Finally, out of all the development jargon I pick
one term which is of special importance: sustainability. It is an
important word because it sums up the real goal of development, namely projects and programmes which have the ability
to continue to exist after the donor has left. As I will show,
achieving this goal is far from easy.

2

THE IMPULSE TO HELP

Driving home from Wexford in August 1994, I stopped with my family in Courtown for a break in our journey. A sign on one of the booths caught my eye:

Proceeds of tonight's bingo will go to victims of the Rwanda genocide.

I have seen hundreds of such notices over the years, as has everybody in Ireland, yet this one sticks in my memory.

A few months earlier I had seen grisly evidence of the Rwanda genocide for myself when I accompanied Minister of State Tom Kitt to Tanzania. We visited camps on the Rwandan border where hundreds of thousands were fleeing the killing. Proof of the horrors still going on in Rwanda could be seen in bodies floating down the river to the Rusomo Falls. Now there was talk that President Mary Robinson would visit Rwanda just as she had visited Somalia two years before.

Somalia had tugged at the hearts of Irish people. The terrible spectacle of children dying on our TV screens drew a generous response as Irish people donated huge sums to charities. Irish aid organisations rushed to help. The Minister for Foreign Affairs of the day, David Andrews, broke new ground by going to Somalia in the summer of 1992. Two months later President Robinson visited Somalia, the first Western Head of State to do so. Those who heard the President speaking at her press conference in Nairobi of the shame she felt and the responsibility of the world community for what was happening will never forget her words.

Now, two years later, came Rwanda. Bad as Somalia was, the deaths were the by-product of a civil war in what was already turning into a collapsed state. Rwanda was different: it was a conscious attempt by hardliners to commit genocide on the Tutsis and moderate Hutus. And it almost succeeded. People reeled back in horror at the appalling cruelty of the death and wounds inflicted – mostly with machetes – and at the murderous intent of the killers.

And here, in a small seaside town, was proof once again of the Irish people's willingness to help a country far away from Ireland of which we knew little. The impulse to help is a phenomenon that recurs so often as to make it a feature of the Irish character.

There is hardly a disaster where Irish people have not been to the fore, often giving far more than our richer neighbours. Somalia, Rwanda, the Indian Ocean tsunami – all saw millions raised in public donations. Going back further, the same story can be told about Biafra in the 1960s and Bangladesh in the 1970s. And the Ethiopian famine of 1984 brought an outstanding response from Irish people: £16 million was contributed to NGOs and a total of £8.4 million to Bob Geldof's Live Aid – more per head of population than any other country.[1]

Why are Irish people so ready to help the developing world? And not only with money, but with their time and services, often in the riskiest of situations? Because it is not just cash which Ireland has provided. People have been ready to drop everything to go out and help – doctors, engineers, even people without special skills – eager to contribute to relief efforts.

Whenever and wherever I have travelled in Africa, the Irish have been present, whether working for Irish Aid, for NGOs, as missionaries or for international aid organisations. Some of the most impressive representatives of the UN and other humanitarian organisations have been Irish. Many have risen to the top of their profession.

The Defence Forces, too, have a reputation second to none for peace keeping and for the humanitarian assistance they have given in countries such as Liberia, Rwanda and Chad.

The first place to look for the reasons behind this extraordinary level of caring for the poorest has to be Ireland's missionaries. Their numbers have fallen but their influence is still felt everywhere. Whenever I met an African official or minister I would be a bit surprised if they did not reveal in the conversation that they had been educated by Irish priests or nuns. At the very least, when they heard I was from Ireland they would refer to the contribution our missionaries have made to educating their countrymen and women.

What are the other reasons? Folk memories of the famine? Some might say that is a bit fanciful. But Jim O'Keeffe, who served as Minister of State for Development in the 1980s, was in no doubt that folk memories play a part:

> Skibbereen, where I grew up, was particularly hard hit by the Famine. My uncle was a local historian and he would speak about the pamphlets, which had been written about the Famine in Skibbereen and the fact that even the London *Times* published some of the accounts. The local football team was known as the donkey-eaters from those times. In my childhood I heard many stories about the workhouse in Skibbereen, the 'soupers' and the prohibition on starving people to fish in the rivers which belonged to the rich.[2]

He recalled his mother's indignation at Queen Victoria donating a mere five-pound note to the victims of the Famine (I told him I heard the same story from my mother!).

Jim O'Keeffe said that he sensed that it was official policy to let the Irish starve; he saw the Famine as having left a 'searing impression' and that in later life when issues like famine and hunger arose his background kicked in.[3]

David Andrews had a similar view. He feels that concern for the underdog came down to him through his family's genes. The Famine taught Ireland a salutary lesson, he believes, and made us understand poverty in its real form.[4]

A more recent memory was the aftermath of the Second World War. Although neutral, Irish people were aware of the toll that the war took and were anxious to help relieve the plight of the victims. The story of the Irish Red Cross hospital at St Lo in France is well known, as is the programme to bring German children to Ireland in the post-war years. My grandmother took in one of those German children, a girl called Christel from Solingen who was four when she arrived and stayed for four years. Christel visited Ireland many years later when she was married and herself the mother of two children.

Another factor is the solidarity that Ireland felt with the newly independent African states as they struggled and achieved independence. A new generation of African leaders emerged in the sixties: Kwame Nkrumah of what is now Ghana, Julius Nyerere of Tanzania, Kenneth Kaunda of Zambia, Jomo Kenyatta of Kenya. Irish people could see obvious parallels between the problems these leaders faced as they got rid of their colonial masters and Ireland's struggle for independence. A colleague spoke to me of the excitement she felt as a student in Canada when Julius Nyerere came to speak at the university she was attending.[5]

The people of the emerging African nations looked to Ireland as a model for themselves. They saw us as closer in terms of development to their own situation than other donors. A Tanzanian Minister said that his memory of a visit to Ireland in the fifties was of rural thatched houses without electricity. But that was changing. Even though we were not a wealthy country, we were managing to achieve what they aimed for: the consolidation of our independence and a reasonable level of well-being.[6]

Apart from word brought back by missionaries, there was little first-hand knowledge of Africa in Ireland of the 1950s and 1960s. I grew up in Drumcondra, and I recall an African medical student who was taken in as a lodger by a family called Turner who were next door neighbours of the future Taoiseach Bertie Ahern. The student was a friendly young man who was studying at the Royal College of Surgeons and he became a popular figure in the neighbourhood. I hope that he forgave us children who stared in open-mouthed astonishment at the sight of a real black person.

The fact that the Irish can empathise with people living in the developing world is an important factor, as is the absence of colonial baggage. The ability to see things from the point of view of the poor – maybe because we come for the most part from modest backgrounds ourselves and have learned through our history what it is to be on the receiving end – made us more suitable partners than donors from rich countries who often talk down to the recipient countries.

When I asked partners in the recipient countries what was different about Irish Aid, they said that we *listened* more than other donors and were able to get on their wavelength. Brendan Rogers, my successor as Director General of Irish Aid, put it well:

> Irish people have an amazing strength to get out of ourselves and connect with other cultures. We have a gut capacity to understand others' situations and to influence them. Humour and emotion play a part. Our development workers have gone outside the capital cities and have lived and experienced poor people's experiences. Perhaps most importantly, Irish people have genuinely wanted to make a difference.[7]

The anti-apartheid movement also played a part. Kadar Asmal and his wife Louise led a successful drive to keep the apartheid issue in the public mind; their supporters included numerous figures who would go on to play a role in political life and on whom the issue of justice for black people in Africa made a lasting impression. The courage of the Dunnes Stores strikers also struck a chord with many people.

The Communist threat was another factor. It is easy to forget how, in the 1950s and 1960s, Ireland saw the world as divided between Communism and Christianity. The suppression of the Hungarian uprising in 1956 reinforced the idea that Ireland had to keep up the fight against paganism, as did reports of the persecution of Catholics such as Cardinal Mindszenty in Hungary. The Communists were seen as trying to push their agenda in Africa and to win that continent over to their cause.

The experience of the Irish soldiers in the Congo during the sixties heightened awareness of Africa. Even greater was the impact of the Biafran war where so many Irish missionaries found themselves caught up. The Irish public sympathised with the Igbos who wanted to secede from the Nigerian state and set up their own country. The war raged from 1967 to 1970. Hundreds of thousands of civilians died of starvation, some think as many as two million. People got their first glimpse of the horrors of famine as images of children with swollen bellies appeared on TV screens. Television itself was still a fairly new phenomenon – it would radically widen our knowledge of what was happening in the developing world.[8]

There is no one explanation. But the overwhelming view of those I interviewed for this book was that it is, above all, the missionaries we have to thank for the interest which Ireland takes in the developing world.

In the age of the Internet it is not easy to cast our minds back to a time when most of the information we got was from the printed word and oral testimony. The missionaries' story came to us through the plethora of newspapers and magazines about the developing world. At my boarding school in New Ross magazines such as the *Far East*, *Africa* and *Catholic Missions* were put out in the recreation rooms, along with *The Word*, the magazine of the Divine Word Missionaries.

Oral testimony came from missionaries at home on leave who were allowed to speak from the altar or in schools about their work.

Everyone of my generation remembers the appeals for 'Black Babies' in school. Here is Mary Holland's account of how it was in Belfast:

> Anyone who has been to a Catholic Primary School will be able to remember paying two shillings and sixpence for a colourful cardboard figure of an African child. You chose a name for your black baby and, for a penny a week; you took him up thirty steps on a cardboard chart to heaven where the child Jesus stood at the top to welcome him. Vast sums of money were collected in this way.[9]

My memory is of a box – a square box surmounted by the plaster figure of a black baby – which was kept in the classroom and brought around to each class at certain times in the hope that donations would be made to support the missions. The baby figure's head was moveable so that when you put in a penny or a halfpenny the head would nod.

Politically incorrect they may be now, but the Black Babies introduced thousands of Irish children to the fact that children in the developing world were a lot poorer than the poorest at home.

The sheer scale of Irish missionary activities is amazing. At the height of their work there were 6,000 in the field.[10] Typical of a missionary career is that of Father Joe Whelan. A Mill Hill Father, he was assigned to Africa because his order felt that African countries which were moving towards independence needed teachers. He went out to Uganda in 1953, taught in a secondary school for a year and then took up a position in a training college for primary teachers, a job he held for 13 years. He worked in Ngora, a remote part of the country, at a time when very few Irish missionaries went to Uganda. The college took students from all over the country. Competition was fierce; almost all the students qualified but only the best were accepted. The students were very motivated and were supported by their clan, which hoped for a return from their success.

In time he became an education adviser to President Milton Obote but he came under suspicion from Idi Amin's regime when Obote was overthrown. The Education Minister tried to protect him, but then he too was arrested by Amin's people. Fr. Whelan was thrown out of the country by Amin in 1972, but he came back later as chaplain and tutor at Ngongere University in Tororo. He spent four years lecturing there in history and helped write new textbooks to replace the old ones, which taught everything from the colonial point of view.

Fr. Whelan found things in ruins after Amin's fall. Soldiers had looted everything they could get their hands on. People lacked everything so his Order arranged to bring in two containers of supplies per month with basic materials such as aspirin, beds and bandages. It was ironic, he says, because Uganda had been quite an advanced country. But the people matured during these bad times and showed great resilience.

He believes that missionaries were very valuable instruments both in helping during emergencies and with long-term development: 'Missionaries were part of the scene and knew it like no other outsider.'

It was not just Catholic missionaries either: the Protestant churches had a strong record of working in the developing world. Christian Aid and the Church of Ireland, Methodist and Presbyterian Churches were actively engaged. Their counterparts in the Protestant churches in Scandinavia were a driving force in the growth of their national aid programmes, which are the most impressive, in terms of both volume and quality, in the world.

Some academics see the reason why rich countries should give aid in terms of geopolitical and security considerations. They argue that it is in the interests of the rich countries not to have instability which can lead to rogue states and the threat of terrorism. Dire poverty can lead to mass migration and be a threat to the developed world's economic well-being. One commentator uses this argument to support the notion that it is in the Western world's interest to help Africa:

> Africa's fragile and impoverished states are a natural haven
> for global terrorists. Porous borders, weak law enforcement
> and security institutions, plentiful and portable national re-
> sources and conflict zones make perfect breeding grounds
> for all sorts of terrorist organisations.[11]

Well, yes, there is something to be said for these arguments. But I never really bought the notion that Irish people see it in that light when the collection box is rattled before them or the fund-raiser event is being set up. It seems to me that the main motivation for Irish people's generosity towards the developing world has more to do with people doing what they feel is right. The Christian injunction to love thy neighbour is, of course, central.

To those who think that such altruism is universal I would re-call a conversation I had with a senior Russian official in 1995. I had just finished my first four-year term as head of the aid programme and was taking up my appointment as Ambassador in Moscow. As often happens, I was still full of the job I had just left and when the official asked me about it, I spoke at some length about Irish Aid. He listened with interest but I could see a puzzled look on his face. Finally he said, 'And what does Ireland gain from this?'

The question flummoxed me, I must admit. The Russian official saw the issue in terms of the relationship between aid and foreign policy. That is an important question, which I will come back to, but I do not think that foreign policy concerns have been the key to our interest in the developing world. While foreign policy can be described as the protection of Ireland's interests abroad, aid and development seem to me to have more to do with the promotion of Ireland's values.

The 1960s and 1970s saw a surge of interest in improving the lives of people living in the developing world, not just in Ireland but internationally. Major reports were published, the two best known being the 1969 Report of the Commission on International Development, sponsored by the World Bank and chaired by the former Canadian Prime Minister Lester Pearson, and the Brandt Report of 1977, named after former German Chancellor Willi Brandt. Michael D. Higgins remembers the excitement of being present at Buswells Hotel in Dublin when Willi Brandt formally handed over his report.[12]

The United Nations declared that the 1960s were to be the first Development Decade, when the richer countries were expected to make a greater effort to bring the poorest countries out of poverty. In 1970 the United Nations set a target for richer countries to spend 0.7 per cent of their Gross National Product on aid to the developing world. (At first the target had been 1 per cent of GNP but 0.7 per cent was felt to be more realistic.)

This was a landmark decision and the 0.7 per cent target has become the benchmark of a country's aid performance ever since. The United Nations' role had a strong impact in Ireland where the UN was highly respected and the centrepiece of our foreign policy of that era.

The UN's Food and Agriculture Organisation called on member states to set up national Freedom from Hunger Campaigns and one was set up in Ireland in 1960. The Irish Red Cross, the oldest of the Irish Non-Governmental Organisations, was initially placed in charge of the Freedom from Hunger Campaign. In 1965 the Government transferred responsibility for the Freedom from Hunger Campaign to a new organisation, which was to be called Gorta.

Gorta, which operated initially under the auspices of the Department of Agriculture, can claim to be the first Third World development organisation in Ireland. It lost no time in funding projects in developing countries, mostly in India and Africa, with the emphasis on small-scale agricultural programmes aimed at meeting long-term food needs. Gorta and the Freedom from Hunger Campaign caught the public imagination and attracted wide support.[13]

One of Gorta's longstanding members was Joe Haughton, Professor of Geography at Trinity College. He recalled:

> I am a Quaker and it was in that capacity that I was invited
> to serve on Gorta's Council. There is a strong sense of justice
> in the Quakers' faith. They believe in the equality of all hu-
> man beings and the right sharing of the world's resources.
> Gorta aimed to be a truly national organisation and lots of
> different interest groups were brought on board. Large
> numbers of people from the different churches, from sports
> organisations, from the farming community, attended the
> early council meetings.[14]

Joe Haughton says that a visit to the US with a group of young Quakers when he was in his twenties made a deep impression on him. They went to a restaurant in Indiana for a meal but when the owner saw that one of their group was a Jamaican girl he refused to serve them. When the group insisted that she be served, he shut his restaurant rather than do so. Experiences such as this offended his sense of justice. Joe's involvement with Gorta continued for 40 years.

Gorta would soon have rivals: this period saw the emergence of more development NGOs in Ireland. Two in particular stand out: Concern and Trocaire. Concern was first known as Africa Concern. It came into being in 1968 in response to the Biafran crisis and quickly became the largest of the Irish NGOs.[15] Trocaire was set up in 1973 by the Catholic Bishops Conference.

A prominent feature of these organisations was the forceful in-dividuals who led them: for Concern there were the brothers Aen-gus and Jack Finucane, Fr. Raymond Kennedy, John O'Loughlin Kennedy and his wife Kay. Trocaire's chair was Bishop Eamon Ca-sey and its first Chief Executive Brian McKeown. (Since the Finu-cane brothers were Holy Ghost fathers and Brian McKeown was a layman, it was said that Concern was a lay organisation run by priests and Trocaire a religious organisation run by lay people!)

Concern and Trocaire developed into flourishing organisations which were and are important partners of Irish Aid, and I will come back to their role in a later chapter.

The Catholic Church's interest in the developing world had a strong influence. One of the outcomes of the Second Vatican Council was the Pastoral Constitution *Gaudium et Spes* (Joy and Hope) which Pope Paul VI issued in 1965. This document called for greater effort by the church to building 'a peaceful and fraternal community of nations' and to 'promote progress in needy regions and international social justice.' A Pontifical Commission on Justice and Peace was set up in Rome and encouragement was given to the setting up of national commissions.

Jerome Connolly became the first chief executive of the Irish Commission for Justice and Peace when it was established in 1970. His first experience of the developing world was classes on community development, which he gave to students at the Overseas Club in Harcourt Terrace. He saw the Commission's task as to look at the broader picture; Gorta was already there but theirs was a specific mandate with an agricultural emphasis. There was a need for public discussion of development issues such as the huge disparity between rich and poor countries and the root causes of poverty. He set about bringing these arguments to public attention through articles and a short book he wrote called *The Third World War*.[16]

The key message from the growing number of people in different walks of life who were interested in development aid was that the Government should do more. People recognised that it was not enough for missionaries and charitable individuals to help: a more sustained approach was needed and the Government should play its part.

Up to 1973, Ireland's Official Development Assistance was extremely small. There were few Government transfers apart from contributions to organisations such as UNICEF and the World Food Programme, and commitments arising from membership of the World Bank. When extra aid was given, it was done in an ad hoc manner, usually in the form of emergency assistance to countries facing disasters or to ease the plight of refugees, channelled through UN humanitarian organisations or the Red Cross. It would often be made by means of a supplementary budget towards the end of the year, which in itself was an indication that it was seen as an add-on rather than a recurring, planned expenditure. One official recalled looking up papal encyclicals for inspiration when making the case for funding to the Department of Finance![17]

Shortage of cash in the public coffers was the obvious reason why Ireland was not more generous. Ireland was a much poorer country then than it is today. The official line was that we would increase our level of ODA 'as resources permit', a vague formula that committed us to nothing. In defending our low level of official aid at the UN and other fora, the argument was also made that the official figures did not include the contribution in manpower of missionaries or the generous private response which the Irish people made whenever called upon. But some of the arguments made in defence of our poor record smack of special pleading.[18]

Pressure on the Government to do more for the developing world was intensifying. I got a flavour of the changing mood myself. I joined the Department of Foreign Affairs in 1971 as a Third Secretary and my first assignment was to Trade Section. I shared a big room overlooking Stephen's Green with other Third Secretaries. For much of the 18 months I spent there I was a supernumerary, which meant that the Department had yet to find a job for me. I did work on the trade side and also for the International Economic Organisations Section. Development aid formed a part of the work of this section, mainly in the form of processing the placement of overseas students in Irish colleges, overseeing payment of Ireland's UN contributions and servicing conferences such as the UN Conference on Trade and Development, then a major event in the development calendar.

Because I was a supernumerary a mixture of jobs came my way. One day the Counsellor, Brendan Nolan, who was in charge of both the trade and international economic organisations sections, called me into his room. He was a tall, bespectacled man with a habit of chain-smoking strong smelling cigarillos. He took a friendly interest in me although he was much too busy to waste time trying to find a role for a supernumerary Third Secretary. That day he pushed some papers towards me and said, 'You could try your hand at that'.

It was a request for a speech on development aid from the office of the Minister for Health Erskine Childers, to be delivered at a function just a week or so away. He said, 'I simply don't have time for this and neither has anyone else. See what you can do.'

There was little to go on – there was no Google or Wikipedia in those days. I was given a few OECD reports on aid and told to look up the files but they were not informative. But I read up on the subject as quickly as I could. It became clear to me that Ireland was giving very little in the way of official aid for the Third World as it was called then. I remember being surprised at that as I had heard so much about what the missionaries were doing. I learned that official development aid was different from what the missionaries did; it was the transfer of resources from the richer countries to the poor ones on a regular, continuing basis and on a scale far higher than what Ireland was doing.

I wrote a speech which set out the facts and which argued that Ireland could do better. Our record compared unfavourably with that of countries like Sweden and Norway, which were making generous transfers.

Brendan Nolan read through my draft quickly and told me to send it off. I thought that that would be the end of it but the following Monday I opened *The Irish Times* to find the headline 'Ireland should do more to help developing countries'. The story said that the Minister for Health had told his audience at the weekend that Ireland lagged far behind other developed countries when it came to official assistance for the Third World. I felt mixed emotions: surprise that the words I had so casually put together should end up in print, and fear that my career as a diplomat was over before it had begun. I need not have worried on the latter point as Brendan Nolan just smiled and said, 'We didn't think this would be put up in lights'.

Clearly the speech had chimed with what others were thinking: that Ireland's official aid performance was not commensurate with our rising living standard and did not reflect the people's deep concern for the least well off in the world.

I also remember from that time contributing to a discussion about whether Ireland should consider joining the Development Assistance Committee of the OECD. The DAC, as it is known, is the elite club of countries which are committed to making substantial contributions in aid. I quickly saw that Ireland's level of funding was so low that there was no question of applying to join the DAC. It would be thirteen years before we actually did so but it is interesting that, even in 1972, the issue was occupying the minds of people in Iveagh House.

In fact, there was an understanding in official circles that raising the level of official aid was desirable and had to be planned for. Discussions took place between officials in External Affairs and Finance in the 1960s and 1970s and memos drawn up.[19] But the biggest pressure for Ireland to have its own aid programme was coming from outside official circles.

A key development was a number of meetings held in Trinity College Dublin in 1971 about the setting up of a volunteer service. Ken Whitaker, who was Governor of the Central Bank at the time, attended the meetings.[20] They were organised by George Dawson, Professor of Genetics at Trinity, described by Dr. Whitaker as 'a very concerned, thoughtful man' who realised that Ireland had no organisation in the area of development such as they had in Britain.[21] Dr. Whitaker thinks that he was invited because of an article he had written in *Administration* magazine about Third World poverty.[22] Like Professor Dawson, he did not have an in-depth knowledge of the issue but they shared a concern to improve Ireland's contribution.

The group which met was impressive, including such figures as Chief Justice Kingsmill Moore, Tom Barrington, founder of the Institute of Public Administration, and Willie Jenkinson of the Irish Missionary Union. A memorandum was drafted and sent to the Department of Foreign Affairs, proposing that the State should foster voluntary service in the developing world. One of those who helped the group in their drafting was Bill Jackson, a Trinity graduate who had worked for Oxfam in Africa and then took up a teaching position in Keele University. He would later become the first Chief Executive of the volunteer agency set up by the Government, called the Agency for Personal Service Overseas (APSO). Ken Whitaker would become APSO's first Chair.

This farsighted group chaired by Professor Dawson had pointed the way forward but their representations at first fell on deaf ears. Correspondence on their proposals went back and forth between the Departments of Finance and Foreign Affairs but no action was taken over the next two years. It was not until the change of Government in February 1973 that there was real movement.

Endnotes

1. *The Irish Times* photo in *Annual Report 1985* shows President Hillery handing over a cheque for £7,176,262 to Bob Geldof. The final total came to £8.4 million. See 'Famine in Africa', *Annual Report*, pp. 39-44. (Note: *Annual Report* is the name used for the reports on the aid programme issued each year by the Department of Foreign Affairs, starting in 1981. The name of the reports changed over the years as the name of the aid programme changed – the generic title *Annual Report* is used throughout.)

2. Jim O'Keeffe, Minister of State for Overseas Development 1981, 1982 to 1986, interview with the author ('Interview' is used throughout where the information is based on the author's interviews with the person under discussion).

3. See also John Waters: 'It's a long time ago I hear you say. Really? Our great grandparents – yours and mine – were adults in the famine period. That we might have been handed on its trauma and grief is but a matter of three cultural transactions, three generations of horrified silence.' 'Confronting the Ghosts of Our Past' *The Irish Times* October 1994 from *Irish Hunger: Personal*

Reflections on the Legacy of the Famine', Ed. Tom Hayden, Wolfhound Press, 1997, p. 29.

4. David Andrews, Minister for Foreign Affairs 1992, 1997-2000, interview.

5. Mary Sutton, Irish Commission for Justice and peace 1976-1979, Trocaire 1982-1992, Advisory Board on Irish Aid 2002-07, interview.

6. Gary Ansbro, Clerk to Oireachtas Joint Committee on Development 1985-87, Charge D'Affaires Tanzania 1987-89, interview.

7. Brendan Rogers, Charge d'Affaires Zambia 1991-98, Uganda 1998-2000, HQ Irish Aid 2000– , Director General Irish Aid 2008– , interview.

8. Kevin O'Sullivan's article 'Biafra to Lomé: The Evolution of Irish Government Policy on Official Development Assistance 1969-75' in *Irish Studies in International Affairs* Vol. 18 (2007), pp. 91-107, gives a good description of the impact of the Biafran war on Irish interest in the developing world.

9. Mary Holland article in the *Observer*, 18 January 1970, 'The Catholics and the Black Babies'.

10. Fr. Joe Whelan interview. Daniel Murphy's masterly account *A History of Irish Emigrant and Missionary Education*, Dublin, Four Courts Press, 2000, reveals just how extensive the work of the missionaries was and how far back it goes – right to the early part of nineteenth century. Summing up their impact in Nigeria he says:

    The most fundamental impact of the mission schools lay in the cultural advancement of the people of Nigeria. Some have seen them as replacing the indigenous cultural values of Africa with the alien, Western-oriented values of Europe. That remains a highly controversial issue...What can be claimed beyond any doubt is their cultural empowerment of the primitive peoples of that country through the provision of elementary and secondary education at a time when the colonial authorities failed completely to do so (p. 251).

11. *Dead Aid: Why Aid is not working and how there is another way for Africa*, Dambisa Moyo, Penguin Books, 2009, p. 151.

12. Michael D. Higgins interview.

13. See *Gorta and the Third World: A History of 30 Successful Years 1965-1995*, Gorta publication. Brian Hanratty, CEO, Gorta sent me this and other documentation on Gorta's history.

14. Joe Haughton interview.

15. See Tony Farmar *Believing in Action: Concern, The First Thirty Years 1968-98*, A&A Farmar, 2002.

16. Jerome Connolly, CEO of the Irish Commission for Justice and Peace 1970-2002, interview. *The Third World War*, Veritas Press, Dublin, 1971.

17. Bob McDonagh, Secretary, Department of Foreign Affairs, 1977-1979, conversation.

18. A good example is the debate on the UN's Second Development Decade where the intervention by the Irish representative attempts to paint a positive picture of Ireland's contribution at a time when the level of ODA was extremely low. See *Statements at the United Nations: Texts of the Main Speeches*, pp. 71-77, DFA publication, 1970.

19. DFA files in the National Archives chronicle the exchanges.

20. Dr. T.K. Whitaker, Secretary, Department of Finance 1956-69, Governor of the Central Bank, Senator, Chairman of APSO, 1973-1977, interview.

21. George Dawson, 1927-2004, Professor of Genetics, TCD, Chairman of APSO 1977-1980, later Chair of HEDCO.

22. T.K. Whitaker 'World Poverty' *Administration*, Spring. 1971. Whitaker argued that 'a substantial increase in our financial contribution . . . is urgently required. Our sincerity about the alleviation of world poverty will be judged in relation to the proportion of our resources which we are prepared to contribute'.

3

STARTING FROM SCRATCH

One of Garret FitzGerald's first acts as Minister for Foreign Affairs in the Fine Gael/Labour coalition government that came to power in February 1973 was to announce that Ireland would be starting its own official development aid programme. To this, as to other areas of his brief, the new Minister brought energy and determination to effect radical change.[1]

In April 1973 he brought home Ireland's ambassadors to a conference in Iveagh House which reviewed Ireland's foreign policy. He told the assembled ambassadors and senior officials that Ireland was not meeting its obligations in regard to development aid and that he was determined to get an aid programme off the ground. This was the first time that development aid had been given such prominence among the Department's foreign policy objectives.

In reality, it could be said that Ireland had no option but to start an aid programme. As well as the groundswell of public support, Ireland's entry into the European Economic Community that year meant that a programme would have to be set up sooner or later.

Europe held out the promise of many benefits to Ireland but, at the same time, it was obvious that changes and sacrifices would have to be made. The advantages were seen as outweighing the disadvantages and the leap of faith proved to be justified. Ireland took to the EEC from the start and benefits flowed in the form of funding for agriculture and infrastructure, access to European markets and membership of a huge economic and trading bloc. But there were financial downsides. Some industries did not survive as Ireland opened its markets to outside competition. And contributing to the developing world was part of the price we would have to pay for entering the Common Market. Difficult though it would be, funding for an aid programme had to be found.

The Treaty of Rome of 1957 provided that the EEC 'would contribute to the campaign against poverty in the developing world' and would assist the developing countries 'with a view to their smooth and gradual integration into the world economy'.[2]

Some of this was based on altruism and a desire to see a new and better world order in the aftermath of World War II. But self-interest came into play too: relations with the former French and Belgian colonies had an important influence on the shaping of Europe's approach to aid.

The main operational effect of the Treaty was the establishment of the European Development Fund. Ireland, like all member states, had to contribute an assessed amount each year to the European Development Fund. The contributions we were to make from 1973 onwards could be counted as Official Development Assistance, as could a portion of our overall contribution to the EEC budget.

The size of Ireland's Official Development Assistance would rise automatically, therefore, once we joined the EEC. But we were expected to do more. Development is one of the areas where the Commission and the member states share competences. As well as contributing to the EEC's effort, targets were set for member states to reach in terms of their own overall aid effort, with the UN's 0.7 per cent as the eventual goal. These were not obligatory as the payments to the European Development Fund were, but they constituted powerful moral pressure. At the time of our entry to the EEC, Ireland and Luxembourg were the only member states not to have a fully fledged aid programme; as a result, we were given a later date as a target for raising our performance. But, just as on a whole range of foreign policy issues, it was not an option to sit on the fence, so by joining the EEC Ireland had to take on the development agenda.

Within days of taking office, Garret FitzGerald was approached by George Dawson about the proposal of his group to set up an agency for volunteers interested in serving in the developing world. Ken Whitaker remembers being asked by the Minister to call to see him on a Saturday morning to discuss the proposal.[3] A working group was set up to get it going.

The new Minister cut through the drawn-out official level discussion of the pros and cons by announcing that an Interim Agency for Personal Service in Developing Countries would be established. The name of the volunteer agency was changed the following year to the Agency for Personal Service Overseas and it would play a big role in the growing aid programme for almost 30 years.[4]

Putting together a full aid programme was a big challenge. In May 1973 Garret FitzGerald told the Dáil that a comprehensive aid programme was intended and the Minister for Finance, Richie Ryan, announced in his budget speech that £1.5 million would be allocated for 1973/74 – double the amount spent in 1972/73. In November of that year the Minister sent a Memorandum to the Government proposing:

- To increase the annual level of Official Development Assistance in absolute terms and as a percentage of GNP, aiming at an annual increase of 0.05 per cent of GNP taking one year with another over a five-year period

- To develop a comprehensive and coherent ODA policy, and

- To establish a permanent Inter-Departmental Committee on Development Assistance.

It was not until April 1974, after more correspondence and memos, that the Government finally approved the plans. According to Garret FitzGerald's memoirs, they did so only by a tight margin.[5]

What was it like to be working for a determined, energetic, well-informed Minister with clear ideas of what he wished to achieve? Officials in the Department of Foreign Affairs who were engaged in the embryonic aid programme painted a picture of a hectic time.

The Department of Foreign Affairs in 1973 was an exciting place to work. A revolution was taking place, although as a new Third Secretary it was only later that I was able to fully comprehend the extent of the changes that were happening. I thought that the expansion and quick promotions which happened at the time were a feature of Iveagh House which would last forever!

The Department was a small place then but over the next few years promotion prospects improved beyond anyone's dreams. My first Counsellor, Brendan Nolan, was typical of his generation in that he returned to Dublin from being a First Secretary in Geneva on promotion as Counsellor, and then was further promoted to Assistant Secretary within a few years.

Expansion was already happening by the time Garret FitzGerald took office but the pace speeded up rapidly. There were two main reasons for this: EEC membership and the explosion in the North. These developments would change and expand the role of the Department for the next thirty years.

Events in the North from the late 1960s on required enormous amounts of attention and skill. The question could have been posed as to how much the Troubles were a matter for Foreign Affairs and not, say, the Department of the Taoiseach? After all, the Constitution clearly stated that Ireland was the entire island and what was happening north of the border involved Irish men and women. As against that, virtually every aspect of the ever-worsening situation involved our nearest neighbour and increasingly other external players such as the United States. In the event, the small group of officials in the Department who dealt with the North soon proved themselves indispensable and the scale of the Department's involvement grew beyond recognition.

Similarly, entry to the EEC made stern demands on Iveagh House, and there was also the question of whether departments such as Finance should not have a greater role vis-à-vis Brussels. But Foreign Affairs again proved its ability to rise to the challenge and played a central role in enabling Ireland to box above its weight in Europe.

The pressures on the department at this time were great: in Brussels diplomats were required, not just to defend Ireland's national interests, but to have a view on all sorts of foreign policy issues, even if they did not impinge on Ireland's concerns. The tiny size of our diplomatic representation abroad was shown up.

Garret FitzGerald quickly moved to fill the gaps by opening more embassies – the scale of what was needed can be gauged by the fact that Ireland still had no embassy at all in countries such as Russia and China.

Expansion benefited me too. I was promoted to First Secretary after only two and a half years in the department. The previous generation had had to wait as long as seven or eight years for promotion. My case was not exceptional – early promotion was the order of the day for most of my intake into Foreign Affairs.

The Department's enlargement was demonstrated also in terms of accommodation: Iveagh House, the city residence of the Iveagh family, which was the headquarters of the Department, was creaking at the seams in every sense. The ever-burgeoning EEC section moved to 52 St. Stephen's Green, a fine building with beautiful ceilings, which formerly housed the Church Representative Body. Less grand offices were rented in 72 St. Stephen's Green and this was where the aid programme would have its first home.

Small wonder, with all these pressures, that Foreign Affairs faced challenges as work began on building an aid programme. Until 1973 Ireland's official aid consisted of occasional funding for disaster relief, support for a modest number of overseas students studying in Ireland and contributions to the UN family – to organisations such as UNICEF, the World Food Programme and the Of-

fice of the UN High Commissioner for Refugees. There was also
funding for the World Bank and its offshoots in Washington, which
the Department of Finance administered.

It really was a case of starting from scratch. There was no dedicated position for aid in the Department up to then, let alone a dis-
tinct division. The trade and economic brief was supposed to cover
that, along with its other responsibilities. Brendan Nolan moved on
from being the Counsellor in charge to Assistant Secretary on the
Administration side, although he retained an interest in aid and
played a big part in shaping policy during the first years. He was
replaced by Paul Dempsey as Counsellor. The growing responsibilities were too much for one First Secretary so a second was assigned.
Eamon Ryan, who joined Jim Flavin, believes he was the first officer
to work solely on aid in the department.[6]

The recollection of the officials is of their Minister breaking new
ground almost on a daily basis. One of them said that he found out
what the policy was by listening to the Minister's speeches (usually
it is the other way round!). In the case of the Interim Agency for
Personal Service, the announcement was made before the details
were decided. Paul Dempsey recalls writing a Memorandum for
Government overnight on the form the new agency would take.
This was a complicated process, as there had to be articles of corporation establishing the agency and a Memorandum of Understanding with the Department of Foreign Affairs defining the relationship.

When it came to the shape the bilateral programme should
take, the tried and tested approach of civil servants was adopted:
Paul Dempsey and Eamon Ryan looked around at what other countries did. They studied aid programmes in comparably sized countries such as the Netherlands, Austria, Sweden and New Zealand. A
model that looked promising was Denmark so they visited Copenhagen in November 1973. Denmark fitted the bill on several counts:
size, experience in the field, a good reputation as a donor. The difference was that the Danes already had a large programme; their

Official Development Assistance represented 0.48 per cent of GNP in 1973 compared to Ireland's 0.05 per cent.

The Danish model was the classic one for those times:

- A mix of bilateral and multilateral aid
- A focus on a limited number of priority countries
- A fund to respond to emergencies
- Technical assistance.

Other aspects of the Danish model which were of interest were that they had produced a White Paper setting out their development aid policy, they held an annual meeting to discuss development issues and they had an external advisory committee.

As regards the structure for running the programme, Garret FitzGerald was not persuaded by the officials' argument that the programme should be run by Foreign Affairs. He wished to have all options examined including that of an agency or semi-state body. The question of the programme's structure led to the biggest tussle that the fledgling programme would encounter.

Meanwhile, though, there was money to be spent and ways had to be found of spending it by the end of the first financial year of the programme – March 1974. This was when the officials discovered what anyone who has worked in development finds out – that spending aid money quickly is not easy. Increasing grants to the UN family of organisations is one way and this was done through contributions to a number of UN Trust Funds. A dedicated Disaster Fund was set up which meant that there would be less scrabbling around for funds after a disaster struck. But identifying bilateral projects, that is, direct contributions from Ireland to meet needs in particular countries, proved more difficult.

One of the first bilateral projects to be funded was a curious choice. A grant of £150,000 was made to the Sophisticated Instrument Centre in Madras in India. The circumstances surrounding this choice tell a lot about the rush to get the programme up and running.

The fact that India was one of only two developing countries where Ireland had a resident embassy – the other being Nigeria – seems to have been a major factor. The Indian authorities were consulted by the Embassy in Delhi and they suggested the Madras Centre, which had as its function research and development of scientific instruments. This was a long way removed from most people's idea of development aid. But there were time pressures: Liam Rigney, who was working in Administration in the Department, remembers pointing out that if the money was not transferred to the project by the end of March deadline, it would have to be returned to the Exchequer.[7] Garret FitzGerald recalled personally handing over the cheque to the Indian Ambassador.[8]

The Danish model of focusing activity on a small number of countries was attractive. Ireland had to focus scarce resources where they would be most effective, especially when the funds were as small as they were in the 1970s.

Choosing the countries on which Ireland would concentrate its efforts was clearly a major decision. Just as when diplomatic relations are established, when a country is chosen as an aid partner care is needed. The relationship is meant to be long term, with commitment by both parties.

The priority countries, as they were to be called, were determined by a combination of policy decision, time pressure and luck. Some of the rationale for them seems to have been applied after the event.

Brian O Ceallaigh, who transferred from the EEC side to the new ODA Section in 1974, recalls a visit to Africa that year with Tom Barrington, Director of the Institute of Public Administration.[9] The IPA had a track record dating back to the 1960s in training public servants from developing countries and Tom Barrington was one of those who had pressed for a strong aid programme.[10] He had brought Zambian civil servants to Ireland for training in administration – something they badly needed as most of the colonial officials left after independence and their replacements had no experience of public administration – and he had plans for the Institute to expand its training activities.[11]

Five countries were visited: Tanzania, Zambia, Sudan, Kenya and Ethiopia. The first three would be chosen as priority countries, along with Lesotho and India.

Tanzania and Zambia were obvious candidates in that they had existing links with Ireland: Tanzania through its President Julius Nyerere, an admired figure who would pay a state visit to Ireland and would host President Hillery in turn; Zambia whose President Kenneth Kaunda was also well known in Ireland and which had already seen cooperation in the training of military cadets and civil servants. Both countries had long-standing missionary presences, and business connections too such as Irish Ropes in Tanzania and Irish Cement's interests in Zambia.

Objectively, they both met the criteria for countries in need of aid: they were relatively peaceful, had recently achieved independence, had large numbers of very poor people, were English speaking, and had the capacity to absorb aid. They also had training needs that matched skills available in Ireland. This was a factor which would play an important role in the early years of the aid programme.

In his autobiography Garret FitzGerald tells the story of how Lesotho came to be chosen.[12] Two fellow passengers on a flight to New York turned out to be a Lesothan Minister and his Permanent Secretary. Garret FitzGerald suggested that if they were in Europe later in the year they should visit the Department and representatives from Lesotho did that and their country became a recipient of Irish aid. That is not to say that the choice was entirely a case of the luck of Lesotho in meeting a sympathetic minister. Lesotho was a landlocked, extremely poor country, entirely surrounded by what was then apartheid South Africa. Its situation and small size appealed.

Sudan was a different story. One reason Sudan was chosen was the argument that it had the potential to be the breadbasket of Africa; helping it would benefit both Sudan and the continent. Others told me its inclusion was largely for foreign policy reasons – to reach out to the Arab world and to forge links with what is a huge, strategically important state. The Euro-Arab Dialogue was at its height then and Ireland needed to show that it was doing its bit. Whatever the motives, Sudan always struggled as a priority country. In 1992 I had the unhappy task of having to recommend that we wind up our programme there.

Tom Barrington and Brian O Ceallaigh were less positive about Kenya and Ethiopia following their visits. The political situation in both countries was volatile. Kenya had advantages: some connections to Ireland, English was spoken and, as a former British colony, their system was familiar. But Brian O Ceallaigh recalls coming upon a square where demonstrating students had been beaten by police and the ground was red with their blood. The country seemed close to revolt. The scale of corruption was also evident.

Ethiopia was in a bad state politically following the recent Communist takeover. Brian O Ceallaigh made the mistake of asking after an Ethiopian diplomat he had known in Germany and regretted it when it became apparent that this would not help his friend's standing with the new regime.

India was the only non-African state among the priority countries. Presumably one reason was not to have all the aid effort in Africa. Also, India was a country held in high regard in Ireland as the largest democracy in the world and a leader among developing countries. Its first Prime Minister Pandit Nehru had won respect for the independent, non-aligned position he took. There were longstanding links with Ireland. Gorta had agricultural projects there. And, of course, millions of Indians lived in dire poverty.

India did not last long as a priority country however. The usual explanation is that it was soon recognised that the challenges there were so great that Ireland lacked the capacity to help. The story was more complicated than that.[13]

Those involved told me that the Indians were not pleased to be bracketed with least developed countries in Africa. Although it was not the economic powerhouse it has become today, India had many wealthy people and has always regarded itself as a player in international affairs. The Indians also felt they had expertise and didn't need outsiders to tell them how to do things – especially not a small country like Ireland.

There was even a row over the funding for the Madras Centre. Dublin regarded the £150,000 as a one-off grant but the Embassy in Delhi sought a renewal and argued that Ireland would look bad if it did not continue funding. The Department declined to do so.

There was no more luck with the sector identified for cooperation between Ireland and India: agriculture. A delegation went out from Ireland including technical experts, among them the Chief Veterinary Officer at the Department of Agriculture. The people they met on the Indian side made it clear that they felt Ireland should just hand over the funding and leave it to them. The delegation felt that conditions for raising cattle in the area they visited were unsuitable, being mainly desert. They held talks with the Swiss Government's aid people who had tried to give support to the agricultural sector but had had to admit failure. When the delegation returned home, the unanimous verdict was that Ireland should not proceed with the Indian programme.

There was a delicate problem in that the designation of India as the fifth priority country had already been announced. There was no wish to offend the Indians (or the Irish Ambassador in Delhi who was a strong supporter of India's claims) so some small projects were funded.

The other four priority countries saw spending increase rapidly over the first years of the programme. In 1974 a grand total of £10,000 was spent on all four; by 1978 the total was over £1 million. Lesotho had the fastest growth: from £21,000 in 1975 to over half a

million in 1978. Expenditure in Tanzania rose from £18,000 to
£195,000 in the same period, and in Zambia the increase was from
£19,000 to £192,000. Sudan had more modest growth to £74,000.

The Inter-Departmental Committee, which the Government
had authorised to steer the aid programme, was up and running.
Interested departments were invited to attend: Finance was the key
player along with Foreign Affairs, while the Department of Agriculture also played a role because of its servicing of the Food and Agriculture Organisation and the World Food Programme and its links
with Gorta.[14]

A big advantage of the Department of Finance's presence on the
committee was that every single proposal did not have to be submitted separately to Finance for approval, as would normally have
been the case. The reports of the Inter-Departmental Committee of
those early years confirm the feeling the officials had that the availability of new funds was attracting a lot of attention. Hundreds of
applications came in from NGOs and from organisations such as
the Irish Management Institute (private sector training), An Foras
Talúntais (agricultural advisory services), the ESB, Aer Lingus and
others.

What strikes me as surprising in retrospect is that more mistakes were not made in the early days, given the lack of experience
in Foreign Affairs. Ad hoc and precarious it may have been, but
spending did take off and the countries identified for assistance began to see projects on the ground.

I got a taste of the challenges those in charge faced much later,
in 2005, when Conor Lenihan, the Minister of State at the time, set
up a programme of mentoring of the new EU member states –
countries such as the Baltic States, Hungary and Poland – who were
setting up their own aid programmes.[15] They were starting with
blank sheets, in some ways even blanker than what Ireland faced in
1973. They accepted that they must make their mandatory contributions to the European Development Fund, but the very concept
of channelling scarce funds from their national budgets to bilateral

projects in Africa or Asia was something they found hard to accept, not to mention the challenge of explaining this to their sceptical publics. Some got hung up on the legal aspect until we explained that Ireland never passed a law setting up the programme but simply began to implement projects and learned by doing.

I saw then that Ireland had had a huge advantage when it started out in that the missionary tradition had built up a real connection, especially with Africa, which resonated with the Irish public. None of the new EU member states had such strong connections.

Another big advantage for Ireland was that in the 1970s our NGOs were growing in strength. Some were becoming major development organisations. Again, this was not a feature of the new member states who had very different historical experiences from us in the twenieth century and whose NGOs (with one or two exceptions such as the Czech Republic) were fairly weak.

The Department of Foreign Affairs' success in finding suitable projects to support so quickly is all the more remarkable in that the work had to be done from Dublin, thousands of miles from the scene of the action. Ireland had no diplomatic representation in the African priority countries and cost restrictions on foreign travel meant visits to the field were few and far between.

Brian O Ceallaigh moved into offices which had been allocated to Development Cooperation in 72 St Stephen's Green with a staff that was still very small though it was growing. The growing importance of aid was symbolised by raising the grade of the head of the programme to Assistant Secretary. Dermot Waldron was the first person to occupy this position. Two Counsellors reported to the Assistant Secretary, one on the bilateral aid side and one on the multilateral side. Much the same arrangement was still in place when I took over the Division in 1991, although the numbers of support staff had increased somewhat.

A feather in the cap of the fledgling aid programme came from the handling of the Irish Presidency of the EEC in 1975.

The Presidency was a huge undertaking for the still tiny Foreign Service and it put great pressure on everyone. Yet there was an exhilaration about taking on a big task and managing to pull it off. I was serving in Brussels by then and had little involvement – the coalface was in Iveagh House and in the committees that had to be chaired by Irish officials on topics of every description. I sat in on a meeting of the Political Committee in Brussels when Ireland was in the chair. This is the committee of officials that discusses the main political issues of the day and seeks to get agreement among the EEC member states on joint action and approaches. The meeting was chaired by Noel Dorr with the assistance of John Campbell (Political Director and Political Correspondent respectively). I remember the feeling of pride that two of our own were able to do it, to steer everyone, small and large countries alike, to agreed positions.

Garret FitzGerald scored a big victory on the development side. Negotiations on a new agreement between the EEC and the African, Caribbean and Pacific countries were at an advanced stage but had not been finished under the French Presidency as had been expected. The Minister had to steer the difficult negotiations through to the conclusion of the new Lomé Agreement. As he describes in his autobiography, there were tough negotiations on what was a vital agreement for these developing countries – it embraces not just assistance but a wide range of complicated trade instruments – but he managed to bring the sides together and tie up all the outstanding issues. The Minister's achievement brought him great personal kudos, put Ireland on the development map and brought home to many people the international dimensions of aid and trade.[16]

Meanwhile, the Agency for Personal Service Overseas was growing. Professor Dawson was closely involved as was Ken Whitaker. Most importantly, the Government agreed to a first grant of £100,000. Funding would be a constant preoccupation of APSO – I was told that Professor Dawson always regretted not having asked for more at the start!

Bill Jackson took up duty as APSO's first Chief Executive. Ken Whitaker persuaded the Hill Samuel Company to provide the new agency with rooms in Adelaide Road and Bill Jackson set about organising its work. The idea was for APSO both to send its own volunteers overseas and to co-fund the sending of NGOs' volunteers. Bill knew that he would have to show organisations such as Concern, Gorta, the Irish Commission for Justice and Peace and the Irish Missionary Union that APSO could provide a valuable service. One of his first actions was to hire a training officer and training would become one of APSO's strengths.[17]

Ireland's official aid programme was under way. But two issues clouded the positive picture: controversy over the Government's delivery on its promised increases in the aid budget and the fundamental question of who should be running the programme.

Endnotes

1. Garret FitzGerald's autobiography *All in a Life*, Macmillan London, Gill and Macmillan, 1991, describes his time as Minister for Foreign Affairs (1973-77) and his two terms as Taoiseach (1981- February 1982, November 1982-1987) in detail. His account of the starting up of the aid programme is on pp. 189-191.

2. Treaty of Rome, 1957.

3. Ken Whitaker interview.

4. APSO, *All in a Life* p. 189. See also DFA file 2004/7/2561 National Archive.

5. Government Decision of 26 April 1974. DFA file 2004/7/2573 contains the Memorandum for Government and related correspondence. See *All in a Life*, p. 190.

6. Interviews with Paul Dempsey, Eamon Ryan and Jim Flavin.

7. Liam Rigney interview.

8. Garret FitzGerald interview.

9. Brian O Ceallaigh interview.

10. The IPA's involvement in training dated back to the Overseas Training Fund of the 1960s, which was set up in response to an appeal for administrative training from President Kenneth Kaunda of Zambia. The training was out sourced to the IPA. Joan Corkery, who worked for the IPA for many years, recalled that the Zambian officials who came in groups knew little about their new post-colonial responsibilities but were well selected. On one occasion she

says that 33 came off the plane even though only 20 were expected! Conversation.

11. Ruth and Anne Barrington showed me their late father's unpublished history of the IPA. It does not refer specifically to the visit with Brian O Ceallaigh, but contains a lot of information on Tom Barrington's and the IPA's extensive connections with the developing world in the 1960s and 1970s.

12. *All in a Life*, p. 190.

13. Dermot Waldron, first Assistant Secretary in charge of ODA, interview. He headed the delegation which travelled to India to explore the possibilities for cooperation. The then Ambassador to India, the late Denis Holmes, pressed for further funding to be made available. An article by his son Michael Holmes is contained in *Ireland and India: Connections, Comparisons, Contrasts*, ed. Michael Holmes and Denis Holmes, Dublin, Folens Press, 1997. Entitled 'A Friend of India? Ireland and the Diplomatic Relationship', it is critical of the fact that assistance to India was ended and argues that an opportunity was lost for increasing contacts between the two countries. Noel Fahey, later Ambassador to Germany, the United States and the Holy See, was First Secretary at the Embassy in Delhi at the time and was present during President Hillery's State visit to India in 1978. He saw no evidence that the discontinuation of aid to India adversely affected relations and said that the Indian side did not raise the issue. Interview. See also file 2008/79/1 in the National Archive on Hillery's visit.

14. Numerous files on the proceedings of the Interdepartmental Committee are in the National Archive e.g. 2005/145/1632-1648.

15. The mentoring exercise was chaired by Helen O'Neill, formerly Professor of Development Studies at UCD.

16. The negotiations are described on pp. 150-153 of *All in a Life*.

17. Bill Jackson interview.

4

PIONEERING DAYS

The 1970s saw aid-related activities and initiatives springing up all over the place. But that was not the main focus of many of the articles and critiques that appeared at the time. They were mainly concerned with what was seen as the Government's failure to meet the promised targets for increasing official development aid.[1]

The Irish Commission for Justice and Peace and Trocaire led the charge, criticising the fact that monies voted were lower than had been promised: 'the worst performance in the EEC . . . abysmal in relation to the UN target . . . Irish efforts are meagre in the extreme.' Much ink was spilled over the meaning of the phrase 'aiming at an annual increase in ODA of the order of 0.05 per cent of GNP, taking one year with another, over the next five years'.[2]

The issue of the size of the ODA budget has dominated discussion and coverage of the aid programme since it began. It deserves special attention and I will come back to the subject in a later chapter. For now, what I will say is that, while it is true that progress on the official targets fell short of what was promised, by 1978 ODA had reached £9.6 million, almost four times the 1974 level of £2.5 million. In terms of GNP the percentage rose from 0.08 per cent to 0.15 per cent. In the decade that followed, the volume of aid remained significant and there is a formidable roll call of achievements over that period. By the mid-1980s the programme had expanded to the highest level to date – 0.25 per cent of GNP – despite severe economic constraints. Most of my interviewees look back on this time as one of steady expansion.

I should stress that during this period I had no connection with the aid programme. I left Economic Division after my few contacts with aid – including serving briefly as secretary of the Interdepartmental Committee – and my career followed the usual diplomatic round of foreign postings as various as Paris and Brussels, three and a half enjoyable years as Consul General in Chicago, back home to Anglo-Irish Division, then two years as Chief of Protocol (a job I hated but I had to earn my promotion to Counsellor!), three years in the newly set up Foreign Earnings Division and four years as Deputy Head of Mission in Germany. Only then did I return to take up duty as head of the aid programme.

During those years my contacts with Development Cooperation Division, now a firmly established part of Foreign Affairs, were slight. Abroad, it was confined to reading press releases about Garret FitzGerald or Michael O'Kennedy or Jim O'Keeffe's visits to Africa and the information material put out by the Bilateral Aid Programme as it was then called, with maps showing the locations of Ireland's aid activities around the world. Very occasionally I was asked by Dublin to make enquiries with my host government about an aspect of aid, such as the situation in the Horn of Africa or their approach to disaster relief.

I would say that my perception of what was going on was typical of my colleagues in the Department who were not working on the aid side. Development Cooperation Division seemed separate, different. The work being done looked interesting but I thought that if I were ever assigned there I would have an awful lot of learning to do (this would prove to be the case when I joined in 1991!).

My account of those years is based on what I learned from colleagues who worked on the programme at that time. As in other areas of its work, Foreign Affairs was fortunate in the quality of the personnel who found themselves running the new programme. Two in particular stand out: Dermot Gallagher, who shaped the fledgling programme, and Martin Greene, who started his career when the programme was in its infancy and would go on to become Director General and one of the main thinkers behind the programme as it evolved over the years.[3]

The question of who should run the programme – the Department of Foreign Affairs or an independent agency – was a question that exercised a lot of minds.

In his autobiography, Garret FitzGerald says that the Department of Foreign Affairs let him down over the agency issue.[4] He says he knew that there were arguments in favour of both an agency and the Department, but what irked him was that the pros and cons of the two models were not set out clearly. Officials, on the other hand, felt that the Minister favoured an independent agency. APSO joined with others in lobbying for an agency and the suspicion was that they saw themselves as the ones who should be in charge. The preference at official level in the Department was that it should run the programme and not an outside agency.

Debate about what was known as 'The Structures Issue' went on and on. Garret FitzGerald suspected foot-dragging; he says he became so exasperated that he enrolled the help of John Kelly, who was appointed Parliamentary Secretary at the Department of the Foreign Affairs in 1975, with the aim of the two of them writing a Memorandum for Government themselves. He even hoped to produce a White Paper on development. But there were so many other issues demanding their attention that they never had the time.[5]

One of the officials' arguments was apprehension about the safety of public monies if the programme was not under government control. And there was a view that development was an integral part of foreign policy, which ought not to be dealt with separately. Others thought the Department feared the NGOs would not follow Government policy if they got independent funding (though in my experience the receipt of large sums of public funding has never stopped NGOs from voicing their views about the Government!).

Some in Foreign Affairs concede that there was an element of territoriality in the opposition to an agency. Feelings were sore that the Department had lost a recent battle to be given responsibility for foreign trade and to have Córas Tráchtála reporting to it.[6] But they stress that there were genuinely strong concerns about accountability for the new funds which were coming on stream, concerns which were shared by the Department of Finance. The debate continued through the four years of the Cosgrave government without a resolution.

When Michael O'Kennedy was appointed Minister for Foreign Affairs after the 1977 elections he made it clear that he did not favour the agency model. A Working Group was tasked with preparing a report on the structures issue. This was chaired by Dermot Gallagher along with representatives from the Departments of Finance and the Public Service.[7] The report was completed in August 1978. It is an important document since its recommendations shaped the way the aid programme would do its work.[8]

The Working Group's report was quite sharp on the lack of a coherent structure:

> The present arrangements for administering development aid show the classical weaknesses and lack of synthesis associated with a too rapid and unstructured growth. Almost all the significant and substantial institutional developments have been crowded into the past five years.

Noting that the Minister had rejected the semi-state model, it took the view that 'there were very strong and valid reasons for retaining the administration and coordination of aid within the Department of Foreign Affairs'. It added that the Department's 'primary, central and coordinating role now seems to be generally accepted, though the argument about a semi-state agency will inevitably surface from time to time'. The second part turned out to be true, but it was some time before Foreign Affairs' role would be generally accepted.

Another major recommendation of the Working Group was the establishment of an Advisory Council on Development Cooperation. This recommendation was based on the recognition that interest in development issues had grown enormously, that the developing countries themselves were making demands of the richer countries and that some of the issues being raised could be sensitive from Ireland's point of view.

> In these circumstances it would seem desirable that there should be some formal mechanism whereby the relevant sectoral interests here in Ireland – such as the farmers' organisations, trade unions, industrialists etc – could advise the Government through the Minister for Foreign Affairs on the entire range of issues arising in the area of development cooperation.

Emphasis was placed on the need for the Council's membership to include strong NGO representation.

Setting up an Advisory Council made up of members from outside the Department of Foreign Affairs could be seen as a quid pro quo for the decision to having the Department in charge of the programme. The report's language also suggests that ACDC (the acronym always raised a smile) was designed to be a substitute for some of the more radical proposals coming from the development community. The aim of the Council was:

> to introduce an element of balance into the views being offered to the Government while at the same time ensuring the maximum participation and involvement of the community at large in our growing development activities and, in general, bringing to the formulation of development policy the range of expert advice available nationally.

The Working Group was critical of the direction the Interdepartmental Committee had taken. Instead of considering policy issues it concerned itself mostly with decisions on individual projects. I was told that its deliberations could last for days. The Working Group felt that interdepartmental coordination was vital for the success of the aid programme but it recommended that the Inter-departmental Committee should have a broader function:

> To be the forum in which development cooperation issues are considered and, where possible and appropriate, interdepartmental agreement reached;
>
> To review annually the programme for ODA, particularly in the light of the international target for ODA;
>
> To consider and recommend the year to year level of contributions for the various elements and sectors of the programme . . .

Meanwhile:

> decisions on the financing and implementation of projects should be delegated to the Department of Foreign Affairs which would report on the progress of the programme to meetings of the committee.

In other words, the Interdepartmental Committee should stop examining individual projects; instead, the Department of Foreign Affairs was empowered to consider these themselves.

These recommendations were put into effect. The Interdepartmental Committee would meet annually, usually in December, to consider the budget for the following year. It was a key financial mechanism in that it approved the overall budget document and authorised payments up to the value of the budget for that year. In addition, and in line with the working group's recommendations on strengthening the programme's mechanisms, a Project Appraisal and Evaluation Group was established in Development Cooperation Division. Pronounced 'PEG' this group was where projects were assessed, then approved or rejected and their impact assessed. PAEG meetings became the key mechanism for the running of the bilateral side of the programme.

These structures formed the basic model in existence when I came to the programme in 1991 and they still exist today.

Much of the credit for bringing order to the aid programme must go to Dermot Gallagher. He says that when he arrived in Development Cooperation Division in 1977 he was taken aback by the diffuse state of the programme:

> I am a clean desk person and I found the filing system chaotic. It was unclear how payments were being made. Questions were being asked in the Dáil as to why this or that country was chosen. There was an outburst of interest in the aid programme, by far the most of it from people genuinely interested in helping the poor, but others perhaps attracted to some degree by the possibility that public funding might be available to their organisations and enterprises. All were clamouring for the Minister's ear.[9]

His aim was to professionalise the aid programme. The core structures at headquarters had to be got right, the Department of Finance had to be brought on board, especially to sanction increased staffing levels, and there was a need to move from ad hoc projects to a more coherent approach.

The India issue had to be resolved. The way Dermot Gallagher dealt with it was to place all the emphasis in speeches and statements on the other priority countries and to let the Indian programme gradually fade from the picture.

Activity in the four remaining priority countries had to be built up and decisions made about where Ireland could make a valuable contribution – agriculture and training were two obvious areas where we had something to offer. As recommended in the Working Group report, the programme got its first economist. John Grindle was recruited in 1980 and became a mainstay during the eight years he spent with the programme and for many years after as a consultant.[10]

As well as the decisions about structures, a significant step forward was the Department of Finance's agreement to making the money allocated for the bilateral programme grant-in-aid, meaning that unspent money could be carried over from one year to the next. Up till then any unspent money automatically reverted to the exchequer. Given the unpredictable nature of spending on aid, it was a big advantage to have some flexibility at year-end.

Even at that early stage, the information gap about what the Government was doing on aid – as opposed to Concern and Trocaire, Gorta and the other NGOs – was apparent. A booklet was published in Dermot Gallagher's time, setting out what was being done with taxpayers' money, an initiative that led to the publication of annual reports which has lasted throughout Irish Aid's history.[11] At the same time, the first grant was given in 1978 to fund development education activities in schools and colleges.

One of the decisions which Dermot Gallagher oversaw was the setting up of Development Cooperation Offices in the priority countries. He remembers being present at a meeting during the State visit of President Nyerere to Ireland when the aid programme was being discussed with the Taoiseach Jack Lynch, and realising that we had to get our presence established on the ground as soon as possible. The system of doing it from HQ was untenable. The first office was opened in Lesotho in 1978, headed by Martin Greene. Offices in Tanzania and Zambia followed shortly after. At the same time, a full resident embassy was opened in Nairobi which meant that Ireland had a presence in East Africa from which aid offices could be accredited.

A significant landmark was reached in August 1978 when Michael O'Kennedy, the Minister who replaced Garret FitzGerald, left for a visit to Africa.[12] A large delegation accompanied the Minister who began his visit in Kenya, then went to Swaziland (where it was hoped to fund projects though in the end little came of this other than technical support by Aer Lingus to the country's airline) and then, unexpectedly, back to Kenya again since one of the giants of Africa's struggle for independence, Jomo Kenyatta, had died. After attending the funeral, the Minister travelled on to Lesotho, Sudan, Zambia and Tanzania. He was impressed with what he saw, and with the aid programme generally. Michael O'Kennedy says:

I thought that targeting a small number of countries was a good
approach as personnel and money were limited. The visit enabled me to see at first hand that this was the right approach.[13]

It was an important moment. Development cooperation had
been strongly identified with Garret FitzGerald and he can justifiably be described as the father of the aid programme. New ministers do not always favour their predecessors' projects; as opposition
spokesman Michael O'Kennedy had spoken favourably about aid
but that did not mean he would give it the same attention as his
predecessor. Storm clouds were beginning to appear over the public finances. The visit to Africa served to confirm the new Minister
in his support for the young programme and to signal cross party
support.

Michael O'Kennedy was especially proud of the successful negotiations on the second Lomé Convention between Europe and the
ACP states which happened to coincide again with Ireland's EEC
Presidency. He found that Ireland's experience of colonialism
helped with the developing countries who recognised that we knew
what it was like to be on the receiving end. One night when he was
chairing the Ministerial Council he had to deal with a difficult Nigerian envoy who harped on about 50 years of colonialism. Michael
O'Kennedy said, 'You only had fifty years; Ireland had a thousand!'

Interest in the Third World reached new heights in Ireland.
This can be illustrated by the fact that in the 1970s *The Irish Times*
ran Development Pages, following the model of their Europe Pages,
which Douglas Gageby had started.[14] Probably the most visible sign
of this interest was the increased profile of the NGOs.

The largest of the Irish NGOs, Concern, was already well established when the Government's aid programme was announced in
1973.[15] (Like Irish Aid, Concern has had a number of name changes:
Africa Concern, then plain Concern and today Concern Worldwide
– not to be confused with Concern International which is a different NGO again). Under the guidance of the formidable Finucane

brothers, Aengus and Jack, by the 1970s and 1980s Concern had developed into a professional, highly respected organisation which was recognised both at home and abroad as a major force. It played a leading role in the international response to a series of disasters starting with the Biafra war, then going on to Bangladesh in 1971 and Ethiopia in 1984.

Concern did not just respond to emergencies; its commitment was to long-term solutions to poverty. Here, too, it had built up an enviable record.

Trocaire's approach has always been different from that of the other NGOs.[16] Its focus was not so much on food aid or disaster relief but on tackling the root causes of hunger and poverty. Trocaire advocated for Ireland to take more radical political positions on Latin America, the Philippines and Cambodia. In this it sometimes found itself at odds with the Department of Foreign Affairs; the level of spending on aid would also become an ever-increasing source of criticism on Trocaire's part with Bishop Eamon Casey a strong voice. But even those who found themselves on the receiving end of Bishop Casey or Brian McKeown's criticisms would acknowledge that Trocaire had a deep knowledge of development and political issues, and that their research activities eclipsed what the Department was doing.[17] A particularly successful fundraising instrument for Trocaire was the Lenten Fasts.

GOAL arrived later than the other two major NGOs. It was set up as a non-denominational humanitarian organisation in 1977 by John O'Shea whose background in sports journalism brought it speedy recognition and support from the sports community. Active in India initially, GOAL soon expanded to Africa where John O'Shea's drive and commitment made it one of Ireland's leading NGOs by the 1980s.

These three are by no means the whole story of Ireland's NGOs. There were many more, large and small. Christian Aid was one of the oldest, dating back to the 1950s when leaders of the Protestant faiths in Ireland and the UK met to discuss the plight of European

refugees after the war. It expanded over the next decades to assisting the developing world and included most of the Protestant
churches among its supporters.

Gorta was still a powerful force. The annual grant it used to receive from the Department of Agriculture was transferred to Foreign Affairs. The Irish Red Cross, established in 1939, was a significant player. International NGOs made their appearance in Ireland –
organisations such as Oxfam and World Vision. UNICEF had a
popular base in Ireland too. And the 1980s saw newcomers arrive
including Self Help and Refugee Trust.

From an early stage, many of the NGOs realised that they
shared common interests. They set up a liaison committee at the
time that the aid programme was being established, called the Voluntary Agencies Liaison Committee. This was replaced in 1976 by a
new structure called CONGOOD – the Confederation of Non-
Governmental Organisations for Overseas Development. CON-
GOOD held its first meeting in February 1977 and by the following
year included 16 organisations. CONGOOD sought to strengthen
NGOs' role in Europe as well as at home. CONGOOD would later
be replaced by Dochas as the umbrella grouping of the NGOs.[18]

One of the first initiatives of the aid programme was a scheme
to co-fund projects with the NGOs. This proved to be very popular
and applications came in thick and fast from NGOs of every shape
and size. In 1978, 69 projects were approved at a total cost of
£440,000; by 1986 the figure was 153 projects with funding totalling
£2.6 million.

It was not just the NGOs that grew over the decade: interest in
development found expression in many ways.

The semi-state bodies organised themselves into an organisation called DEVCO, short for State Agencies Development Cooperation Organisation. The aim of DEVCO, which was funded by its
member organisations, was to ensure that the semi-state bodies
were systematically involved in providing training to opposite
numbers in developing countries. DEVCO's founder was Brendan

O'Regan, head of the Shannon Free Airport Development Company. It was given office space by the Institute of Public Administration, which, as mentioned earlier, was first among those to recognise the potential for Ireland to share expertise with the Third World under its Chair Tom Barrington and his successor Colm O Nuallain.

John Shiels, who spent five years as Chief Executive of DEVCO, recalls the attitude of DEVCO's members:

> There was great enthusiasm to get involved. Big semi-states like Aer Lingus and the ESB were already doing business in Africa – Aer Lingus was managing three national airlines on the continent at one stage – in Lesotho, Swaziland and Botswana. They knew that there was funding available for training and technical assistance from the EEC and the World Bank.[19]

An array of semi-states signed up: likely ones such as Córas Tráchtála and the IDA, which aimed to help developing countries market their exports better and increase foreign investment; An Foras Talúntais, which offered agricultural expertise; and the Irish Management Institute and the IPA, whose forte was training public and private sector people to improve their administrative and management skills. Plus some less likely ones, such as the Institute for Industrial Research and Standards, which helped to develop the Lesotho Handknits project, and Bord na Mona, which advised Rwanda and Burundi about how to get value from their peat bogs.

The academic community was not to be outdone. At first there was the Higher Education Consultation Group; then many third level colleges came together to form Higher Education for Development Cooperation (HEDCO), an umbrella group aiming to increase participation by these seats of learning in Ireland's development cooperation programme. A permanent secretariat was set up by HEDCO in 1978 and in 1981 it became a limited company.[20] HEDCO was funded by the Department of Foreign Affairs and also successfully competed for EEC funding. It was chaired by Professor

George Dawson who had spearheaded the first drive to get the Agency for Personal Service Overseas going.

Meanwhile APSO itself was increasing the number of volunteers it recruited and co-funded with NGOs and missionaries. By 1985 its budget had risen to over £2 million. There was close cooperation with the UN Volunteers programme. The agency extended its sponsorship to more specialised volunteers, introducing new categories of semi-professional and professional volunteers, depending on age, experience and qualifications.

An important initiative was APSO's support for development workers on their return to Ireland.[21] It encouraged the setting up of Comhlamh, a body that grew from its beginnings in 1975 to be an important forum for returned development workers and enabled their experience to find a voice. The returned volunteers were losing out in terms of employment and superannuation rights, and a campaign to secure better conditions ended with the Department of Social Welfare allowing them to earn social welfare credits while abroad which enabled most of them to qualify for the normal PRSI benefits on their return.[22]

APSO's decision to lobby, together with the Institute for Public Administration and the Irish Commission for Justice and Peace, for an agency to run the aid programme instead of Foreign Affairs must have caused friction. Bill Jackson, who was then Chief Executive of APSO, says that relations between APSO and the Department of Foreign Affairs were 'by and large easy'.[23] But he acknowledges that Iveagh House did not favour APSO's semi-state status and there do appear to have been tensions between the two, especially in the early days.[24] This is hardly surprising given the question about ownership of the programme, which surrounded it from the start. Even years later, when the respective roles of APSO and Foreign Affairs were pretty clear-cut, I would still hear stories that APSO had designs on taking over the programme – while APSO personnel would tell me that they felt the Department wanted all along to abolish them!

The Advisory Council on Development Cooperation was duly set up in 1980. Tom Walsh was the first Chair; he was succeeded by Helen O'Neill. The Council did useful work: it carried out a survey of attitudes towards aid and found a high percentage of those surveyed considered that aid money was being well spent or very well spent. In the wake of the Ethiopian famine it carried out an in-depth study of food security in Africa.

An event which would have an enduring impact on the aid programme was the setting up of an Oireachtas Committee on Development Cooperation in 1981. A proposal to establish a Foreign Affairs Committee ran into difficulties with the result that that committee was not established for another six years – well after the Development Committee was up and running. Nora Owen, the first chair of the Development Committee, was only in her new role briefly when the Government fell. The chair should have then gone to Fianna Fáil but no member was interested so she went forward and was elected to a post she held until 1987. She feels that the lack of interest in the position reflects the low level of interest in development issues in the Oireachtas at the time, other than individuals such as Michael D. Higgins, Brendan Ryan and Niall Andrews. After the Ethiopian famine more members of the two Houses began to take an interest.[25]

Nora Owen saw her role as to bed down the aid programme and she made sure that the delegations got a full picture of what Irish Aid was doing in the field. She organised visits for TDs and Senators to the priority countries and held meetings to discuss their findings and the development issues of the day. One of the visits included seeing the situation in Ethiopia after the famine.

The outcome of all this activity was that a significant number of people in Ireland had become involved, in one way or another, with development. This was a change from the days when missionaries were the only link. It had the effect of creating a development community who would put pressure on the Government to spend more and carry forward debate about how aid should be done.

A final word about the agency issue.

The argument that Irish Aid should be run by an agency continued to be active in the 1970s and 1980s with many in the NGO community in favour. It has even surfaced again from time to time, for example during the Ireland Aid review of 2002. Whenever the issue has been considered the conclusion has always been that the Department of Foreign Affairs should continue to run the programme. But the fact that the question has been looked at so often deserves attention.

Is an independent agency the best way to do development? This was a question that arose for the new EU member states and one which they often put to me. I pointed out that there are numerous ways of running an aid programme and no perfect way. The Netherlands, one of the most respected donors, does its aid through its Foreign Ministry; the UK has a full separate ministry, the Department for International Development, with a Secretary of State who sits at the cabinet table; the Swedes set up an agency called SIDA, which is highly regarded; and the Norwegians had a separate agency called Norad, but have recently brought aid back into the Foreign Ministry.

In 2006 the OECD invited me to Istanbul to speak at a conference of newly emerging donors in the region – countries such as Turkey, India and South Korea – and I researched the question again. I found that the verdict of most studies is that there is no 'one size fits all' model for doing development. Countries have to decide which model works best for them and which suits their particular circumstances.

Generally speaking, I think that keeping the aid programme in the Department of Foreign Affairs was a good decision, having regard to the need to account for large sums of public money and the risky circumstances in which aid is delivered. I say this from a practical point of view, in terms of delivering an effective and accountable aid programme. There is a bigger issue of where and how development and foreign policy fit together which needs to be examined more deeply.

It hasn't been perfect or easy. Inexperience and lack of expertise within the Department made for a rocky start. Staff changes which are invariably part of diplomatic life can disrupt development work. Getting suitable candidates for postings in the field could be difficult. But I believe that the approach taken and the choices made as regards how, where and when to spend the aid budget have been justified in most respects. Ireland's aid programme has consistently received praise from the external bodies that look at aid programmes. The lack of specialist experts was the biggest ground for criticism but, as we shall see, that gap has been filled over the years.

Endnotes

1.   Jerome Connolly feels that the tone of the discussion was so sharp because there was a feeling that, while Foreign Affairs might want the aid programme to continue, the Department of Finance were not on board. If the Government did not feel that there was a strong, vigorous constituency out there in favour of development, the budget would be cut. Interview.

2.   *Irish Government Aid to the Third World – Review and Assessment*, Mary Sutton, Joint Trocaire/Irish Commission for Justice and Peace publication, 1977, p. 63. Another joint Trocáire/ICJP publication *One World*, 1976, also criticises the Government's failure to meet the annual 0.05 per cent increases and deplores the fact that no forum to discuss development issues has been set up.

3.   Other key figures in those years were Frank Cogan, who spent six years in charge of the bilateral side and eight in all with the programme; Denis O'Leary, who succeeded Dermot Waldron and Paddy Power as Assistant Secretary in charge; he was followed by Michael Greene and in turn by John Swift. Pat O'Connor, Etain Doyle and John Neary were other senior officials working for the programme at headquarters. And there was a growing cohort of diplomats heading up operations in the field: those who served in the first Development Cooperation Offices, people like Frank Sheridan, David Barry, Pat Curran, Bill Nolan and Gary Ansbro.

4.   *All in a Life* p. 191.

5.   Interview.

6.   The Report of the Public Service Organisation Review Group (known as the Devlin Report), Dublin, 1969 recommended that Foreign Affairs have responsibility for trade and that Córas Tráchtála, the Export Board, report to it rather than the Department of Industry and Commerce. But this, like many of the Report's recommendations, was not implemented.

7.   Michael Guilfoyle and Colm Gallagher, respectively.

8.   Quotes that follow are from *Report of Working Group on Development Aid and Cooperation*, 6 August 1978. The text can be found in the National Archive, DFA file 2008/79/1636. As well as being important for the setting in place of the structures to run the programme, this document gives a detailed description of the main developments in the evolution of Government aid up to that date.

9.   Dermot Gallagher, Secretary General, DFA 2001-2009, interview.

10. Later Sean Hoy and Fintan Farrelly, rural and agricultural specialists respectively, brought much needed expertise, as did Mike Scott who had a business background and had lived for years in Africa.

11. *Development Cooperation: Ireland's Bilateral Programme*, DFA publication, 1979.

12. Accounts of this important visit were given to me by Michael O'Kennedy, Dermot Waldron and Dermot Gallagher. Also on the delegation were Declan Connolly, Bobby McDonagh and Martin Greene.

13. Michael O'Kennedy interview.

14. Denis Kennedy edited *The Irish Times* Developing World page which appeared on a Monday and ran from 1981-84 and he recalls the wide public interest in the issue. Interview. A personal friend of Brendan Nolan, he praised the latter's role in building up the programme, describing him as 'a lone apostle for development' in the early days and determined that it should remain a central part of foreign policy. Bill Jackson sent me a copy of a supplement on Ireland and the Third world carried in *The Irish Times* 22 June 1977.

15. Tony Farmar op cit.

16. See Brian Maye's *The Search for Justice: Trocaire A History*, Veritas Press, Dublin.

17. An example of Trocaire's research capacity was the publication of an annual Development Review. Begun in 1985, it is still published and claims to be the only Irish academic publication dealing with development.

18. *A History of Dochas 1974-2004*, Dochas publication, tells the story of VALC, CONGOOD and the formation of Dochas.

19. John Shiels interview. DEVCO, like HEDCO, ACDC and other development organisations, published annual reports and other publications in its day though these are no longer easy to track down.

20. *HEDCO Annual Report 1981*, p.4.

21. Bill Jackson interview. I am grateful to Donal McDonald for showing me his unpublished account of APSO's history.

22. *Comhlamh.org* the organisation's website, contains a brief history.

23. Bill Jackson interview.

24. John Daly, APSO interview.

25. Nora Owen interview.

26. See DAC publications *A Comparison of Management Systems for Development Cooperation in OECD/DAC Members,* Chang, Fell, Laird and Seif and *Managing Aid: Practices of DAC Member Countries,* OECD 2009.

5

ALL KINDS OF EVERYTHING

If the mid-1970s were a groundbreaking period, the 1980s saw the programme bedding down. Established projects were consolidated and new ones begun in the four priority countries – to differing degrees, with Lesotho seeing the strongest activity and Sudan the weakest.

There was a blip at the start. The aid budget was reduced in 1980 as part of a round of public expenditure cuts. This was all the more serious as the promised annual increases of 0.05 per cent of GNP had only been achieved once in the first seven years of the aid programme's existence.

But the Labour/Fine Gael coalitions which governed for much of the 1980s made serious efforts to keep the budget on track. The budget increases still fell short of the optimistic targets set when the aid programme was first announced, but they marked a solid achievement nonetheless.[1]

The aid programme got a fulltime Minister of State in Jim O'Keeffe, who served both in the short-lived 1981 Government led by Garret FitzGerald and again in the Government that took office in November 1982. He was succeeded in 1986 by George Bermingham.

What sort of projects were funded during this period? The answer is that it was a large and very mixed bag of small and big (but mostly small) projects. Not surprisingly, agriculture, education and health were to the fore, as well as training in all sorts of professions, but some unexpected projects were tried out too. Here are four of the more interesting examples of the types of project funded.

The Basotho Pony Project

Probably the best known of the first projects was the scheme to improve the pony breed in Lesotho through the introduction of Connemara ponies.[2] Irish Aid workers who served there at the time say that Ministers were always asking them how the pony project was doing.

It was the Lesotho side that asked for help with this, probably because a love of horses is one thing which Ireland and Lesotho share. The Basotho pony is a hardy animal, which copes well with extremely tough conditions. Lesotho is a mountainous country, so much so that it is known as the Mountain Kingdom. We are talking high mountains – up to 3,400 metres or three times the height of Carrauntuohill. The country overall is at a high altitude; it is the only independent country in the world which lies entirely above 1,000 metres. Even the capital, Maseru, is 1,200 metres above sea level. The mountainous parts are freezing cold in winter and virtually inaccessible except on foot, by pony or by helicopter. Extreme poverty is the lot of most people living in the mountains.

The native ponies had been around for 200 years but the strain had declined, it is said, because the best ones were taken for use in the Boer War, first by the Boers and then also by the British once they saw how hardy and useful the animals were. One of their advantages is that they have a particular gait between trotting and cantering called 'tripling' which makes the rider's job easier. This skill was being lost in the breed.

The Irish project started in 1978 and had as its goal to preserve and improve the native breed of pony. It aimed to do three things:

- Set up a national stud
- Establish a system of registration for Basotho ponies so as to identify the best stock
- Establish a marketing centre for selling ponies.

The approach was the classical one for many projects at that period: an Irish manager together with expatriate support staff went out to run the project in its first phase; at the same time, training was provided for Lesotho workers with a view to their taking it over in due course. All funding was provided by the Irish side.

The project made good progress to begin with. The Irish manager was assisted by agricultural specialists who came out from Ireland. Two top class Connemara stallions, called Milford Hurricane and Croc an Oir, were shipped out on what was a long and arduous journey from Ireland via Southampton and Capetown. They were based at the breeding centre, which was located in the mountain village of Thaba Tseka. There was a hitch when only one 'performed', but this stallion (Croc an Oir) proved his worth and sired many foals. The training of Lesotho counterparts in Ireland took place at our National Stud and was a success for the trainees. As John Grindle, who monitored the progress of the project, put it, 'They could sink or swim and they swam'.[3]

The high point of the pony project was probably the opening of the National Stud in 1980 where the ceremony was performed by the Queen of Lesotho with the Prime Minister, Chief Jonathan, and the entire cabinet present.

But problems appeared. Local practice did not favour registration of ponies; the custom was to exchange and buy and sell them informally. This put a roadblock in the way of the registration idea. The marketing centre at Mulimo Nthuse also emerged as a difficult proposition: the Irish model of a horse fair where people came to buy and sell in one place was not the Basotho custom.

What did work was pony trekking from a lodge near the marketing centre; tourists took to this and it brought in revenue. One colleague in Irish Aid recalls trekking with the Irish cross ponies in 1998 and still finding them incredibly strong, capable of scaling almost sheer mountain paths.[4]

The pony project carried on until the 1990s but with ever growing doubts about its sustainability. A private investor became interested and this might have worked but the Lesotho authorities did not favour it as they valued the revenue they got from the trekking.

Pat Curran, who was in charge of the programme in the early 1990s, visited Thaba Tseka in 2009 and found little remaining evidence of the breeding station, and there is no trekking any more at Mulimo Nthuse. On the positive side, the practice of pony trekking by tourists is alive at other lodges and you could say that that was one legacy of the Connemara pony project.

Pat Curran believes that it and other novel Irish projects had another beneficial effect in that they helped to get the Irish public to buy into the aid programme. 'It was Fr. McDyer of Glencolmcille writ large,' he says.

George Bermingham, who visited the project in 1986 when he was Minister of State, agrees: 'Projects of that kind served to arouse people's interest not only in the projects themselves but in the aid programme generally.'[5]

They also served to give other Government Departments – in this case Agriculture – and organisations like An Foras Talúntais a role in the programme.

Lesotho Knitting Project

Just as unlikely at first sight as the pony project was a scheme for knitting Aran jumpers in Lesotho! Although, whatever image the country might have outside Africa, the high altitude and cold weather conditions do explain the thinking behind the scheme.

In this case, the initiative came from the Irish side. The Institute for Industrial Research and Standards first proposed a plan for a knitting factory in 1975 and a feasibility study was carried out. The project took on a cottage industry shape with a focus on training Lesothan women to knit the jumpers in their villages. Fashion designer Cyril Cullen from Carrick-on-Shannon was asked to go out to Lesotho to see if the model he had developed in Ireland, whereby women knitted articles in their own homes, could be replicated there. By 1979 the programme was under way and six women came to Carrick for training. Their presence caused a considerable stir. Cyril Cullen incorporated local motifs as variations on the traditional Aran pattern to make the articles more sellable.[6]

Over the following decade the knitting project expanded with as many as 1,500 women involved in the home knitting activities. As well as enabling the women to earn some much-needed money, there was a social side as most of the knitters lived in isolated rural villages. They would come together in small groups, which were irreverently known as 'stitch and bitch sessions'! A central workshop was supervised by a succession of Irish managers who by all accounts threw themselves wholeheartedly into the project.

Two significant obstacles dogged the project over the years and hindered its success. One was the price of wool. Initially this came from South Africa at a reasonable price. But the supply dried up and wool had to be bought from Australia at a higher cost. This dealt the project a big blow. The other big obstacle was the difficulty in marketing the jumpers and other items. Sales in Lesotho itself were too small to sustain the project and strenuous efforts were made to find outlets elsewhere. South Africa was the obvious target and some sales were made there. Attempts were made to interest markets in the US and Germany, but results were disappointing.

Pat Curran told me that one of the project managers stayed on after his contract ended and used the same model of local women knitting and making tapestries. He continued to do business for almost twenty years, selling through an outlet he had in Capetown. Pat also saw local handknits which were separate from the Irish-sponsored ones in recent times. So it could be said that the skillsets which the women learned in the mountains had an impact.[7]

Bord na Mona's Peat Projects

We don't tend to think of peat and turf in an African context but two small countries in the middle of the continent, Rwanda and

Burundi, have extensive boglands. Burundi had and still has a semi-state organisation called Onatour whose mission is to develop the use of peat. Rwanda also grows papyrus which was the subject of research into its possible use for fuel.

In the 1970s the Catholic Relief Services, a US charity, sought funding for a project to develop peat production in Burundi from USAID, the development arm of the US government. USAID in turn asked Bord na Mona for help as they were the recognised leading world authority on turf.

There was a strong motivation to find alternative fuel supplies in the light of the severe degradation of forests by a population that relied on wood to make charcoal for cooking. (Interestingly, the United Nations hosted a conference in 1981 in Nairobi on new and renewable sources of energy, long before it became the pressing issue it is today.) USAID agreed to purchase the capital equipment while the Irish Aid programme funded the secondment of engineers and technicians from Bord na Mona. APSO was responsible for recruitment of the technical staff. At the height of the activity in the two countries, in the mid-1980s, funding from Ireland reached almost £200,000 per year.

Eamon Maher still works for Bord na Mona and he told me of his experiences on the Burundi project.[8] He went out in 1983 with two colleagues to survey a large bog in the north of the country, design a drainage plan and carry out trials using turf cutting machinery. Bord na Mona was quite active in Burundi by then, mostly in the south.[9]

The countryside where Eamon and his partners worked was wild and remote; they were the first white people many of the inhabitants had seen. The only Irish person he came across in his time there was a Sister Teresa who was in her sixties and had been in Burundi for many years. He recalls that when she went home it was her first visit to Ireland in 15 years. There was close cooperation with USAID and the Peace Corps. Eamon would go to the capital, Bujumbura, every few weeks for supplies and the US ambassador would allow him and his colleagues to use the embassy facilities including the swimming pool and tennis court – a welcome break.

At that time three or four bogs were being worked in the south of Burundi. When the Bord na Mona personnel arrived they found everything being done by hand – collecting the peat, packing it into square containers and storing it. They taught people how to use the slean, then sent out tractors suitable for bogs and turf cutting machines. They also helped to build sheds to store the turf. Trainees came to Ireland to learn how to maintain the new equipment.

They encountered problems you would not find in Ireland. For example, the heat of the sun was so intense that there was a risk of the turf drying too quickly. Also, peat produced more heat than charcoal so the traditional cooking pots would burn through. USAID, who was in charge of the marketing side, had to produce special stoves that were more heat resistant.

In the north, where Eamon Maher was based, there was a particular difficulty in that, while there were much bigger bogs there, severe drainage problems existed. There was also a conflict in the local community between the relative merits of peat extraction and agriculture. The Bord na Mona personnel demonstrated that crops could be grown after the turf was removed. But agriculture eventually won the day and the work on peat extraction did not proceed to the same extent as in the south. However, drainage of the bogs was of huge benefit in making more land available for crops.

It was different in the south. When Eamon returned in 1990 he found that turf production had reached around 12-15,000 tonnes a year. Controls had been introduced to slow the drying process. It was still a labour intensive job with lots of people employed turning turf manually, carrying it in sacks to storage hangars and loading it onto lorries for transport to Bujumbura.

The papyrus project was the work of a TCD botanist, Michael Jones, who received funding from the aid programme to explore the use of papyrus as a source of biomass energy.[10] He visited Kenya and Rwanda a number of times and wrote papers based on his research, which indicated that it was worth carrying out trials. His counterpart in the University of Nairobi visited Ireland. But by 1989 funding dried up and the project was not pursued.

Turf is still produced in Burundi though not on the scale of the earlier years. Bord na Mona gets occasional requests for spare parts which it sends out as a goodwill gesture. It seemed fitting that, when the Board hosted the 13th International Peat Congress in Tullamore in 2008, Burundi sent a senior official from Onatour as their representative.[11]

Chilanga Cement

Production of a different kind was the objective of the Chilanga Cement project in Zambia, which received Irish funding from the mid-1970s until 1991. The factory was set up in the 1950s while Zambia was still a British colony and one of its achievements was to provide the cement for the hydroelectric Kariba dam between Zambia and Zimbabwe, one of the largest dams in the world. It was the sole producer of cement in the country and as a result it occupied a key position in Zambia's economy.

There were two factories: one in Chilanga outside Lusaka, the other in Ndola in the Copperbelt region near the border with the Democratic Republic of Congo.

Chilanga had a connection with Irish Cement that dated back to the 1960s, before the aid programme started. Contacts originated through a Danish firm, F.L. Smidth, an international engineering company which supplied cement-making equipment both to Irish Cement and to Chilanga. Irish Cement sent engineers for training to F.L. Smidth in Copenhagen and they in turn would send the engineers to their contacts in different parts of the world. One of these was Chilanga Cement.

I spoke to Eamon Geraghty, who was Acting General Manager/ Technical Director of Chilanga Cement for six years and now holds a senior position with CRH, the parent of Irish Cement. I also spoke to Chris Matthews who was at the Ndola plant for 14 years.[12]

Chilanga was originally privately owned but was then nationalised. Zambia was hit hard by the oil crisis of 1973. Copper prices fell and oil prices rose. The company fell on bad times; it let a lot of expatriate staff go and this resulted in a loss of expertise. Irish Cement's Sean Tangney and Ray Lund carried out an audit of the company's needs and concluded that training was the top priority, with rehabilitation of the productive units also crucial. Eleven Irish Cement staff went out in 1978, including Chris Matthews who started off like the others on a three-year contract but ended up spending 14 years at Chilanga. The salaries of the experts were partly paid by the Irish Aid programme.

Chris Matthews had qualified as an engineer in UCD and worked at the Irish Cement plant in Limerick. His motivation for moving his family out to Zambia was a combination of taking on a new challenge, helping Third World development and financial incentives.

The problems he encountered were the standard ones you would face in any cement factory, he says. The main equipment was okay but the ancillary machinery was a constant headache. Getting spare parts was a big problem: very little was manufactured locally and foreign exchange hard to come by, even for a semi-state company like Chilanga. Applications had to be made via head office and it took a long time to get the parts.

Eamon Geraghty found the same problem with equipment that needed updating. While the Irish Aid programme was subsidising salaries and paying for training, it did not cover capital costs. The Danish aid agency Danida was involved and Eamon says he was 'always knocking on their door looking for money for spare parts'. He found ways of making foreign currency by exporting cement and had a significant success in selling product to Zimbabwe.

Training of staff was a key part of both Chris and Eamon's role. The quality of the Zambian staff was high but they lacked experience. Zambia had a good school of engineering because of the country's mining industry but no practical experience of running a cement factory. A valuable aspect of the project was that Zambian engineers were funded to go for training at Irish Cement's Limerick and Drogheda plants. They came to Ireland in ones and twos and when they returned they gradually replaced the Irish experts.

Eventually Chilanga Cement was privatised. Ireland's aid involvement ended then but Eamon was asked to stay on for three further years during the transition. The Commonwealth Development Corporation was the successful bidder for Chilanga. They packaged the business with a Malawi operation and sold it to the French group Lafarge. Today, Chilanga Cement is very much a going concern and part of the Lafarge family of companies.

Eamon returned to Chilanga in 2008 for a visit.

> To go back after 15 years and see an ultra-modern kiln system in place using raw materials they developed with Ireland's help is quite a feeling. Also to see people trained by Irish Cement in management positions not only in Chilanga and Zambia but in other countries in the region is very satisfying.

He also made an important, more general point:

> There is a need for sustainable jobs to be created if a country is to succeed. A serious problem for developing countries is a lack of venture capital, which hampers entrepreneurship. There is scope for development aid to play a role in industrial projects. Aid organisations cannot help an industry that is not viable and there are plenty of examples in Africa where that was tried and failed. But if an industry is viable – as Chilanga Cement was – aid can help it to move forward and to develop much faster than if such help was not forthcoming.

The pictures above are but four out of many projects, probably a hundred or so when counted up, which the aid programme was funding wholly or in part by the 1980s. They are typical of the variety of initiatives and the different directions the programme was taking in those years.

By then, projects were mostly driven by the Development Cooperation Offices, which were opened in each of the priority countries: Lesotho in 1978, Tanzania and Zambia in 1980, Sudan in 1986. It proved what Dermot Gallagher and others involved at the early stages had realised: a presence on the ground was essential both for identifying projects and for monitoring their progress.

A number of features of the early projects can be identified:

- They were for the most part small scale

- Many were the result of requests from the partner countries

- There was heavy reliance on technical assistance from Ireland

- Projects were not tied to the purchase of goods from Ireland but many projects were linked closely to the availability of Irish expertise

- Grants and not loans were involved; this was a distinctive feature which set Ireland apart from many donors

- The big question about aid raises its head in many of the projects: whether they were sustainable in the long term by the partner country once assistance was removed.

Not all projects were small. Examples of more ambitious initiatives included the Hololo Valley scheme for strengthening agricultural cooperatives in Lesotho, the Kilosa District programme in Tanzania and a programme to improve water supply and agriculture in Zambia's Northern Province. But they were predominantly small and the amounts of money involved were modest.

In the middle of the decade, the Ethiopian famine caught the world's attention. It took time for the full scale of the disaster to become known. Droughts were not uncommon in Ethiopia, but a series of recurring droughts built to a disastrous situation, worsened by the presence of a dictatorial, centrally controlled Marxist system. The usual sources of information – NGOs and journalists – were lacking as the Government restricted their movements. Information was slow to get out.

When it did, the reaction was shock and revulsion. People of my generation will always remember the first BBC reports by Michael Buerk and the pictures of the terrible tragedy unfolding in that country. They will remember the huge outpouring of money which people gave, the impressive number of Irish nurses and volunteers who went to help the starving Ethiopians. And of course they will remember the role played by Bob Geldof in organising Live Aid. (My two strongest memories of the concert are Bob Geldof's emotional haranguing of the viewer – 'give us your ****in' money!' – and in America Jack Nicholson introducing 'a young band from Dublin –U2').

The Ethiopian famine resulted in a big upsurge in financial support for the NGOs; record sums were collected at church gates and in all sorts of fundraisers – £7 million was collected in one day from the public. Perhaps more importantly, Ethiopia demonstrated that volunteer workers could make a difference, even in the grimmest of emergencies. Television was the key to showing the public what was being done by aid workers from Ireland and around the world, just as it had brought attention to the tragedy in the first place.

The Government played its part. The famine is remembered by Jim O'Keeffe, who was Minister of State at the time, and by Frank Cogan, then head of the bilateral programme.[13] The Minister visited the drought stricken region on behalf of the EU as 1984 saw Ireland once again holding the EEC Presidency. He says that the ground looked like an endless dust bowl. Yet when he met the Ethiopian President, Mengitsu, he found him tough and unconcerned about what was happening.

After he reported back to the Government Jim O'Keeffe managed to get an extra £250,000 in food aid which was a lot of money at the time. He is especially proud of the fact that Live Aid was granted a sum equivalent to the amount of the VAT paid on the Live Aid CD and video which were best sellers.

This was the era when Guinness Peat Aviation was a leader in aviation leasing. GPA offered the use of two planes, which were duly filled with supplies, particularly by Concern, and flown out to Ethiopia. Frank Cogan remembers overseeing the packing of the supplies at the airport with Mary Humphries of Concern. An Irish plane was the first to arrive in Addis Ababa with relief supplies. The IFA got involved and Leinster Shipping provided a ship at reduced rates, which took out foodstuffs including wheat. In addition, Ireland was instrumental in getting the EEC to make a massive food aid donation to Ethiopia.

Ireland's contribution to Ethiopia was described as 'one of the best and one of the quickest international responses'[14] – not to mention the incalculable contribution which Bob Geldof made through his passionate activism.[15]

Another landmark for the aid programme was reached in 1985 when Ireland joined the Development Assistance Committee of the OECD. Long promised, this step confirmed Ireland's determination to be numbered among the top echelon of donors and to submit its aid programme to scrutiny by its peers.

In 1986 the programme was reviewed for the first time by the DAC and the quality of its activities was praised.[16] Development Cooperation Division moved to new, bigger premises in Harcourt Street. But the following year, just as everything seemed to be progressing well, the programme suffered a major blow.

Endnotes

1. See Table 1 in the Appendix showing ODA figures from 1974-2010.

2. I am grateful to Pat Curran, one of Irish Aid's longest serving officers, for his assistance with the sections on the Basotho ponies and the handknitting project. Pat spent 16 years in all on aid postings, including as head of mission in Uganda and Zambia and head of development in South Africa. He served two stints in Lesotho, from 1990-1994 and from 2008-2010.

3. John Grindle, the programme's first economist and author of numerous reports and evaluations for Irish Aid, interview.

4. Nicola Brennan, Senior Development Specialist, served in South Africa, Uganda, Zambia, head of HIV/AIDS unit 2003-09, interview.

5. George Bermingham, Minister of State for Overseas Development 1986-87, interview.

6. The story of Cyril Cullen's involvement with the Lesotho handknits project is told in the book *Knot Sure: The Life and Work of Fashion Designer Cyril Cullen* by his daughter Margot Cullen, Blackwater Press, Dubli,n 2005, pp. 164-9, which includes a dozen photos of the knitters, designs etc.

7. Interview.

8. I am grateful to Eamon Maher, Bord na Mona, for his assistance with the section on BNM's peat projects in Africa.

9. Quite a large number of BNM employees worked in Burundi. Those mentioned by Eamon Maher included Patrick Keating, Noel Craven, Justin McCarthy, Jim Martin, Patrick O'Rourke, Frank Carolin, Sean Casey, Gerry Carroll and John Maher.

10. Michael Jones interview.

11. Eamon Maher interview.

12. Thanks to Eamon Geraghty and Chris Matthews for their assistance with the section on Chilanga Cement.

13. Jim O'Keeffe, interview; Frank Cogan head of bilateral aid programme 1978-1986, interview.

14. Frank Cogan interview.

15. A detailed account of Ireland's response to the Ethiopian famine can be found in the *Annual Report 1985* pp. 39-44. See also Bob Geldof *Is That It?*, Sidgwick and Jackson, London, 1986. Tony Farmar's book on Concern (pp 124-44) and Brian Maye's on Trocaire (pp 138-53) give these organisations' perspectives. Michael Buerk's account of his reporting from Ethiopia is in his memoir *The Road Taken*, Hutchinson, London, 2004, pp. 274-362.

16. DAC Peer Review of Ireland, 1986, OECD publication.

6

SHOW ME THE MONEY

In the 1980s the aid programme was going strong. Yet, when I took over responsibility in 1991, what I found was a demoralised, dysfunctional division.

People working there wanted out; elsewhere in the Department people ran a mile from Development Cooperation Division. The new head of the bilateral side, Hugh Swift, who took up duty on the same day as me, recalls that the atmosphere in Harcourt Street at that time was one of despondency and low morale.[1]

What happened in the previous few years to bring this about? There had been no scandal over unaccounted funding – the greatest risk for any aid operation – and the programme was regularly praised for the high quality of its work, even if the scale was small. What had caused the change of fortune?

The answer was simple: money. Or rather the lack of it. From 1987 to 1990 the programme suffered the worst cuts in its history.

It was not just aid that was cut. This was the era of 'Mack the Knife'. All public spending was being chopped to bring the country's spending under control. After the elections in 1987 Ray McSharry was appointed Minister for Finance with a brief to knock the country's finances into shape. Charles Haughey, once a big spender, had seen the light and gave his Finance Minister his backing.

No one could deny that the economy was in a bad way and that radical measures were needed. It was clear even before 1987 that something had to give but the Fine Gael-Labour coalition was unable to agree on the drastic steps that were needed.[2]

No area of expenditure was spared by the new Fianna Fáil Government. But the aid budget was hit harder than most. The figures tell the story:

	£ Million	% of GDP
1986	41	0.25
1987	39	0.22
1988	32	0.18
1989	35	0.17
1990	35	0.16

The key benchmark, aid as a proportion of GNP, saw the trend of earlier years reversed. The cuts dwarfed the previous occasion the programme had suffered cuts – in 1980 – which was also the result of a need to cut back public spending generally.

Money had continued to be tight in the 1980s and the targets the Fine Gael/Labour coalition set themselves proved hard to meet. But the momentum had been maintained when Garret FitzGerald was Taoiseach. Now all of that was in question. The goal of Ireland having a decent-sized aid programme seemed to be fading.

When I took up duty the impact of the cuts was everywhere to be seen. The Development Cooperation Office in Khartoum had been closed in 1987, less than a year after it was opened. The embassy in Nairobi, one of only three missions which Ireland had on the entire African continent, had also been closed, the only time until then that an embassy has been closed on financial grounds. HEDCO, the body which sought to expand links between third level institutions in Ireland and the developing world, had ceased to function because funding was no longer available.

I remember thinking that if cuts of the order of the previous four years continued it would mean the end of the programme. We would be back to the pattern of the early 1970s – a few payments to the UN plus our compulsory EEC contributions and scrabbling for some money for disasters.

The nature of the job to which I was assigned symbolised the decline: I was to be in charge not only of aid but also Foreign Earnings, a vamped up version of the old Trade Section that I started out in. The two jobs had been separate but now they were combined.

The Minister of the day made it clear to me what his priorities were:

> 'You have two jobs. One involves spending public money; the
> other is about bringing money into the economy. I expect you
> to concentrate on the one that brings in money.'

Newly promoted, I was undaunted by the challenge of taking on two roles. I had worked in the Foreign Earnings Division before and liked the work. It had a small but dedicated staff, the only drawback being a long-running feud between the Departments of Foreign Affairs and Industry and Commerce about who should be in charge of trade. I visited Brazil, China and Japan wearing my trade hat and made two visits to Iran amid efforts to try to get a ban they had imposed on Irish beef exports lifted.

But I soon found that there were formidable obstacles to doing the aid job well.

One of the first documents that landed on my desk was a report by the Advisory Council on Development Cooperation.[3] It was highly critical of most aspects of the aid programme. It argued for a board to be set up to oversee the aid programme, reviving the old issue of an agency. It claimed, in effect, that as far as development was concerned, the Department of Foreign Affairs was not up to the job. It was a comprehensive, well-researched report and therefore not to be ignored. I queried, and would still query, a lot of its findings but it did point up shortcomings – and not only in the declining budget. A central point it made – that there was a serious absence of any policy document setting out the programme's objectives – was something I took on board and sought to rectify.

Reading the Council's report years later brings back memories of the mood of the day. The newspapers were full of Bishop Casey's fulminations against the Government for its failure to keep ODA spending on track. I stood in for the Minister of State at a public panel discussion of the Council's report and I can vividly recall the angry mood of the audience over the cuts and the Department's perceived supine reaction.

It didn't help that a decision had been taken to abolish the Advisory Council on Development Cooperation. The development community simply did not believe the reason given – cost grounds – and linked it to the critical report the Council had written. They saw it as a case of shooting the messenger. They probably had a point.

Given the profile which success or failure in increasing the aid budget has for those who follow the development agenda, it is worth pausing to look at this aspect in some detail.

The 0.7 Per Cent Target

Spending 0.7 per cent of a country's Gross National Product on development aid is the ultimate goal of all donors. The figure of 0.7 per cent emerged at the UN in 1970 when the international drive to help poor countries was at its height.

Reaching the target is a formidable challenge. For many years only four countries managed it: Sweden, Norway, Denmark and the Netherlands. One or two have even gone further and achieved 1 per cent of GNP. In recent years Luxembourg has joined the select group to reach the 0.7 per cent target. The UK and Spain have seen big rises too. But even the best performers have experienced falls as well as rises.[4]

Setting a benchmark in GNP terms is fair as it takes account of the donor country's size and wealth. If the rating were to be in volume terms only, the US would be at the top. But, in GNP terms, the US comes well down the donors' list, as it is not as generous as other countries in relation to its wealth. Where the US does make a big difference is in emergencies. America's logistical capacity, with its Hercules transport planes and Chinook helicopters, is second to none. Other donors that are large in volume terms are Germany, France and Japan, but they usually sit in the middle of the list in terms of percentage of GNP.

A Moving Target

A problem with the 0.7 per cent target is that it is a moving target. Gross National Product does not remain static. It usually increases although, as we have learned in Ireland in recent years, it can also decline.

There is a paradox in that the trend towards increasing aid is likely to be strongest when a country is faring well economically and hence it needs more money to show a GNP percentage increase. As the percentage is the main barometer for judging performance, it can look as if the Government is not making a great effort even though the volume increase may be substantial.

Similarly, if GNP is declining, a country's record can look better than it is. The recent crisis in Ireland's public finances has resulted in a substantial cut in the aid budget, yet the percentage figures have continued to look quite good because GNP has declined!

What is Ireland's Record on the 0.7 Per Cent Target?

Ireland has made enormous progress from a very low base of £1 million, representing 0.04 per cent of GNP in 1973, to a high point of €920 million or 0.59 per cent in 2008. In 2007, Ireland was the sixth biggest donor in the world on a per capita basis.[5]

Who Decides What Counts as Official Development Assistance?

The Development Assistance Committee of the OECD – known as the DAC – is the arbiter of what is and is not to be counted as Official Development Assistance. The DAC secretariat is located in Paris at the OECD headquarters. Its meetings are attended by the 24 biggest government and multilateral aid donors. The DAC secretariat measures the donor countries' performance according to agreed criteria and reports on this every year.

For a country to join the DAC it must demonstrate that it has a substantial aid programme, the institutions and policies necessary to manage an aid programme and the necessary statistical capacity. The DAC tries to encourage new members to join and it has a halfway house for observer donors. But the entry criteria are strict and that is why it would have been difficult for Ireland to join in the 1970s when the programme was still in its infancy. Ireland finally joined the DAC in 1985.

The DAC's statistical department examines returns made by donors to confirm that they are genuine aid; it also rules on which countries qualify as aid recipients. Ireland has never had a problem with this as our partner countries are some of the poorest in the world. But some DAC members assist what are known as Middle Income Countries – typically in Latin America and Asia– which may not be eligible to count as aid.

Equally, there is debate among the DAC members – sometimes a fierce debate – about what kind of aid should qualify. For example, some countries argue that the cost of peacekeeping activities should count as ODA on the grounds that conflict prevents the delivery of aid and peacekeeping therefore is part of the overall aid effort. Opponents say the lines between the two should not be blurred and so far that argument has won out. Another issue that has come forward is whether costs involved in accommodating refugees and asylum seekers should count. Like peacekeeping costs, these can be very considerable, as they were for Ireland in the Celtic Tiger years.

Another important role of the DAC is its peer reviews of donors' performance. Conducted every four to five years, these reviews do not pull their punches if they find shortcomings, yet they are seen by donors as a fair, independent assessment of performance.[6]

The Budget Process: How it Works

Back home, the budgetary process starts early, much earlier in fact than most people realise.

It begins in the early summer when the Department of Finance sets out its Review and Outlook for the year ahead. Once the Government signs off on this, Finance sends out an Estimates Circular asking departments to send in their bids for the following year – nowadays usually with a deadline of around end September – with guidelines about the state of the public finances. Finance looks at bids to see if there are any howlers, then meet departments at official level after which they report to Government on progress.

A crucial stage is what are called Ministerial Bilaterals which normally take place in the autumn. This is when the Minister, accompanied by his or her officials, sits down with the Minister for Finance who is also accompanied by officials who deal with the relevant departmental vote.

Having accompanied the Minister for Foreign Affairs and the Minister of State for Development at quite a few of these meeting, I can say that the dynamic at the Ministerial Bilaterals is very different from meetings between officials. The nature of the meeting is political. Ministers are judged by their capacity to bring in a good departmental budget but they also have to take account of the bigger picture: Government policy on spending, the state of the public finances and the competition from departments which have just as strong a claim as theirs.

So it is a case of horse-trading. I would like to have brought some of my more idealistic staff to these meetings to see how the world works!

The most common issue raised about the aid budget was the lack of visibility of the work of Irish Aid. There was some talk too of whether Ireland should not get more economic benefits from the expenditure on ODA. But the general tone was one of endorsement of the programme; the big issue being how much should be allocated for the coming year.

Obviously, the prospects of an increase in a Department's allocation are much brighter if the economy is booming. But it is never easy. Overall, it comes down to the question of how to slice the national cake, which is limited even in the good times.

Outstanding issues go back to the Cabinet for decision. Nothing is finally decided until the budget speech. Even then, there can be changes, for example if exchequer returns are less good than expected. One piece of advice I gave my successors was to keep a close eye on the budget allocation money right through the process. I have seen figures agreed only to be cut very late in the day.

The Oireachtas Foreign Affairs Committee considers the estimates before they go on to the final stage which is the passing of the Appropriation Bill.

Representations arguing for the aid budget to be increased often came in too late to make a difference. I remember one NGO asking me if there was still time to write to the Minister the day before the Minister for Finance made his budget statement. I was told that 'the Minister for Finance can change his mind right up to the moment he enters the Dáil chamber'.

This may theoretically be true, but the chances of influencing the Minister to change his or her mind after a long, and usually difficult, budget process are remote.

Foreign Affairs Has Two Votes

The Department of Foreign Affairs belongs to the small number of Government departments which have more than one vote. Vote 28 is Foreign Affairs while Vote 29, International Cooperation, is the heading under which a lot of the aid is allocated. The bulk of Vote 28, Foreign Affairs, goes on salaries and the cost of running embassies and consulates.[8]

There can be some tension between the two Department votes when it comes to arguing the case for more money. In the early days the International Cooperation Vote was modest and it was a case of asking the Government of the day to do its best for ODA after the Foreign Affairs needs had been seen to. In more recent times the budget under Vote 29 has increased until it dwarfs the Foreign Affairs Vote.

The nature of the discussion of the two votes differs. Pressure on individual Foreign Affairs lines of spending is very strong. The approach to Vote 29 is not to enter into detail but to consider the overall total and how it fits with Government commitments. It could be awkward sitting there as hundreds of millions were being considered for ODA while detailed arguments took place about relatively small sums for the Irish abroad or culture or the opening of a new embassy.

The Vote for International Cooperation is Not the Only Source of ODA

Vote 29 – International Cooperation – provides the bulk of spending on aid. But significant amounts come from other sources.

The biggest items not included in Vote 29 are the part of Ireland's contribution to the EU budget which is calculated as being for development cooperation; Ireland's contribution to the European Development Fund; monies contributed to the World Bank group of organisations by the Department of Finance, and contributions made by the Department of Agriculture to the World Food

Programme. 'Other ODA', as these figures are called, can amount to a considerable total. In 2008, for example, 'other ODA' amounted to €160 million.[9]

Two technical points are worth mentioning. One is that the main funding for the World Bank group (mainly the Bank's soft loan arm which is called the International Development Association) is set by statute and comes out of central funds so it is not included in the Estimates. Debate on these contributions takes place when legislation relating to the World Bank is being renewed.

The other issue that provides a headache for those monitoring spending is that uncertainty exists about a number of the elements of spending and it can be late in the year before the picture is clear. The EU contribution is only an estimate and the contributions to the World Bank/IDA, like those for the European Development Fund, rise or fall depending on how much money these organisations draw down. If the variations are big enough they can change the percentage of GNP achieved in a given year.

Do Targets Have a Value?

Targets have featured prominently in the aid debate from the start. The overall 0.7 per cent figure was accepted early on by all political parties as the ultimate goal. The days of saying that Ireland would aim for 0.7 per cent 'when resources permit' ended in 1973. So it is the interim targets which the Government of the day sets on the road to reaching 0.7 per cent that are seen as the real benchmark of how committed a Government is to development.

Ever since Garret FitzGerald set up the aid programme, interim targets have been set. In the 1970s the aim was to increase funding by 0.05 per cent of GNP per year. For a time in the 1980s the target was lowered to 0.015 per cent per year, reflecting the fact that money was very tight. In the 1990s the earlier annual target of 0.05 per cent was reinstated. In the Celtic Tiger years the targets became

much more ambitious as the goal of reaching 0.7 per cent looked
feasible.

Reaching interim targets has proved problematic. So why set
targets at all? The answer is that Government-set targets are the
only argument which cut ice with the Department of Finance. If
they were not there, aid increases would be reduced to a pious aspi-
ration. The politicians I spoke to all agreed on this. As one put it:

> If there were no targets there would be no incentive to raise
> spending. The catch cry is 0.7 per cent and it is well known
> even if people may be uncertain as to what it means. The target
> goes higher with economic growth but its existence forces us to
> make a greater effort.[10]

From time to time there have been calls for the aid budget to be
ring-fenced, even covered by legislation, which would require the
Government to raise it annually by certain percentages. I think that
Governments have to be in a position to decide priorities when
public money is being allocated. It would tie their hands if legislation were to protect one area of spending. Also, by putting aid into
a special category, it would imply that it was of greater importance
than any other area of spending, which could alter the generally
positive public attitude towards the aid budget. Public support is
essential.

ODA needs champions in the cabinet, or at least some who are
well disposed. The ideal is if the Ministers for Foreign Affairs and
Finance and the Taoiseach are all on board but that is a rare con-
juncture. The best example I can think of is in the UK when Tony
Blair was Prime Minister, Gordon Brown was Chancellor and Clare
Short and Hillary Benn Secretaries of State for International Development. (I am sure it helped that the Secretary of State sits at the
cabinet table.)

Garret FitzGerald undoubtedly favoured the aid vote both as
Minister and as Taoiseach. 'Cabinet colleagues knew that there

were two issues I would not be budged on,' he told me, 'Northern Ireland and ODA.'[11]

Jim O'Keeffe and George Bermingham both remember going directly to Garret when the budget was under threat during their time as Minister of State. Later, Bertie Ahern would be a consistent supporter of the aid programme.

Champions of Vote 29 were thin on the ground at the time of the 1987 cuts. Charlie Haughey showed no interest in aid other than very occasional grants for assistance following high profile disasters. The programme had never seen such cuts as in the late 1980s, which explains my dismay when I came in.

Those in charge during the lean years sought to maintain the programme as best as possible.

Sean Calleary served two terms as Minister of State in charge of development, from 1987 to 1989 and from 1989 to 1992. He travelled to the priority countries and earned respect for the interest he took in the job. An engineer by profession, he brought his skills in that field and his knowledge of local government to bear. 'Even though money was tight,' he says, 'we managed to scrape together funding somehow.'[12]

He was struck by how little people wanted – a roof to be repaired or a supply of rubber gloves in a hospital. He had tremendous respect for the work done by the missionaries. And he was impressed by the way the programme focussed on women's role in development. 'I believe that Irish Aid was one of the first aid agencies to focus on this and to design a number of programmes specifically for women.'

The Development Cooperation Offices were proving their worth. One of their tasks was to oversee the Technical Cooperation Agreements between Ireland and the priority countries. These agreements were drawn up at the start of the aid relationship; they spelled out which areas and projects would be developed during the period covered by the agreement. In reality the agreements were expressions of good intentions and were not legally binding.

But the argument could be made that projects committed to under them had to be completed.

Etain Doyle was head of the Bilateral Programme during the difficult years of the cuts. In 1987, her first year on the job, the budget cut was huge and then there were further cuts every year until she left in 1991. Etain came to Foreign Affairs from the Department of Finance as a result of a service-wide competition, one of John Boland's efforts to increase mobility across the public service. She found that she had to manage on less and less money; she saw her task as to try not to let the programme disappear, 'just not to fall over the edge'.[13]

She used her Finance training and the fact that she is a Certified Accountant to improve systems and structures which were still very basic. She was aware that Africa had numerous half finished aid projects and resolved to make everything the programme dealt with as sustainable as possible. She strengthened the review and evaluation capacity by bringing in Mike Scott with his business background; she reorganised the NGO co-financing scheme; as the Disaster Relief allocation had been sharply reduced, she wangled money for unexpected emergencies from anywhere she could including Lotto funds.

But it was hard going. Relations between the Department and the NGOs were overshadowed by the cuts. The Advisory Council's Report revealed the development community's frustration and anger at the turn the programme's fortunes had taken.

Despite my doubts about the viability of a programme where funding was falling sharply, there was no alternative but to go on. My first year saw an increase of £10 million in the budget. This was deceptive in that it was due to unusually large draw downs of EU and World Bank funding as well as a one-off contribution to states affected by the first Gulf War. But it was a change from the picture of the previous four years.

I began to visit the priority countries. Zambia and Tanzania were suggested for my first visit but these sounded like success stories and it seemed to me more important that I saw one of our troubled places. I went instead to Sudan where I was shown our projects in Wad Medeni by Niall Toibin, who was flying the flag after the Development Cooperation Office was closed by the cuts. Our Ambassador in Cairo, Eamon O Tuathail, was accredited to Sudan and he visited there often and devoted much time to ensuring that the programme was kept alive.[14]

Niall was the perfect host (although the tour of the butchers' market he brought me on would turn anyone into a vegetarian!) and it was obvious that he was giving his all to make the agricultural, forestry and educational projects work. He had an uphill task. Sand blew through the classrooms of the little schools we were funding. The biggest project was the Gezira dairy where I learned the value of asking direct questions. Everyone was being very positive but the place seemed unusually quiet and by dint of persistent questioning I learned that the dairy was producing only 10 per cent of its planned output. (By a tragic irony two of Irish Aid's stalwarts, Niall Toibin and Sean Courtney, both of whom served in Sudan, died much too young.)

The strongest impression I took back from that visit was not from Wad Medeni but a camp for displaced people outside Khartoum. The Sudanese Government did not want the refugees from the civil war in the south close to the capital so they issued a decree expelling them with any meagre possessions they had to a barren place miles from Khartoum. I visited the camp for the displaced with young volunteers from Concern and GOAL. 'Biblical' is the word I would use to describe the scene as thousands of people tried to organise their belongings and find a space to exist. My naive thought was: what is the plan for these people? Where are they supposed to go and how can they survive? The answer was that the Government didn't care – they were offering them no alternative; this was it.

Yet here were Irish men and women helping as I always came to expect in such situations. One GOAL volunteer, a young midwife newly arrived in Sudan, told me how she had treated a baby who needed a spinal tap, a simple procedure back in Ireland but here there was no equipment available. She used her free day to go to Khartoum and search for it. Her search was in vain and when she told a Sudanese doctor about it he told her sharply that she should stop playing God, they did what they could with the instruments at their disposal and that was what she should focus on.

I have seen much worse scenes in places like Somalia and Rwanda and the *favelas* in Rio, but for some reason that picture of the thousands of families huddling on the desert is one that has stuck in my mind.

Many of those I interviewed for this book recalled similar individual experiences that lodged in their memory.

Nora Owen recalled a visit to the Philippines in 1982, driving down the main street of Manila which was well built and lined with Chinese lanterns put up at great expense by Imelda Marcos. Then there was a bump as the good road ended and it turned into a rutted track. Here people were living in abject poverty with sewage flowing and people in cardboard boxes. The thought that came to her mind was that just one of Imelda Marcos' Chinese lanterns would have paid for 10 houses. 'It was like moving from heaven to hell. If ever I needed persuasion about the plight of the poor, this confirmed it.'[5]

Rodney Rice, who presented his popular *Worlds Apart* programme on RTÉ radio for 14 years, saw the dire effects of poverty and the denial of fundamental rights so often that it became less shocking. But he singled out the *favelas* in Rio and poverty in West Africa as two recent examples that shook him. And he was shocked from the start by the poverty in the South African townships. 'It was not just poverty, it was dehumanisation. During apartheid the black people were kept down by a battery of laws that were meant to dehumanise them.'[16]

The visits I made to see other examples of Irish Aid's work gave a more positive picture. In fact, the mood in the field was more upbeat than back at headquarters. Brendan Rogers, who took charge of the Zambian programme in 1991, told me that even with only £2 million he found that there was plenty he could do.[17]

In the priority countries in those days I would be met by a phalanx of Irish technical assistants (TAs as they were known), hydrologists, agricultural experts, medical specialists, teachers and lecturers, engineers, the people hired to run the many projects which existed then.

I saw some of the bigger projects that were under way. One that I did not see was the earliest – the Hololo Valley project in Lesotho. This was an ambitious programme on the model of integrated rural development programmes, which aimed to bring people living in rural areas above the poverty line by providing funding to a range of agricultural and other sectors. The project had mixed reviews. John Grindle, the economist who was more or less single-handedly in charge of evaluation at that time, thinks that the programme was not well planned or executed. But we had entered into a five-year commitment with the Lesotho Government and felt we had to see it through. Some on the ground in Lesotho felt it had an impact.[18]

I did visit the biggest programme of the day, the Kilosa District Development Programme in Morogoro region in Tanzania. It began modestly with a carpet factory and a farm but it 'growed' like Topsy: there were road improvements, advice was given on agriculture, trees were grown in arid places, local dispensaries were built and health training given, a large trade school was built in Mikumi and training provided for carpenters, electricians and mechanics. The range of activities carried out with Irish funding was extraordinary; it was hard to say what activities Irish Aid was not involved in throughout the district.

I also visited Northern Province in Zambia, another large-scale programme. It was really remote; you felt that just a few steps from a village would bring you to the Africa of childhood with jungles and wild animals. Water was one of the great issues for this very poor district and the drilling of wells was one of Irish Aid's first achievements. Donal Denham, the first head of the Development Cooperation Office in Zambia, believes that simple technology which did not require expensive maintenance was the key to success.[19] Villagers were taught how to make concrete rings for wells with simple pump mechanisms. Over 100 wells were eventually drilled in the Kasama district. The visitor would be shown the huge improvement that a low-tech well could bring to a village and how it eased the burden on so many, women in particular.

There were plenty of other projects in the programme to be proud of: maternity clinics in Zambia run by a remarkable nun, Sister Mona Tyndall; the Centre for Accountancy Studies in Lesotho; medical laboratories in Zambia and Lesotho; agricultural projects in Pemba; all sorts of areas where training and consultancy advice were being funded.[20]

I came back from seeing these projects and programmes convinced that the aid programme was delivering real value to poor people. But money was the key and there we were on the back foot.

Then help came from an unexpected quarter. Just when it seemed that aid was no longer a high priority, Somalia happened.

Endnotes

1. Hugh Swift, head of the bilateral programme 1991-94, later Ambassador to Egypt, South Africa and Singapore, interview.

2. 'In the 1980s the Irish economy was in crisis. During a prolonged recession, the unemployment rate approached 18 per cent in spite of massive emigration. The spectre of national insolvency loomed as the debt to GNP ratio approached 130 per cent.' *Principles of Economics*, Turley, Moloney, O'Toole; Gill and Macmillan, Dublin, 2001, p. 285.

3. *Ireland and the Third World: An Official Overview of ODA*, Advisory Council on Development Cooperation, 1991.

4. See Table 2 in the Appendix showing DAC figures for member states' ODA performance in 2010.

5. See Table 3 in the Appendix for performance in cash and as percentage of GNP.

6. The *OECD.org* website spells out the DAC's role.

7. Thanks for help on the budget process to Phil Furlong, Assistant Secretary, Department of Finance (later Secretary General of the Department of Arts, Sport and Tourism and Chair of the Dept of Foreign Affairs Audit Committee) who dealt with the DFA vote.

8. Estimates are published annually with the breakdown of DFA's two votes.

9. Irish Aid's *Annual Reports* include detailed statistics on expenditure including the breakdown of Other ODA.

10. Bertie Ahern interview; all other politicians I spoke to took a similar line.

11. Garret FitzGerald interview.

12. Sean Calleary interview.

13. Etain Doyle, head of bilateral programme 1986-91, interview.

14. Eamon O Tuathail sent me an interesting memo on his experiences in Nigeria during the Biafran war and in Sudan and his time as Ambassador to South Africa.

15. Nora Owen interview.

16. Rodney Rice interview.

17. Brendan Rogers interview.

18. John Grindle, interview. Gerry Gervin, Ambassador to Lesotho 2010, said that people on the ground still speak well of it.

19. Donal Denham interview.

20. The late Mona Tyndall's maternity clinics were a must for visitors to Lusaka in the 1980s and 1990s. Helen Labanya, who trained under Sister Mona, spoke glowingly about the impact her mentor's approach made in improving the quality of perinatal care in Zambia. Mona's aim was sustainability and this was achieved in that the clinics are now wholly run by Zambians and Mona Tyndall's model has been followed by other donors. Helen Labanya interview.

7

SOMALIA

My first spell as head of the aid programme coincided with horrors in Somalia and Rwanda, in 1992 and 1994 respectively, on a scarcely credible scale.

It would be inappropriate to call what happened in these two countries disasters. The dictionary defines a disaster as 'a sudden event, such as an accident or a natural catastrophe that causes great loss of life or damage'. It is something that *befalls* us. The 2004 Tsunami was a disaster, an act of God if you will. What happened in Somalia and Rwanda was not an accident or a natural catastrophe: it was very much the work of man.

Events in Somalia and Rwanda have much in common, though there were big differences too. The direct cause in both cases was political in the form of struggles for power. The origins of these struggles were deeprooted and complex. The malign legacy of colonialism played a big part, not only in sowing seeds of division within the two countries but also in stirring up the explosive issues of land and resource ownership. Some countries – rich ones but African too – continued to play politics even as the death tolls of the civilian populations mounted. Arms suppliers from both the Soviet Union and the West made their usual deadly contribution. The outside world gave generous humanitarian help but only after their publics were alerted by the NGOs who led the way. The capacity of the international community, and the UN in particular, to address such extreme crises was tested and found wanting.

Somalia and Rwanda also have in common the positive role played by Ireland. On both occasions the Irish people maintained their reputation for generous giving, not only in cash but through the service of hundreds of volunteers who went out with Concern, GOAL, Trocaire, the Red Cross and numerous other NGOs. The Defence Forces played a blinder, as they can be relied to do in every emergency. At political level, Ireland was active in highlighting both tragedies at an early stage and in pressing the international community to do more.

The stories of Somalia and Rwanda could fill up volumes on their own. Indeed, the literature – books, UN reports and resolutions, articles, even films – is immense. I have listed a few for those who wish to get a better understanding of what happened, but they are only a fraction of the works that have appeared.[1]

The story of Ireland's contribution, too, has been told often. Media coverage at the time was extensive and memoirs and accounts have since appeared. What follows is how it looked from my perspective.

Somalia changed the fortunes of the aid programme radically and I will come back to that in the next chapter.

August 1992 was when the crisis in Somalia first really came to the forefront of public attention, not that it could be said to have come out of the blue. The World Food Programme had been warning of the danger of famine in the country for over a year. Charlie Bird sent back reports for RTÉ.[2] Concern started operating feeding stations in Baidoa and Mogadishu in April of that year. The NGOs warned the Minister for Foreign Affairs, David Andrews, that an already grave situation was deteriorating rapidly.

There had been a changing of the guard in Iveagh House: Albert Reynolds succeeded Charles Haughey as Taoiseach in February of that year; David Andrews was now Minister and Brendan Daly Minister of State for Overseas Development.

Ministers for Foreign Affairs tended to leave the development side to the junior Minister, especially when funding was low. David

Andrews took a different approach. His record shows that he took
an interest in people on the receiving end of injustice. He took up
causes like the Birmingham Six and East Timor long before they
became mainstream issues.

In the summer of 1992 the clamour about the situation in Somalia had reached the stage where it was clearly a tragedy out of the
ordinary. The NGOs, Concern in particular, were sounding the
alarm bells in the face of what seemed like an indifferent international response.

The immediate cause of the famine and deaths was a bitter fight
for control of the country between former allies who had ousted
the Marxist regime of Siad Barre. There was an interim government
headed by Ali Mahdi Mohamed, which was opposed by General
Mohamed Aideed. Both sides were armed to the teeth. Bloody
fighting cost thousands of lives and left the capital Mogadishu and
other towns in ruins. The capital itself remained a major theatre of
the fighting with a battle line running through the ruined city. Civilians fled, across the border to Kenya and other neighbouring
countries, to centres such as Baidoa and Afghoi. Food supplies
could not get in because of the fighting or else were hijacked by the
fighters.

David Andrews decided to travel to Somalia to see the situation
for himself. He says in his memoirs that he did so against official
advice.[3] I cannot remember being asked for advice; I daresay that if
asked I would have advised caution. In any event, it was a courageous decision as the conflict in Somalia was severe and the UN
presence there fragile. Hugh Swift, the head of the Bilateral Programme, was in South Africa with Minister of State Brendan Daly
and he recalls me ringing him from Dublin and asking him to go to
Somalia to prepare for the Minister's visit. This he did, basing himself in Nairobi and linking up with Concern to arrange the visit.[4]

David Andrews found things even worse than he had been led
to believe, with thousands dying of starvation and disease every
day. As he puts it in his memoirs:

What I witnessed was a horror story of the first order: people
dead and dying on the sides of the streets in the various towns
to which I went, famine and chaos everywhere. I vividly remember one particular sight outside a Baidoa feeding station.
There was an area as big as a football field with rows and rows
of bundles of rags, which were in fact starving people. The feeding station could take in only a few people each day. What
struck me most – in addition to the smell – was the silence.
With that number of people there should have been children
running round, laughter and indeed crying, and lots of noise;
instead there was only the awful silence as so many waited to
die.[5]

The Minister followed up on his visit in a pattern that was to
become familiar: he reported to his EU colleagues at a meeting of
Foreign Ministers in September, he briefed the UN Secretary General, Boutros Boutros-Ghali, when he made the annual visit to New
York for the General Assembly later that month and, instead of the
usual tour d'horizon of issues of the day, he devoted much of his
speech to the General Assembly to urging member states to do
more to help the stricken country.

Then, within weeks of David Andrews' visit to Somalia, came an
even more dramatic development. President Mary Robinson said
that she wished to visit the country. The shockwaves in the system
were great. The Head of State wished to go to a country where the
rule of law had collapsed and armed factions were locked in a deadly struggle. Even leaving aside the dangers involved, what about the
appropriateness of the President making such a visit?

It is hard to bring the mind back to the days before the Presidency has become the engaged, high profile institution which Mary
Robinson created and which it still is today.

In her predecessors' time the office was largely ceremonial with
functions such as Ambassadors presenting credentials and occasional meetings of the Council of State. I had some personal experience of the nature of the office as Chief of Protocol in the early
1980s. Among my responsibilities was to organise State visits in liai-

son with the Aras, which had a very small staff. Such visits were few and far between then. This was not just down to President Hillery's style, which reflected the fact that he was a private person; it was how the Presidency worked at the time.

Mary Robinson changed all that. Even before her election she made it clear that she would be a proactive President who would take the office to new places. Already, her term in office had seen some tussles with the Taoiseach's Department and Iveagh House. Now the Government had to decide on whether to approve a visit to Somalia.

A crucial factor was the attitude of the Taoiseach. Albert Reynolds' approach was positive; if the President wished to go to Somalia, he would not stand in her way. This was courageous on his part, as he would have been justified in taking a cautious line.[6]

But still the security question loomed. Was it safe for Mary Robinson to travel? I was asked by the Taoiseach's Department to prepare a security assessment. I had the sense that advice to rule out a visit on security grounds would not be unwelcome. I could understand that – there was no doubt that the visit presented risks and nobody would wish to put the Head of State in danger. Those clamouring loudest for the visit would be nowhere to be seen if things went wrong. I asked Hugh Swift to go out in advance and to make contact with the UN people on the ground.

We had great luck in that the Special Representative of the UN Secretary General in Somalia was an exceptional person, a former Algerian diplomat called Mohamed Sahnoun. He told Hugh Swift that the security situation in the capital Mogadishu and in Baidoa, a town where some of the worst starvation was happening, was somewhat improved. He said that a sizeable contingent of Pakistani UN troops was due soon and in the meantime he would arrange security with the local factions. He undertook to personally accompany the President throughout her visit.

This enabled me to make a recommendation on the security aspect: yes, I said, the situation was unstable and unsafe but the risks could be controlled with the UN's assistance and the fact that the President would be accompanied throughout by Ambassador Sahnoun. Some still had doubts about the wisdom of the visit but there was a surge of public support in favour and the Taoiseach's attitude cleared the way.

One lesson I had learned in protocol was that every step of a visit by the President has to be planned. Clearly Somalia was going to be a different story but the principle still applied. I liaised closely with Bride Rosney in the Aras. Transport and accommodation were key issues that had to be nailed down. But, unlike normal State visits, the emphasis had to be on keeping the ceremonial aspect to the minimum. And security had to continue to be the top priority. Here, the calm assurances we continued to receive from Ambassador Sahnoun were a great help.

The days before the visit were hectic. Press interest was unprecedented; it was a real media frenzy. Twenty-nine Irish journalists were accredited for the visit (by way of comparison, for most African visits when I accompanied Ministers, we were lucky if two or three journalists showed interest and could get their bosses' agreement to travel). The NGOs were in constant touch, anxious that their projects and activities would receive their fair share of the President's time.

The party flew out to Nairobi on 2 October and straightaway faced a sensitive issue in that the Kenyans were conscious that a Head of State was visiting and departing from their territory and expected that their Head of State would have a meeting with her. This was not the purpose of the visit and President Moi was facing charges of corruption. In the event, we managed to keep their meeting to a low-key, courtesy call.

The first stop was Baidoa where we flew in a small hired plane. As David Andrews had reported, there were scenes of death and dying all around. Now, as he accompanied the President, she could see the horrors for herself. The sight of people lying down, so weak that they can hardly move, all hope gone from their eyes, is some-

thing that never leaves you. Human beings at the end of their teth-
er in every sense. Seeing children in this condition was the worst of
all.

Mary Robinson has left a graphic account of what she witnessed
in her diary of the visit. Here is one quote:

> I walked with the Somali interpreter towards lines of children
> sitting in the heat, in row upon row, each holding flimsy plastic
> bags or the occasional cup or bowl. Just beyond them were fur-
> ther rows of skeletal men and women – predominantly women
> – with emaciated children. It was explained to me that the cen-
> tres were open from 7 am to 4 pm and that the women and
> children would sit patiently throughout that period waiting for
> food... I knelt down beside one woman and asked her to show
> me her baby. She was almost too weak to lift the small bundle
> but I saw the sores on the scalp and flies crawling over the ba-
> by's eyes and mouth.[7]

Mary Robinson visited all the places where the Irish NGOs –
Concern, GOAL, the Irish Red Cross – were working, and the many
volunteers of Irish and other nationalities working for organisations
such as CARE, UNICEF, Medecins sans Frontieres, Oxfam, Save the
Children, USAID and World Vision. The Irish, as ever, were prominent even in the non-Irish organisations: Geoff Loane was in charge
of the operations of the International Committee of the Red Cross
while Vincent O'Reilly was leading the UNICEF effort.

The NGOs wanted the President to see everything; not only the
people lucky enough to be receiving meagre rations but the worst
cases, those in an advanced stage of malnutrition who were close to
death. She showed amazing stamina to be able to remain composed
in the face of such terrible misery. I must confess that I ducked out
of some of the worst scenes. At least the President had her ever-
reliable husband Nick alongside her as well as her trusted aide
Bride Rosney. David Andrews consciously held back so as not to
intrude on the President's schedule but he was a constant supportive presence.

One image that has stuck in my mind was outside a tent where people in the last stages of starvation were being – comforted I suppose is the best word since they looked beyond help. I came across a young boy of about nine or ten, curled up in the foetal position, just outside the tent. He was not dead but was clearly in a bad way. I wondered how he came to be out there alone. I wished I could do something but he was surrounded by so many thousands as badly or worse off that it was useless to think that possible.

The scenes in Baidoa would be replicated wherever we went – in the capital Mogadishu and again when the President visited Afghoi and Mandera.

I was worried about our arrival in Mogadishu. It would have been grotesque in the circumstances to be met at the capital by the usual fanfare that accompanies a visit by a Head of State and we stressed this to the Somali side. I thought at first when the plane touched down in Mogadishu that we had achieved this goal but when the convoy of UN vehicles drove around the tarmac to the airport what should we find awaiting us but a military band. There was nothing for it but to wait while they played some music and then move on.

We picked up an escort of armed Somalis, the people known as 'Technicals' who hired themselves out at great cost and without whom movement was impossible. They were bristling with all sorts of military hardware, some mere youngsters brandishing weapons almost as big as themselves, many high on a drug called *tchat*. We drove through scenes of utter destruction. There was hardly a building in the city that was not badly damaged or flattened altogether.

After visiting a feeding station, the cavalcade would move on and you had to be alert for when that happened. Sometimes on official visits I found that people got lost or missed the vehicles – not in Somalia. Nobody had any wish to be left behind.

There was particular tension when we crossed the firing line between the warring factions. We swapped one set of Technicals for another but the sense of threat and danger was similar whichever side you were on. And the wholesale destruction continued on all sides. It was on the other side of the line that the President met the acting President Ali Mahdi. Here the first sight that confronted us was a military guard of honour. We ignored it.

Everyone – journalists, officials, aid workers – had to find their own accommodation. I shared a room at one of Concern's houses with Hugh Swift and David Andrews' Private Secretary Conor O'Riordan. Nobody got much sleep after the sights they had seen.

The President overnighted at Ambassador Sahnoun's residence, what was once a fine villa, a reminder of the fact that Mogadishu once had boasted many such buildings, some displaying the style of Somalia's Italian colonisers. Briefings were arranged by Ambassador Sahnoun with the heads of the aid organisations and he himself gave a detailed account of how he saw the situation.

A meeting with the other contender for power, General Aideed, was not confirmed until the eleventh hour but it gave the President a chance to meet the man who was held most accountable for the carnage all around.

President Robinson used the meetings with Ali Mahdi and General Aideed to highlight the toll which the conflict was taking on the civilian population, and the proliferation of weapons, and to plead with them to allow help to reach those in dire need. I cannot say that either gave any assurances or even displayed much concern about the misery their actions were causing. Only once did I see Aideed flinch, when Mary Robinson appealed 'as a mother' to do something about youngsters going around with machine guns.

Before returning to Nairobi the party stopped to see what was happening to the Somali refugees in Mandera camp across the border in northern Kenya where Trocaire were playing a lead role. Away from the actual conflict we expected a less grim situation but the camp, where the UN High Commission for Refugees was in charge, turned out to be another awful scene: 50,000 refugees huddled together in miserable conditions with no clean water or latrines and an imminent risk of cholera.

Back in Nairobi Mary Robinson gave an emotional press conference. Watching, I willed her to get through her statement without breaking down and she did but the raw emotion showed clearly and at times she was close to tears. Shame was the word she repeated, shame on behalf of the international community at what was happening in Somalia. 'The suffering I encountered in Somalia offended all my inner sense of justice.'

Afterwards it was said that she regretted that she did not remain objective and faithful to her barrister training.[8] Difficult though it was to watch, I thought that her presentation of what she had seen, which was transmitted in full on RTE, starkly conveyed the sense of the visit. Sometimes emotion and gesture speak more eloquently than words alone. When Willi Brandt sank to his knees at the site of the Warsaw Ghetto uprising, it said more than a dozen speeches. Seeing the normally reserved President visibly moved was a more eloquent message for people at home than a restrained statement.

Some surreal moments from the visit stick in my memory: the band at the airport and the motley group of soldiers lined up for the guard of honour, for example. And the fact that the first person to greet the President in Mogadishu was Michael D. Higgins. He walked across the runway in the blazing heat. He told me later that he was in a dishevelled state because his clothes were on the other side of the dividing line! He had been to Mandera and Baidoa where he recalls that the trucks had taken away 132 bodies already that day.[9] It was fitting somehow that this indefatigable supporter of the developing world should be the first to greet the President.

The first jeep I got into at Mogadishu airport contained a man who introduced himself as the Minister for Posts and Telegraphs. What his functions could have meant among the death and misery was hard to see. The 4-wheel drive in front of us was filled with Technicals, one of whom had a mortar, which for some reason he kept pointed straight at our windscreen. My chief concern on that journey was that his vehicle might hit a jolting bump in the pitted road; if it had we could have all been blown to kingdom come.

On another occasion we drew abreast of a Technical who stood with his weapon in both hands at the roadside. One of the Irish photographers was travelling with me and started taking photographs of the man. The Technical made it clear that he did not welcome the attention but the photographer kept snapping away. Then the Technical lifted up his gun and fired a shot into the air; going off a few inches away, it made a deafening sound. The photographer stopped snapping.

In spite of the problems I felt that the visit had achieved its objectives:

- The President had visited the main famine areas and met key figures.

- We managed to include all the NGOs to ensure that tribute was paid to their work; this called for a complicated juggling act but it worked.

- The President met the two leaders of the warring factions and made strong plea for them to take account of the humanitarian catastrophe taking place. Nobody could believe that that would make them change their ways but at least they were left in no doubt as to one Head of State's view of their actions

- The President was able to pay tribute to the work of Irish (and other) aid workers; in a brief visit we saw what they had to cope with daily; it enabled her to raise specific issues such as conditions in Mandera camp and the absence of an EU presence in Mogadishu.

- The visit paid tribute to the Irish public's concern and generosity.

- It enabled us to gather material for the meeting with the UN in New York.

Those accompanying the President and David Andrews moved on to New York for a meeting with the UN Secretary General

Boutros Boutros-Ghali. It was a gruelling flight with a stop in Paris and we were all in bits. Bride Rosney gave me a sleeping pill, which worked in the short term but made me disorientated when we got to New York. In fact, the few days in New York had an air of unreality. How to juxtapose what we had seen with the hot dog stands, the coffee smells, the air of people bustling about their business. I went into a McDonalds at one point and remember seeing a stand called The Fixings where ketchup, relishes and bacon bits were set out and thinking how can this be happening on the same planet as the lines of starving people we had just seen.

The meeting with the UN Secretary-General was not encouraging. He was welcoming to the President and thanked her for taking an interest in Somalia. But the thrust of what he had to say was that Somalia was just one of many tragedies he had to deal with. In Africa alone he said that there were half a dozen situations that were equally bad; he instanced Mozambique as one which he considered worse. He spoke of all the challenges he had to face and the reluctance of UN Member States to respond to calls for peacekeeping troops and equipment and aid. He seemed overwhelmed by the problems as he reeled them off – the war in the former Yugoslavia, Cambodia, the Caucasus . . .

But interest in the Somali tragedy was growing in the United States. Mary Robinson was interviewed on the prime time CBS Morning News programme. Although she was cut off while quoting Seamus Heaney, the message had been communicated to a huge audience about how bad things were in Somalia.

Nor did the President let matters rest there. On her return to Ireland she sent letters to a large number of Heads of State around the world including President Bush. The replies she received were in many cases much more than polite responses. It was clear that her courage in going to Somalia and bringing the country's plight to world attention struck a chord with other leaders.

There was a blow a few weeks later when we learned that Mohamed Sahnoun had resigned as UN Special Representative in Somalia. Boutros-Ghali was blamed by many for the falling out which led to Sahnoun's departure and for not really trying to persuade him to stay on. The criticisms made – that Sahnoun exceeded his authority by proposing a meeting of the warlords outside Somalia and that he should not have been buying off the Technicals – were hardly convincing given the parlous situation Sahnoun found himself in. The pressure group Africa Watch blamed Sahnoun's departure on the Secretary-General and internal UN intrigues.[10]

Looking back, I believe that Mary Robinson's visit did have an effect on the situation in Somalia, especially on US attitudes. Before the year was out President Bush (senior) decided to send a strong US force to support the UN's operations in the country. His decision reflected the US public's concern at the deaths appearing on their TV screens each night and the realisation that the small, poorly equipped UN peacekeepers were no match for the heavily armed combatants in Mogadishu and elsewhere.

In December 1992 the existing UN force, known as UNOSOM, was replaced by a much larger force of 38,000 men called UNITAF (Unified Task Force) with America the main troop contributor. UNITAF was authorised by the UN General Assembly under what is known as Chapter 7 provisions. The difference between Chapter 7 and other peacekeeping missions is that the new force had the power to *make* peace by military action as opposed to merely *keeping* the peace. While the UN was formally in charge, the operation was under US command, the new Special Representative of the Secretary-General being a retired American Admiral, Jonathan Howe.

To begin with, the strategy of deploying a massive force worked. The factions stopped fighting and aid started to flow into the country. Operation Restore Hope, as it was called, was making a visible difference when I accompanied the new Minister of State, Tom Kitt, on a visit to Somalia in March 1993. As we flew in, we saw a dramatic change from the time of the President's visit. Scenes reminiscent of the Normandy coast in the days after D-Day saw an array of US ships offshore and a huge range of military equipment

and personnel in the beach area and at the airport. UNITAF soldiers were visible everywhere while most of the Technicals had
gone into hiding. We even started funding a seed project to encourage farmers to start producing crops again.

But there were ominous signs too. The weapons were still
around and the Technicals had not gone away – only dropped out
of sight. In fact, some of them were still providing 'protection' to
the aid workers – at a hefty price. One of the chief reasons for Tom
Kitt's visit was to convey our deep concern about the safety of Irish
aid workers who were increasingly targeted by the factions, now
less able to loot the food supplies. In January Sean Devereux, a
UNICEF official in charge of relief operations in Kismayo, was killed
and in February Valerie Place, a Concern volunteer, was shot dead
when bandits attacked the convoy she was travelling in. The Minister of State visited the spot where Valerie Place was killed; it was a
remote, lonely scene, which summed up the great sacrifice which
the (predominantly young) Irish NGO volunteers made for the
people of Somalia.

We met the UN Special Representative Admiral Howe, the US
Ambassador and the military leaders. Admiration was expressed by
all for the Irish contribution to the aid effort and we were assured
that every effort would be made to ensure the workers' safety. But
there was criticism, too, of the attitude of some aid workers towards the military. For their part, the NGOs told us of their unhap-
piness with the constraints they had to work under. And the fact
that Technicals were still being paid protection money led to inevitable friction.

Admiral Howe came across as a thoughtful man who was ex-
ploring all possible ways to handle what was still a nightmare situation. He said he would welcome Ireland's participation in the UN-
OSOM II operation, which was to take over from UNITAF once the
security situation allowed. Ireland had indicated that we were prepared to send a transport contingent of sixty Defence Force personnel (this would be the first time that Irish troops operated un-

der UN Chapter 7 and legislation had to be passed to allow this). Security was Howe's top priority but he was pursuing possibilities for political progress too. There were few signs then of the obsession about removing General Aideed from the picture and the disastrous consequences which this would have.

Tom Kitt's visit and the offer to send 60 personnel to UNOSOM II demonstrated Ireland's continuing interest in Somalia. David Andrews returned later in the year, having moved from Foreign Affairs to be Minister for Defence. He visited Baidoa where the Irish troops would be deployed. On his return through Nairobi he met separately with Aideed and Ali Mahdi but found that neither was willing to concede ground to the other.

Around seventy-five Irish volunteers, including some seconded from the Defence Forces, continued working in Somalia with various NGOs in spite of the security problems, and Ireland pressed our EU colleagues to keep Somalia on the agenda. Hugh Swift and I attended conferences on Somalia in Geneva, Nairobi and Addis Ababa where improvements were sought in aid delivery and the search for a political agreement continued. Ireland contributed to the UN Trust Fund for Somalia and we waived landing charges at Shannon for aircraft involved in Operation Restore Hope.

Unfortunately, everything changed later that year when the incident known as Black Hawk Down took place in Mogadishu.[11] It sprang from the determination of Admiral Howe and the US commanders to remove General Aideed whom they had dubbed Public Enemy Number One. They had good reason to see Aideed as the enemy; his followers were responsible for a series of attacks on US and UN personnel, the worst being the murder of 24 Pakistani peacekeepers in June. But the use of heavy force in the densely populated city turned people against the Americans. An over ambitious daylight raid and a fatal underestimation of the vulnerability of helicopters (and of local support for Aideed) led to a fierce fight in which 18 US personnel and at least 500 Somalis were killed. TV images of dead American servicemen being dragged through the streets filled the United States public with revulsion and led them to question why they were in Somalia at all.

In his memoirs President Clinton describes Black Hawk Down as 'one of the darkest days of my Presidency'.[12] Despite having endorsed his predecessor's policy, Clinton drew a line under America's involvement in Somalia more or less immediately after the fight.

The UN continued its peacekeeping work under the UNOSOM II framework and Ireland honoured its promise to supply 60 transport personnel. The Defence Forces' performance was highly praised. But the security situation deteriorated further. The NGOs had to reluctantly accept that their work could not continue. One of the Defence Forces personnel seconded to work for GOAL, Declan O'Brien, gave me a vivid account of the perils of trying to deliver aid in Baidoa and Mogadishu at that time. The people working for GOAL in Baidoa were supporters of Aideed, which did not go down well with the Americans. GOAL had to pay as much as $100 per day per vehicle which was plain bribery. Eventually he and his colleague Mick Kiely decided that they had to work on an exit strategy, but they had to speed up their exit as things turned bad rapidly. They were lucky to get out alive.

The US completed the withdrawal of its soldiers in March 1994; later that year, after fruitless efforts to restore peace by the remaining UNOSOM forces, the UN Security Council unanimously voted to withdraw from Somalia. The troops' final departure took place in March 1995.

Why did Somalia exert such an influence over Irish peoples' consciousness in 1992? I think a combination of factors were at work.

- First and foremost were the TV images of dying children, which stirred people's hearts. Boutros-Ghali had a point about the number of deaths in that the total for Somalia was around 350,000 whereas the Mozambique civil war is estimated to have cost 800,000 lives and that in Angola 600,000. But Somalia came into our living rooms and the pictures conveyed the classic images of famine and starvation.

- Somalia brought back memories of the Ethiopian famine when the world reacted with an outpouring of help. Famines on that scale were not supposed to happen again but here was evidence to the contrary.

- The Irish NGOs proved that they could make a real difference. Concern was a key actor in Somalia. GOAL made its presence felt. Somalia was a watershed for Trocaire. It showed that the model of political engagement and working through local partners was not sufficient in the face of starving thousands. Under the leadership of Justin Kilcullen, who became CEO in 1992, Trocaire put more personnel in the field.

- David Andrews' visit played a major role. Other European Foreign Ministers had been slow to go until he did, and then it was often a case of a quick in and out. Mary Robinson's visit tended to overshadow the earlier one but it is hard to imagine the Government agreeing to the President's visit if David Andrews had not shown that it could be done.

By going to Somalia Mary Robinson brought about a complete change in the international role of the Presidency. If some queried the practical results they were in a small minority. The overwhelming reaction of the media was positive, seeing the visit as a fitting gesture of solidarity with the efforts to help a starving people in a highly dangerous setting. It would lead the way to further humanitarian visits by the President, endorsing the value of Irish volunteers and of the development cause generally.

Hard lessons were learned in Somalia. One of the hardest was the question it raised about the relationship between military intervention and aid. The death rate was so awful in the summer of 1992 that most NGOs strongly believed that only the intervention of a major power such as the United States could bring improvement. But the relations between the military and the NGOs proved to be decidedly uneasy. People who work in development have traditionally been wary of the military. In one way, they have good grounds to be as they cannot afford to be seen to be taking sides and the aid worker's role is very different from that of a soldier. The Red Cross in particular has always fiercely defended its neutrality. But some of the NGOs showed an arrogance towards the military which ignored the fact that they could not have done their work without protection. The payments to the Technicals were not only ruinously expensive; they raised the spectre of prolonging the conflict. Some have even argued that shipping in food aid to such lawless situations can give the combatants a vital weapon.

For the US, Somalia was a salutary experience, even if its casualties were minuscule compared to previous military engagements such as Vietnam. The humiliation of Black Hawk Down made the Clinton Administration extremely wary of further engagements, however worthwhile the cause: it would play a big role in the failure to act when the massacres started in Rwanda.

For Ireland there were lessons too. Proud as we were of helping to bring Somalia's plight to world attention, the experience revealed the limits to our capacity to help. This struck me forcibly when we were sounded out about the possibility of Ireland chairing the Somalia Donor Coordination process based in Nairobi. Ireland no longer had an Embassy in Nairobi and we had no presence on the ground in Somalia. It just wasn't on and we had to say no.

Even with our EU colleagues there was a limit to what we could get them to do. I always felt that interventions by our Ministers were listened to with respect because of the high reputation of our military personnel on peacekeeping duties, because we were seen as having no axe to grind and because of the high standing in which Irish aid workers were held. But the EU, like any organisation, has a lot on its plate and soon moves on to the next crisis.

One of the tantalising might-have-beens is to wonder whether things would have worked out better if Mohamed Sahnoun had been allowed to continue in his post. He struck everyone who met him as ideally suited to a well-nigh impossible job. He knew the Horn of Africa intimately, had served 10 years with the Organisation of African Unity, understood that the clan and sub-clan structures in Somalia were the key to a resolution of the conflict and that rebuilding anything resembling political life would take a long time. The loss of his low-key, subtle approach to this most complex of problems is something only the historians can gauge.

Those who lost out most were, of course, the people of Somalia. Today, 15 years on from UNOSOM's departure, the country is still in a collapsed state with an interim government that is more a name than a reality and factions still fighting for control. Some NGOs, including Trocaire and Concern, still work there but with great difficulty and amid tight security.

I asked Mary Robinson for her thoughts on Somalia 18 years on. She said:

> I think a lot about it still. I have a friend who is head of one of the clans and who keeps me informed about what is happening. She paints a very grim picture. I would love to help women's groups in Somalia as I feel they are key to a solution but sadly it is not on, it is not secure enough. It was a tragedy that just as the UN and the US began to move to help Somalia you had a strange CNN atmosphere with film of the troops coming ashore. Too high a profile was given to that dimension and too little to the work being done on the ground to prevent the situation worsening. Then, after the appalling, humiliating killings (of Black Hawk Down), Somalia was frozen out of aid.
>
> It is a tragedy that Somalia has been neglected for so long. There was too little thought, too little caring after the Americans withdrew – official indifference really. Now we are reaping the bitter fruits of failing to have a sustained response with the Somali pirates and the Ugandan bombings and alienated Somalis around the world.
>
> One thing is certain: I will never get Somalia out of my system.[13]

Endnotes

1. Somalia: there are numerous accounts of Somalia's tragic story. For the Irish perspective, in addition to my own papers and recollections and interviews with those concerned, I have drawn on a range of sources including David Andrews, *Kingstown Republican: A Memoir*, New Island Books, 2007; Mary Robinson *A Voice for Somalia*, O'Brien Press, 1992; Olivia O'Leary and Helen Burke, *Mary Robinson The Authorized Biograph,'* Hodder and Stoughton, 1998 pp. 249-55; Chapter on Somalia in the *Annual Report 1992*; chapters on Somalia in Michael D. Higgins, *Causes for Concern: Irish Politics, Culture and Society*, Liberties Press, 2006, pp. 246-56; in Tony Farmar's book on Concern and Brian Mayes' on Trocaire.

2. Charlie Bird, *This is Charlie Bird*, Gill and Macmillan, 2006, pp. 124-6.

3. 'The officials were generally sceptical: they argued that we had already contributed money and there was nothing further we could do. Conor O'Riordan (private secretary) was the only one who supported me.' *Kingstown Republican*, p. 198.

4. Hugh Swift interview.

5. Op cit, 198-9.

6. See O'Leary and Burke, op cit, p. 250.

7. *A Voice for Somalia*, p. 16.

8. O'Leary and Burke, op cit, p. 254.

9. Michael D. Higgins interview.

10. Africa Watch press release 29/10/92.

11. See Mark Bowden, *Black Hawk Down*, Random House, New York, 1999.

12. Bill Clinton, *My Life*, Knopf, New York, 2004, pp. 550-4.

13. Mary Robinson interview.

8

THE SOMALIA EFFECT

It is no exaggeration to say that Somalia marked a turning point in Irish Aid's history. The budget freefall of the late eighties ended. There would be small hiccups along the way, but the next fifteen years would see annual increases on a scale that the aid programme had not experienced since the first years of its existence.

An important factor in the change of fortunes was the entry of the Labour Party into coalition with Fianna Fáil after the November 1992 elections. Labour had a deep-rooted commitment to development and the party pushed for new commitments and targets in Dick Spring's negotiations with Albert Reynolds on the formation of the new government.

Some might argue that, with Labour in government and rising prosperity, the increase in funding for development would have happened even without Somalia. I believe it would have taken much longer and the budget would have been more vulnerable. While the health of the economy is obviously key, the size of the budget is also influenced by external factors, most importantly images of dying children on our TV screens. Somalia had a deep effect on public perceptions of aid. It redirected people's attention at the scale of needs in the developing world, just as Ethiopia had and before it Biafra.

Fianna Fáil also showed renewed interest in the 0.7 per cent target after Somalia. I assumed that when he returned from Somalia David Andrews would thump the table and demand more ODA funding. But he took the view that the issue should speak for itself and that this would be more effective than pressurising the Minister for Finance during the Estimates for 1993 when money was still tight. This strategy worked. Martin Mansergh, who was a senior adviser to Albert Reynolds at the time, asked me to provide figures with a roadmap towards reaching the 0.7 per cent target within a manageable period. (This was a task I would become very familiar with as I was asked to sketch out models for different scales of increase umpteen times over the following years!) He said that a reference would be made in the Taoiseach's Bodenstown speech to the need to increase ODA funding. Even though it was only a brief reference, it was an important step.

When Labour entered coalition the issue was decided. The Programme for a Partnership Government contained the most promising commitments in a decade: Official Development Assistance was to rise to 0.2 per cent in 1993 and by 0.05 per cent each year until 1997.[1] The target for 1993 alone was challenging: the figure had fallen back to 0.16 per cent in 1992 after the flattering outturn of 0.19 per cent the previous year. This meant that funding would have to increase by a third in one year, once GNP growth was taken into account. That increase was indeed delivered, with total ODA rising from £40 million to £54 million, one of the very few occasions where such a commitment was fully met. In 1994 funding went up by a further £16 million to a record £70 million.

These were huge increases for a programme which had become used to cuts or at best stagnancy. Suddenly there was a job to be done. It was great to have more money coming on stream but ways had to be found to put it to good use.

One of the changes brought in by the new Government was that the trade work for which I was responsible was transferred to the Department of Industry and Commerce. I was sorry to lose this work and believed, as I still do, that the Department of Foreign Affairs, with its network of embassies, has an important role on foreign trade. But the decision was made and was not negotiable. The people affected by the change behaved professionally as they always do. Some transferred to Industry and Commerce while others were assigned elsewhere in Foreign Affairs.[2]

Ironically, the change worked to my advantage, as there would have been too much for one Assistant Secretary to take on both aid and trade after the aid funding began to climb.

Planning the programme's expansion was exciting. I arranged for the heads of our Development Cooperation Offices in the field and key people at home to come together for a meeting to discuss the future. The Minister of State Tom Kitt briefed them on the changed situation, particularly the commitment to increase the funding. Some of those who met in the ballroom of Iveagh House were a bit sceptical to begin with. They had heard many promises before.

A clear message from discussions with colleagues was the importance of setting out our plans for the future in a strategy document. The absence of a statement of intent was something that the NGOs and development community had criticised for years. We started the work straightaway and, if my memory can be relied on, it was finished fairly quickly. The approval of the Tanaiste Dick Spring as well as the Minister of State was secured. Then it went to the Government for approval.

The document, which was published in July 1993, was called *Irish Aid: Consolidation and Growth, A Strategy Plan.*[3] It was the first document of its kind since the 1979 booklet. In 1982 an attempt had been made to write a White Paper but it did not go ahead. In the late eighties the focus was on the programme's survival; it would have been strange to plan ahead when the very existence of the programme was in doubt.

The Strategy Plan had a dark green cover and was referred to often as the Green Book. It wasn't a lengthy document – 60 pages in all – and it did not lay claim to be a White Paper or the last word on development aid. But it set out the main elements of what we were trying to achieve. People have told me that the Strategy Plan was a good guide to those in the field as well as at home, especially in setting out the lines on which the expansion would take place and that it served its purpose for a decade.

There was a sense that now was the moment to expand and to open up new areas for the programme. As it happens, one of the very first decisions in the Strategy Plan was to name the programme Irish Aid, thus ending the confusion that had existed about the programme's identity (although there was to be more confusion over the name later!). The main operational features of the Strategy Plan were:

- As well as expanding the programmes in the existing priority countries, new priority countries would be identified starting with Ethiopia and Uganda and possibly Mozambique if peace held there.

- Greater assistance would be given to countries that fell short of priority status; specific mention was made of Somalia, Zimbabwe and South Africa. A fact-finding mission was to be sent to Vietnam and Cambodia. The Palestinian Occupied Territories and Eastern Europe were to get more funding.

- Negotiations were to start with the NGOs on a new funding scheme.

- More funding to be provided for disaster and emergency relief.

- APSO to ramp up its recruitment of volunteers. A target of placing 2,000 volunteers overseas was set.

- An increase in Ireland's voluntary contributions to UN bodies, notably the UN Development Programme, UNICEF and the Office of the UN High Commissioner for Refugees; at the same time, a pledge was made to support UN reform.

- More attention to be paid to areas such as the environment, debt, AIDS, women's role in development, population, children, human rights and democracy.

- A new advisory body to be set up in place of the Advisory Council on Development Cooperation. Also a special Forum

would be established to encourage public discussion of aid issues.

Attaining these objectives would require huge effort and getting
the necessary staff to carry out the changes proved difficult. The
staffing issue would become one of the biggest headaches for me
and my successors running the aid programme. The Department of
Finance had no option but to accede to the Coalition's pledge to
upscale the programme but they fought the battle for extra staff
with gusto. I have sometimes wondered why this was. If spending
was increasing dramatically, it stood to reason that more people
would be needed to do the job, especially as aid is delivered in a
risky environment. I suspect that Finance, having seen the level of
funding fall on several occasions, were never fully convinced that
the aid programme was there to stay.

Nevertheless, the people in Harcourt Street and in the field
were enthusiastic about the expansion and threw themselves into
the work. A great boost came in the return of Martin Greene to the
Division. Martin had served in Lesotho and Sudan and he brought a
wealth of development experience to the job.

Deciding on which should be the new priority countries was a
big undertaking. A list of candidate countries was compiled using
criteria such as poverty level, capacity to absorb aid, capacity of Ireland to meet some of the country's needs, existing links including
missionary or business presence, relative stability and governance.
After the list was narrowed down to half a dozen, scoping missions
were carried out to the countries concerned. The aim was to meet
all the relevant players on the ground from Government representatives to NGOs and from fellow donors to multilateral actors such
as the UN and the EU. In some cases, return visits had to be made
to check further on whether we could commit to the country in
question. We had to be careful not to raise expectations since not
all of the countries visited would end up being partners for Ireland.

I participated in visits to three of the candidate countries: Mozambique, Angola and Malawi.

Mozambique fitted the bill as one of the world's poorest countries which was emerging from a civil war that took a huge toll both in human lives and in destruction of the infrastructure. Landmines had been spread indiscriminately which resulted in high numbers of amputees and thousands of unexploded devices posing a grave risk to the population. A strong Ireland-Mozambique Solidarity Group, led by Niall Crowley, had kept the country's trials in the public eye.

But Mozambique would mark a new departure and was the subject of much debate in the Division. There was no guarantee that the fragile peace would hold, which is why the wording in the Strategy Plan is less firm about the commitment to Mozambique than to Ethiopia and Uganda. And there was the language problem. Irish Aid had hitherto focused on countries where English was spoken although from time to time there had been discussion about including a Francophone country. Now here was a country where Portuguese was the lingua franca. Was it a doable task?

After the first scoping programme I wanted to see the country for myself. Witnessing the poverty and the toll that the war had taken, it was hard not to feel that Mozambique should be helped along the road to peace and true independence.[4]

The approach we took was for each of the visiting group to have separate meetings so as to use the time to gather as much information as we could. An interesting thing happened during my visit when I met the British Ambassador in Maputo. After lunch at the Embassy, the Ambassador said: 'I'd like to show you something that as an Irishman you will be interested to see.'

A series of framed pictures of his predecessors hung along the wall. The more recent ones were photographs, the earlier ones portraits or drawings. One of the early ones was of Roger Casement! I had thought of Casement in connection with his exposure of Belgian atrocities in the Congo but of course he had also been British

Consul in Lourenco Marques, the Portuguese name for Maputo, from 1895 to 1898.

Angola, like Mozambique, was a former Portuguese colony, a very poor country and was emerging from a bloody civil war. The difference, though, was that Angola had still a long way to go before peaceful conditions would prevail. This became clear in the course of my visit.

Collecting the key to my room the first night in a hotel in the capital Luanda, the man at the desk said: 'Don't worry if you hear noises in the night, sometimes there are arguments about food shipments at the docks. It's a long way from here.'

Sure enough, in the small hours came noises of men at the port shouting and then the sound of gunfire, which continued for some time. Clearly these were not small arguments!

The next day I flew with Barbara Jones, a First Secretary who had recently come to work in Development Cooperation Division, in a food aid cargo plane to Quito. Angola had been independent since 1975 but now, 20 years later, the conflict still raged between the MPLA-led government and UNITA which refused to accept the government's writ. Atrocities and massacres were committed by both sides. Quito had been the site of some of the worst fighting.

Sitting in the back of the plane among food sacks with the World Food Programme logo I tried not to think of the landing ahead. The pilot had told us that, to be on the safe side, he would make what was called a corkscrew descent. This entailed flying around in circles instead of coming straight down so as to lessen the risk of being fired at. Back in Luanda (after a corkscrew take off) we met Mike McDonagh of Concern who was working on the supply of food aid to the beleaguered civilian population. It was striking how the Irish could be relied on to be present even in such dangerous conditions. At one stage Mike McDonagh placed a small round plastic box on the table. 'If you want to do something to help this country you could start with these,' he said.

The innocent looking container – not unlike a pill box – was the destructive load of an anti-personnel mine; filled with ball bearings it was the instrument that was causing so much misery, not just to the fighters but to farmers in their fields, to women going to fetch water, to children playing . . .

With regret we concluded that Angola was not stable enough to be considered as a priority country. (Fighting continued and it was only in 2002 that a truce was finally signed between the two sides.) However, we were able to find money for the work of Halo Trust, a brave NGO that was doing good work on de-mining in the region. I met some of their people, mostly ex-British Army, who had the strange job of seeking to reverse the damage that their former profession promoted. Ireland would go on to take a leading role in efforts to ban mines and would host a major conference on cluster munitions in 2008.

I also visited Malawi, which was a much calmer place and came across as a strong candidate. We did not include it at that time as the thinking was that three new countries would pose a sufficient challenge. It would be a decade before Malawi became one of Irish Aid's priority countries and I was glad to be in the job again for my second tour of duty to see that happen. We took a look at Asia too, but not in a very serious way at that stage as I recall.

A sad aspect was the recognition that Somalia was too insecure to be included. There was pressure at home to assist Somalia, not surprisingly given the number of Irish people who spent time in the country during the famine in one capacity or another. Occasionally signs would emerge that the different factions might be on the verge of a breakthrough in the ongoing talks. But Somalia was collapsing ever further into chaos. In the end we confined ourselves to humanitarian assistance and events there proved this to have been the right decision. It said something that Concern left the country in 1994, even though they were never afraid to engage in difficult situations.

My visit to Angola took place in January 1994 after accompanying the Tanaiste, Dick Spring, on an official visit to South Africa.
This was primarily a political visit, as evidenced by the presence in
the delegation of the Political Director Ted Barrington, and it included a memorable meeting between the Tanaiste and Nelson
Mandela. It was when Nelson Mandela was still President-in-
waiting and we met him in the Shell Building in Johannesburg
which was being used as the headquarters of the ANC. Mandela
was as charismatic in the flesh as on television and his warmth towards Ireland was obvious. So, too, was the regard in which he held
Kadar Asmal, the veteran anti-apartheid activist who would become a minister in the government after the change of power. We
broke the protocol rule that visitors do not interfere in local politics
by attending an ANC rally in a football stadium. It was worth it to
share the exuberant feelings of a people who finally could see that
the rotten regime they had to endure was on its last legs and that
better times were about to begin.

Even if politics were to the fore on the visit, we made sure that
the delegation went to see conditions in the townships. It was impossible not to be shocked by the contrast between South Africa's
First World buildings and roads on a par with Europe and the conditions of people living in Soweto. Here, dwelling places were little
more than corrugated or plywood sheds and the lack of water and
sanitation was on a par with the poorest parts of Africa. The only
bright spot was the sight of Irish nuns braving the dangers around
them to bring education and healthcare to the people of the townships.

One nun we met was proud of their success rates in the state
exams. When I asked her what happened to students who failed
she said, with a steely look: 'None of our students fail. We see to
that.'

I felt uneasy about South Africa then and on my subsequent visits to the country. It was so unlike a country such as Zambia where
deep poverty is everywhere to be seen and the vast majority are in

the same boat. The sense of insecurity was ever present in South Africa, arising from the huge gulf between the haves with their fancy homes and the have-nots outside the gates. We had a glimpse of the capacity for this division to boil over into violence when the Tanaiste and the group were leaving Shell House. In spite of the joy and celebration surrounding Nelson Mandela's imminent installation as President, ugly scenes were taking place in the foyer of the building – for reasons that were not clear – and we were advised to make our way without delay to the cars. A few months later there was a serious incident at the building when guards fired on Inkatha demonstrators and 19 people were killed.

Dick Spring was the ideal boss in that he supported the development agenda and let his Ministers of State get on with the job. That applied both to Tom Kitt, who was a member of his coalition partners' party, and later to Joan Burton of Labour. Just as for Peter Barry in the 1980s, the North dominated Dick Spring's concerns as Minister for Foreign Affairs, though there was plenty to do on EU affairs as well. He also had to carry the responsibilities of Deputy Prime Minister and leader of his party.

The two countries which Irish Aid 'adopted' first in this phase of expansion were Uganda and Ethiopia. By 1994 Development Cooperation Offices were set up in both countries. Uganda and Ethiopia had much in common in that they were extremely poor countries emerging from troubled recent history, Ethiopia from the Mengistu era and the terrible famine that ravaged the country and Uganda from the depredations of Idi Amin and, later, Milton Obote.[5]

Though poverty is widespread, Ethiopia is a most important country in terms of its size and political weight: home to the headquarters of the Organisation of African Unity among other things. In 1993 it was enjoying its first period of peace for 18 years. There was a good fit with Irish Aid's expertise in that years of maladministration and civil war had seen food production and the systems for delivery of water, health and education breaking down. Initially Irish Aid's efforts focused on two area-based programmes – in the

Tigray region in the north of the country and the Sidama region in the south.[6]

Uganda had once been a relatively prosperous country but its history since independence was a tragic one. Years of dictatorship and upheaval had left the basic infrastructure in a lamentable state. To add to its woes, the recent phenomenon of AIDS hit Uganda especially hard. The first focus of Irish Aid in Uganda was in the Kibaale District, a remote part of the country near Lake Albert with roads which were often washed out by rains making it particularly inaccessible. Like Ethiopia, its health and education systems were also in dire need of improvement.

On the negative side, this period saw the final closure of the programme in Sudan. It would have been desirable to resume work in Sudan but politically it had stopped being possible. The government of Omar Bashir was already set on the path of repression and tyranny which would manifest itself most clearly in Darfur. Virtually all the bilateral donors had left by 1991; Sudan's declaration of support for Saddam Hussein's invasion of Kuwait was the last straw. Our programme in Wad Medeni lingered on for a few years, then we wound it up and confined our activities to humanitarian assistance.

Not that our connections with Sudan ended there. Sudan was still on the radar because of the civil war raging in the south, which was taking a terrible toll on the local population. I accompanied Tom Kitt on a visit to southern Sudan in 1994. We were particularly impressed by the work being organised by an Irishman, Philip O'Brien of UNICEF, known as Operation Lifeline Sudan. This operated out of Lokichokio in northern Kenya and saw shipments of food and supplies flown in to the starving civilian population.[7]

I have good reason to remember that visit because Tom Kitt and I got a violent attack of dysentery in the course of it. We had arranged to stop off in the Netherlands and Sweden on the way back for talks about the expansion of the programme and, foolishly in retrospect, we persevered only to find ourselves getting progres-

sively weaker. On our return to Dublin the Minister was driven off
to Mount Carmel Hospital while I was admitted to St Vincent's. It
took me six months and numerous visits to Vincent's to get clear of
the bug. We could only blame ourselves I suppose but I did feel
that the advice given by the people who gave us our jabs – don't eat
or drink anything you can't be sure of – was easier said than done
in our line of work. We were usually offered hospitality on these
visits, often out in the bush where you had no idea about the origins of the food but where local people had gone to great trouble
and it would have been impolite to refuse.

Work proceeded on all the initiatives in the Green Book. It was
very pleasing to be in a position to tell the NGOs that more funding
would come on stream for their work. A new departure was the introduction of Block Grants for the bigger NGOs such as Concern,
GOAL and Trocaire. These grants enabled the NGOs to plan and
gave them discretion as to how the money was spent. Not surprisingly, relations with the NGOs improved greatly.

One of the most formidable challenges was the pledge to increase the number of volunteers in the field to 2,000. Going from
400 placements a year to 2,000 was no easy task. Hugh Swift recalls
how he proposed raising the number to 800, I said it should be
1,000 and when we got the decision back from government it was
2,000! APSO did their best and in 1993 the number of assignments
exceeded 800. The following year, over 1,000 volunteers were funded.[8]

I attached a lot of importance to finding a replacement for the
Advisory Council on Development Cooperation. The programme
needed to draw on the expertise available in the development
community and it was with this in mind that the Irish Aid Advisory
Committee was set up.

Getting a committee like this up and running is no easy matter:
identifying good quality members, securing their agreement to
serve, ensuring a balance between different NGOs and interest
groups and the gender balance, getting political approval. Professor

John Kelly of UCD, who had long experience in educational links with developing countries, agreed to chair. The job was finally completed and the Tanaiste announced the new Committee and its members. The contrast between the reaction to the setting up of the IAAC and the abolition of its predecessor was striking. The demise of the Advisory Council was the subject of extensive coverage including editorial comment while the setting up of the IAAC was ignored.

The aim with the annual Forum on Development was to stimulate regular discussion of the issues surrounding aid and the Government's role. Ministers were still very conscious that, outside of dedicated development-watchers, people knew little about what the Government did in this field. An organisation to increase public awareness about aid, the Development Education Support Centre, had been set up in 1986 but its main work was giving professional help to development education projects generally. The Forum was intended to fill that gap.

The programme suffered a blow in 1994 when it emerged that we had an overspend in the previous financial year. The overspend grew out of eagerness to ensure that the increased allocation was fully spent and confusion between accounts in the field and the main account in the Division. It did not mean any loss to the Exchequer as the money was made up from the following year's budget, which was growing fast. But an overspend is a mortal sin in accountancy terms and the Public Accounts Committee took a very dim view. It was a most painful experience for all concerned, especially as the Department of Foreign Affairs had a good accounting record up till then.

Looking back, the overspend bears the classic hallmark of a rapid increase in spending when the financial and accounting systems have not kept pace. It brought home the obvious truth that a bigger aid programme required better systems. We were fortunate to get the services of Joyce Duffy, a young accountant, who came to the programme and oversaw the updating of the accounts with a new computer system.

The overspend had a salutary effect in that it made everyone conscious of the need for closer attention to financial management to avoid such an event recurring. It reminded me of something I heard the glassmaker Simon Pearce say. He was asked if any of the people working with the molten glass ever got burned. 'If they ever do,' he replied, 'it only happens once.'

Along with planning for expansion and handling such major tasks as responding to Somalia and Rwanda and overseeing the humanitarian and refugee dimensions of the Balkan wars, the 1990s also saw a series of UN conferences.

The ones that I was involved with were the UN Conference on Environment and Development (commonly known as the Earth Summit) held in Rio de Janeiro in 1992, the Cairo Population Conference of 1994 and the Copenhagen Summit on Social Development of 1995. The fourth major conference of that period was the Beijing Women's Conference, which took place shortly after I moved on from the Division.

I approached these conferences with doubts about their value and about the UN's role in development generally. Since Irish Aid had more funds available, bigger contributions could be made to the UN bodies so I called on them whenever I was attending meetings in New York or Geneva. UNICEF and the Office of the UN High Commissioner for Refugees were the most impressive; what is more, they understood that the price of Ireland increasing funding was greater interaction about their policies and what was happening to the money we gave them. Others which were doing a good job were the World Food Programme and the UN Relief and Works Agency which helped relieve the dire situation of the Palestinians. But some of the other bodies gave the impression that they would simply like us to sign the cheque and leave them to it.

The main forum for discussion of development issues at the UN is the Economic and Social Committee, or ECOSOC as it is called. It is a poor relation of the bodies on the political side, namely the Security Council and the General Assembly. It was difficult to explain ECOSOC's relevance to ministers, or to justify attendance, even when Ireland was elected to the board as we were in 1994. EU meetings had a point to them, even if a lot of the issues were 'pre-cooked' by the officials. ACP/EU meetings were substantive affairs with vital decisions on access to markets, which had a real effect on developing countries' economies. The DAC meetings in Paris were more discursive but you were always aware that the DAC was dealing with serious issues: what would or would not qualify as Official Development Assistance, how the donors could improve the effectiveness of what they were doing. Debates at ECOSOC were long-winded and, worst of all, inconclusive.[9]

Big UN conferences have a common format. Preparatory meetings, known as Prepcoms, are held, often in far-flung capitals, and the issues thrashed out months before the conference proper. These Prepcoms are usually serviced by middle- or even junior-ranking diplomats who are described as experts but who may know little about the subject. Yet the way they carry out their work can exert a big influence on the outcome. There are regional and special interest groups, the biggest of which is the Group of 77, the heirs of the old Non-Aligned Movement and the most difficult to work with. (Not that the EU can complain. When a tricky issue arises you will see whichever country holds the Presidency rounding up the member states to seek an agreed position. The sight of the EU delegates trooping out – and holding the meeting up until they have agreed – is guaranteed to exasperate everyone else.)

There is a hothouse atmosphere at the official level discussions. Closeted in a hotel or conference centre, all sorts of committees are set up – the Committee of the Whole, Working Groups A, B and maybe C and D, Drafting Committees, the Friends of the Chair etc. The meeting organised by the NGOs are usually more lively and down to earth than the official meetings – and more in touch with the reality of the subject under discussion.

Summits are prone to intrusion by political events which have no bearing on the subject matter but which can cause havoc. Years later, when I was working for Mary Robinson in her capacity as Secretary General of the World Conference against Racism, the Middle East issue almost wrecked the discussion about the worthy goal of reducing racism and discrimination in all parts of the world.[10] There can also be examples of the Law of Unintended Consequences. The Cairo Population Conference saw an example of this where a summit devoted to the urgent question of the world's exploding population turned into a bitter dispute over abortion.

The goal of such conferences is for the pieces to fall into place and the final text to be agreed. One of the sayings I learned when I worked in the UN was that there is no such thing as an unsuccessful conference. By this was meant that somehow or another the last day will see some form of agreement on the text being accepted to applause from the delegates. But that often means that the lowest common denominator has prevailed and an empty text has been adopted. For all that, the UN Summits of the 1990s dealt with important subjects and achieved some results.

The Earth Summit in Rio was the first gathering of world leaders at the highest level to address the connection between the environment and development.[11] The hope was that the poor countries would agree to do more to slow down the alarming pace of environmental degradation while in return the rich countries would make stronger commitments to reaching the 0.7 per cent ODA target and make 'new and additional funding' available for global environmental protection. Unfortunately, the Earth Summit coincided with a period when many donors were not in a position to pledge higher funding. Ireland was one of those which had a difficulty. This was pre-Somalia and the most that the Taoiseach, Albert Reynolds, who led the delegation, could say was that we hoped to raise our funding.

But the Summit did adopt what was called Agenda 21, a comprehensive blueprint for global action in all areas of sustainable development. The conference also adopted new UN Conventions on Climate Change and Biodiversity and agreed to set up a standing committee on sustainable development. These initiatives would play a role in the evolution of the environmental debate, which has since become such an urgent priority.

The Cairo Population Conference also posed problems for Ireland, but of an altogether different sort.

It was clear from an early stage that the more liberal minded countries in Europe and North America saw the opportunity of breaking new ground at Cairo on reproductive rights and health. This was code for issues such as contraception and abortion and it created battle lines between those seeking new language and conservative Catholic and Muslim countries. Within the EU, Ireland was in a minority position on abortion, reflecting our unique national position. We were sometimes joined by Malta in seeking less specific language but most of the time we had to fight our own corner. When I attended the New York Prepcom I found the temperature of the negotiations at boiling point with countries such as Sweden and the Netherlands on a crusade and Ireland in their sights. The tone of the discussion was harsher than anything I had come across but I made it clear that we could not agree to language that suggested the right to abortion on demand when our laws and Constitution did not provide for this.

I was puzzled that the Dutch and Swedish proposals did not cause problems for other EU member states. I recalled from my years in Germany how controversial the abortion issue was there and wondered why their representatives said nothing. Then one of the delegates said to me, 'The Germans are hiding behind Ireland'. It made sense.

One of the stars of the Cairo Conference was Diarmuid Martin. As head of the Vatican delegation he had an extremely tough position to defend. The Vatican had some unenviable allies in the shape of Iran and Saudi Arabia. But, whether you agreed with his positions or not, you could not fail to admire the clear, unfazed way Diarmuid Martin fought his corner.[12]

Copenhagen had less of the sense of a big occasion. John Bruton was Taoiseach and by 1995 Ireland's ODA was on a steady upward graph so we could hold our head up. The main outcome of that conference was the focus on poverty alleviation and the adoption of the 20/20 initiative, which promised that 20 per cent of developing country resources and 20 per cent of aid expenditure by donors should be devoted to basic social programmes.[13]

The Beijing Women's Conference took place in September 1995. The press had grilled us (rightly) over the absence of women from the delegation for the Cairo Conference; naturally this mistake was not repeated at Beijing where the majority of the large delegation of officials, NGOs and parliamentarians were women, though the delegation was led by a man, the Minister for Equality and Law Reform, Mervyn Taylor. Niamh Breathnach, the Minister for Education also attended. Helen Keogh, who was the PDs spokesperson on Equality at the time and later head of World Vision Ireland, was one of the parliamentarians to attend the Beijing Conference. She was somewhat disappointed at the lack of a role for the parliamentarians but she concluded that it was great to be at Beijing nevertheless:

> With hindsight it has to be said that Beijing was a totem and its recommendations an important benchmark. Just to be there marked an occasion when the movement for women's equality made advances. And events of that kind give you creative space for exchanges of views and debate.

Do big UN conferences justify all the time and resources spent on them? The costs involved might make sense where progress towards important goals is being measured, as is the case with the Millennium Development Goals. But in many cases the follow-up meetings keep on going long after the momentum has gone out of the topic in question.

For all their drawbacks, I do think that they serve a purpose and that the ones I attended broke new ground. From a development point of view there was the bonus of Irish Aid working with other departments such as the Department of the Environment at Rio and Health at Cairo. We developed close relations with the officials from these departments and were glad that they experienced the development agenda close up. And the NGOs were members of the official delegation for the first time, which strengthened our relations with them.

Probably the biggest advantage of summit meetings is that they focus attention on important issues at the highest level and, hopefully, advance thinking on better ways of dealing with those issues. But it was good to leave the artificial atmosphere of the conferences.

My most vivid memory of the Earth Summit in Rio was when I accompanied the Minister of State, Brendan Daly, on a visit to the *favelas*. These sprawling shantytowns, almost as populous as Rio itself, are home to the poor and desperate, a striking contrast with the wealth and beauty of Copacabana and Ipinema. You had the feeling that you were taking your life in your hands by just being there. We were the guests of two Irish priests, Fr. Ted Nealon of the Holy Ghost Fathers and Fr. John Cribbin of the Oblates, who were able to operate in this highly dangerous environment because of the respect in which they were held. They had been working among the people of the *favelas* for decades.

Both priests asked for some funding for their work; in Fr. Cribbin's case he wanted to replace sewing machines for women who used them to make clothes for their own use and to sell. The amount he was looking for – £3,000 – was on the low side and I said that more money might be available. I was impressed by his answer: he said that £3,000 would cover the costs of what he had in mind and that he didn't want to give people the impression that money was too freely available.

Would that all our other partners had the same approach!

Endnotes

1.   Programme for a Partnership Government 1993-97.

2.   Ironically, the coalition government elected in March 2011 has reversed this decision and the current Minister of State for Overseas Development, Joe Costello, also has responsibility for trade.

3.   'Irish Aid: Consolidation and Growth, A Strategy Plan', DFA publication, July 1993.

4.   Mozambique duly became a priority country in 1996.

5.   The Annual Reports from 1994 onwards trace the evolution of the programmes in Ethiopia and Uganda just as they do for the other programme countries.

6.   The Annual Report 1996 describes the Tigray and Sidama programmes in Ethiopia (pp. 10-11) while the Annual Report 1998 has a lengthy article on the Kibaale District Programme in Uganda (pp. 36-7).

7.   Philip O'Brien interview.

8.   Figures in the Annual Report 1994 show that APSO funded 1,143 assignments in 1994 in 60 countries, p. 27.

9.   Ireland was elected to a three-year term 1994–1997.

10. The Durban Conference became the target of the American right for perceived anti-Semitism and Mary Robinson was attacked (unfairly in my view) for not doing more to combat this even though (a) the member states were the ones responsible, (b) she was not the chair – South Africa was, and (c) she made her rejection of some of the delegates' actions clear publicly.

11. The Annual Report 1992 includes an account of the Rio Conference (pp. 27-28.)

12. Then Monsignor Diarmuid Martin, the Vatican's head of delegation at Cairo, now Archbishop of Dublin. Diarmuid Martin was an invaluable help to Mary Robinson in mediating some of the bitter disputes at the Durban Conference where he also headed the Holy See delegation.

13. There are short pieces on the Copenhagen and Beijing Summits in the Annual Report 1995 (p. 36) plus further coverage of the Rio Conference.

9

DEVELOPMENT AID AND FOREIGN POLICY

A mantra that is often repeated is that development aid is an integral part of foreign policy. It has appeared in numerous policy and strategy statements of the Department of Foreign Affairs over the years. As early as the first 1979 booklet on the aid programme, development was described as 'an increasingly important element of our overall foreign policy'.[1] The principle was spelled out in greater detail in the first (and so far only) White Paper on foreign policy which was overseen by Dick Spring and published in 1996.

The decision to publish a White Paper on foreign policy was brave. Foreign policy can change quickly in the light of events outside a country's control. A good example is 9/11, an event that brought about seismic changes for every country in the world; the fall of the Berlin Wall another. And the evolution of the EU's approach to foreign policy has influenced, and will continue to exert a powerful influence, on the shape of Ireland's foreign policy.

Nevertheless, the idea of setting out the fundamental lines on which our foreign policy is based had been considered often over the years. Dick Spring's adviser, Fergus Finlay, says he encountered resistance at first at official level on the grounds that there could be hostages to fortune.[2] But he and the Tanaiste felt that it was important to set out where Ireland stood in the area of foreign policy and to show that it had an ethical basis, that a neutral Ireland would stand on the side of the oppressed. A think-in chaired by the Tanaiste in Tralee proved a pivotal moment in that the senior officials who attended came on board for the idea and worked hard to make it a reality. A series of public consultations took place around the country which helped to bring the issues before the public.

In 1996, after much discussion and drafting, the White Paper appeared.[3] Reading it today, the White Paper seems very much of its time, reflecting issues such as Ireland's first engagement with NATO under the Partnership for Peace initiative and the debate on the Intergovernmental Conference on the future of Europe. There is a solid chapter on development with reference to the Strategy Plan for detail on the direction which development aid would take. The White Paper notes that

> Irish Aid and Development Cooperation is a practical expression of Ireland's foreign policy commitment to peace and justice in the world. . . . The Government will continue to ensure that the Bilateral Aid Programme is fully situated within the framework of Ireland's overall foreign policy.[4]

But how true in practice is the orthodoxy on the link between foreign policy and development?

On a day-to-day basis the two blocks of work tend to run in parallel lines in the Department of Foreign Affairs. Political and Development Cooperation Divisions are physically separated in that they have been located for many years in different buildings (and today in different cities since much of Irish Aid has been decentralised to Limerick).[5] The business culture in the Department also plays a role. Political Division is one of the oldest parts of the Department; located in Iveagh House, it has traditionally been regarded, along with Anglo-Irish Division, as the best place to work and the likeliest assignment to involve contact with the secretary general and the minister of the day, and hence the chance for advancement. Development Cooperation Division on the other hand is seen as being at something of a remove from the rest of the Department, even if in recent years its stock has risen.

Ireland is far from being unique in this respect. From my contacts with heads of other development programmes in Europe I could see that it is common for Development and Political to do their own thing and to have different work cultures, even when under the same roof as is the case in the Netherlands. This is also reflected in the Brussels system where the Foreign Affairs Councils (now the General Affairs and External Relations Councils) and its working groups are serviced by people from member states' political divisions, while the development mechanisms are serviced by development people. Even when the two sides meet, there is the strong impression of different approaches, different mindsets even. There is a similar separation of the functions of development and foreign policy at the UN.

But the concerns of the two sides are, obviously, connected and in some cases closely intertwined. Two examples where foreign policy and development concerns came together in a highly visible fashion can be seen in the first half of the 1990s: the international response to the genocide in Rwanda and the war in the former Yugoslavia.

In my case, the first sight I had of Rwanda was on the borders of the country. The memory is vivid:

> I am standing at a waterfall on the border between Tanzania and Rwanda in May 1994. It is a place that should be a beauty spot with the water cascading down into a pool. Instead, it presents a vision from hell. Bodies of Rwandans murdered in the genocide have floated down the river. By some trick of the current, half a dozen of the bodies cannot follow the river onwards and are trapped in the pool. They float round and round like a scene from Dante; one of them, the corpse of a middle aged man with arms outstretched as if still hoping for mercy, is so bloated by decomposition that it resembles nothing more than the Michelin Man . . .

There was no secret about the background to the grisly scene at the Rusomo Falls. The reason that Minister of State Tom Kitt was visiting this part of Tanzania was to see for himself the work of Irish NGOs assisting some of the estimated 350,000 Rwandans who managed to escape the killings and were living in makeshift camps at Ngara near the Rwandan border.

If the tragedy of Somalia developed over months and took time to come to the attention of the world, nobody can claim to be ignorant of what was going on in Rwanda.[6] A carefully planned massacre of Tutsis and moderate Hutus had been organised by hard line Hutus opposed to a peace deal between the government and the Rwandese Patriotic Front. Urged on by the radio station Mille Collines, whose slogan was 'kill the cockroaches', the victims – men, women and children – were hunted down and brutally murdered, in many cases with machetes.

The actual day that the killings began can be pinpointed: April 6th, after the plane carrying the Presidents of Rwanda and neighbouring Burundi was shot down, the extermination plan was put into effect. The Presidents had been negotiating the Arusha Accords, which were supposed to bring a resolution to the longstanding conflict in Rwanda. The hardliners did not want to share power and saw the opportunity not merely to defeat their opponents but to exterminate them. There had been fierce spates of killing already in Rwanda's recent history in the struggle for power. But nothing could compare to what followed the shooting down of the two Presidents' plane. Within three months some 800,000 Tutsis and moderate Hutus were dead.

The sequence of events that followed is also well known. The exiled Rwandese Patriotic Front, led by Paul Kagame, struck back at the Hutu killers, known as the Interahamwe, and drove them out of power and out of the country. Hundreds of thousands fled across the border, for the most part to camps around Goma in Zaire where a new phase of tragedy unfolded as contaminated water supplies brought on cholera and thousands more died.

Rwanda is a story unlike any other. Those I interviewed who were there in the aftermath of the genocide still spoke of it in almost hushed tones. Anne Clery, who was in charge of GOAL's operations helping refugees in Goma, said that Rwanda became a part of everyone who worked there.[7]

A firsthand memoir can be found in the book by General Romeo Dallaire, *Shake Hands with the Devil*.[8] This Canadian general who was in charge of the small UN force trying to cope with an appalling situation in the face of New York intrigues and international indifference paid a high price for his courage but has given us a riveting account of what he witnessed.

Dallaire is one of very few people who come out well from the Rwandan genocide. International indifference to the plight of the country meant that the UNAMIR force sent to supervise implementation of the Arusha Accords was woefully under strength. The UN in New York compounded the error by reducing its presence to a skeleton staff of 270 once the killings got under way when it should have been increasing the number of troops to a realistic level. This happened under the watch of Kofi Annan who was head of the UN's Peacekeeping Department. The United States, burned by the Somalia experience, did nothing. President Clinton made a heartfelt apology to the Rwandan people years later but the damage was done. France played a murky role with Operation Turquoise, allegedly aimed at stopping the killing but in many people's eyes a mission to rescue their allies in the ousted government – among them leaders who were responsible for the genocide.

The Irish NGOs, as ever, were quick to get operations under way to assist the refugees and the displaced, both in Tanzania and in Zaire. The Oireachtas Foreign Affairs Committee played a valuable role in arranging hearings from an early stage, which brought the genocide to broad public attention.

Irish Aid moved promptly by providing £1.25 million to the relief effort in the first months. Then, in July, the Government, having received Tom Kitt's report on his visit to the region and reports from the NGOs about the extent of the problem, decided on a series of measures:

- A further £2 million was allocated for emergency needs.

- APSO was to coordinate arrangements for the release of 35 public servants with relevant skills – particularly doctors and nurses – on special leave without pay to work for NGOs.

- Members of the Defence Forces would be seconded for service with the Office of the UN High Commissioner for Refugees, the lead UN agency dealing with the refugees in Zaire who by then numbered 1.5 million.

The first of these actions should have been easily done but there was a blazing row over the £2 million with the Department of Finance who felt that we should have found savings elsewhere instead of looking for new money. Nevertheless, the funding went ahead and was quickly disbursed. APSO arranged the secondment of the personnel to the NGOs, which was a pressing issue owing to the unprecedented scale of the refugee crisis. The deployment of military personnel in a civilian role raised legal and procedural issues which had to be overcome. It helped that David Andrews was now the Minister for Defence and favoured the step. He visited Rwanda and Goma in August, met the President and Vice President Paul Kagame, and supported the involvement of the Defence Forces.[9]

Around that time the question of a possible presidential visit to Rwanda began to be discussed. President Robinson was due to make State visits to a number of countries in Africa in October and the suggestion was that she could fit in a visit to Rwanda. Somalia showed that such a visit was possible and that it could have a helpful effect in focusing world attention.

Two problems arose: whereas a visit to the Rwandan capital, Kigali, seemed feasible, the main activity of the Irish NGOs was across the border in Zaire. The other question was the old one of the President's security. This proved to be a tougher nut to crack than I expected, given that the Somalia precedent was there.

I accompanied the President on the first two State visits – to Zambia and Zimbabwe. Tanzania was to be the third port of call. Two of the three destinations were priority countries for Irish Aid and the visit, the first to Africa since President Hillery went to Tanzania 14 years earlier, was seen as recognising the assistance which Ireland was giving. The visit went well with Zambia especially laying out the red carpet in every sense, the field artillery at the airport firing off a 21-gun salute in the old style being a good example. Zimbabwe was more of a political visit, a tribute to a country which had a difficult emergence from colonial rule and had suffered as a frontline state in the struggle against apartheid. This was before Robert Mugabe turned his country into an international pariah but all did not run smoothly during the visit and the President himself came across as truculent and unpredictable.

While the party was in Harare, we received a report from Barbara Jones who had gone on a reconnaissance visit to Rwanda and Zaire accompanied by a Garda Inspector, John Feeley. On the flight to Kigali she found herself sitting next to the Tanzanian Ambassador to Rwanda who gave her a good briefing on the history of the Arusha Accords. He warned her that the Rwandan government would be very sensitive to a visit by the Head of State that focused on the refugees in Zaire and did not pay tribute to the appalling sufferings which the country had suffered and which the new government was seeking to address.[10]

President Robinson was met in Kigali by representatives of Concern and Trocaire, had meetings in the capital and drove to Goma. Irish army personnel had by now been deployed in Goma under the UNHCR umbrella and were very helpful there. Among those she met were representatives of the charity CARE who had just lost one of their workers. But the verdict was that, while Goma was dangerous, the Interahamwe were in control and they would not want anything to happen which would divert attention from their political objectives – which focused on presenting themselves as the victims rather than the Rwandans they had slaughtered.

Barbara Jones's conclusion was that it was logistically feasible for the President to visit both Kigali and Goma. But, for some reason that we were never able to establish, it was felt back in Dublin that this assessment was not enough. The view was that I should go to Rwanda and double check the situation. This I did, dropping out of the Tanzanian visit.

Barbara Jones and I flew in a small hired plane to Kigali and after the meetings there we flew on to Goma. Once again I was struck by how dependent we were on the help of people on the ground: the Honorary Consul in Nairobi, Joe O'Brien; Brian McKeown, the former head of Trocaire who had based himself in Kigali and was focusing on the human rights dimension and had lots of contacts; Dominic McSorley of Trocaire; the army personnel who put us up in Goma; the Concern and GOAL and UNHCR staff who showed us around the camps.

The situation in the refugee camps was ghastly, every bit as bad as Barbara had reported. Hundreds of thousands of human beings were perched on volcanic rock, clutching their meagre possessions and with no idea what the future held for them. The fact that leaders of the genocide were among them and that many ordinary people had participated in murdering their neighbours could not take away from the dire situation they now found themselves in.

In Kigali we met the new President, Pasteur Bizimungu, a moderate Hutu, and the Vice President and Minister of Defence Paul Kagame. As in Somalia, we were extremely fortunate in that the UN Special Representative Shaharyar Khan, an experienced Pakistani diplomat, was most helpful, as was the head of UNAMIR, General Tousignant, who had just replaced Romeo Dallaire. All of them made it clear that they welcomed the idea of a visit by the President, indeed were eager for the Head of State of a neutral, respected country to witness their plight and bring it to the world's attention.

On the security aspect we were told that Kigali would be no problem, but some were doubtful about Goma. The US Ambassador assured us, however, that Goma was safe to visit and our own experience on the ground, especially with the presence of the Defence Force personnel, reassured us.

The atmosphere wherever we went was grim. Bodies were still being buried and stories of the genocide were everywhere to be found. A huge mass grave was marked by the roughest of crosses at the entrance – two branches tied together. One of the terrible sides to the killings was that thousands were slaughtered in Catholic churches, in some cases with the active involvement of clergy. We visited one such church in Kigali where the evidence was still all too clear with blood on the walls and bullet and shrapnel holes in the roof. A Polish priest had served there and I asked if I could see him. I was told: 'He will not see you. He has lost his faith.'

The only place we could find for the party to stay was the Hotel Mille Collines, close to the site of many killings and still in a chaotic state. With the stories we heard it was the last place anyone would want to stay but there was no alternative.

We flew back to Nairobi, taking off over the wreck of a transport plane which had not made it and lay beside the runway. We experienced one more shock to the system when our small plane was caught in a thunderstorm over one of Rwanda's volcanoes and we were buffeted back and forth. I wondered if we were to meet our end. We happened to have a bottle of whiskey left over from several we brought as gifts to smooth our way – it is the only time I drank whiskey straight from the bottle!

But I succeeded in sending off a report from Nairobi saying that, in my view, the visit could go ahead.

Mary Robinson was magnificent during her visit to Rwanda, which took place on 12-13 October. She had substantive meetings with the President and Paul Kagame and received briefings from the UN Special Representative and General Tousignant. In Goma she attended a meeting of the heads of all the humanitarian organisations and went to the camps where the Hutu refugees were being assisted by the Irish NGOs, avoiding the Interahamwe leaders who could be plainly seen. (They showed no sign of remorse; rather had looks of hatred and regret that they had not finished the job.) GOAL had distinguished itself by taking on the task of burying thousands of victims of cholera. The burial site was not as awful as on our advance visit in that earth now covered the bodies in an enormous mound. But the eerie silence and the sight of the mountain of earth were as bleak as you could find and it was no surprise when the President shed tears. The emotional impact of everything seen and heard in Rwanda was overwhelming.

It is hard to describe the tensions and pressures around the visit – the worries over the logistical arrangements, the President's security, making sure all of the NGOs got their due attention, getting the President and her party out of the country to the next stop, Uganda, which was not a formal visit but where she had a useful meeting with President Museveni. And all in the shadow of this awful event which had happened only a few months before.

The humanitarian disaster that overtook the vast number of Hutu refugees and displaced persons in Zaire became the focus of media attention in the months following the genocide. The coverage almost overshadowed the genocide itself and Paul Kagame's government had the toughest of tasks in re-building the shattered country.

Barbara Jones paid a return visit to Kigali in the Spring of 1995 to check on Irish Aid's expenditure and to decide if we should contribute more. She found that Ireland was one of the very few countries helping Rwanda to recover, apart from the US and the UK. Donors were divided over whether to support Kagame; the European Commission first gave assistance and then suspended it. It meant that Kagame's government was starved of support it badly needed to get the wrecked administration up and running again.[11]

Mary Robinson would make two further visits to Rwanda as President, in 1995 and 1997, and since then she has visited the country often, both as UN High Commissioner for Human Rights and after she left the UN.

I think that Rwanda, with the human rights issues it raised, was more her line of expertise than Somalia. It could be argued that the main issue in Rwanda, both before and after the genocide, was human rights. Rwanda saw the first serious efforts to monitor and strengthen human rights in a post-conflict situation. As such, it was a situation where development aid and foreign policy came together. Human rights had always been an issue in conflicts, of course, and abuses often were at the heart of conflicts, but it was only after the Rwandan genocide that considered attempts were made to put human rights centre stage. Both the UN and the EU launched major programmes in Rwanda aimed at ensuring that the rights of all, and not only the Rwandese Patriotic Front who had 'won', would be respected. Monitors were dispatched to all parts of the country.

In the years that followed, Ireland played a positive role in seeking to help this troubled country and to resolve the complex problems that the genocide posed. We supported Brian McKeown in his appointment as head of the EU monitoring mission. Irish Aid provided £1 million in funding for basic equipment to get ministries going again. During President Robinson's 1995 visit she was appalled by the conditions in which prisoners suspected of involvement in the genocide were being held, as was Minister of State Joan Burton who accompanied her. Ireland provided funding for a prison-feeding programme.

It was essential that the culture of impunity for mass killings, which were a feature of Rwanda and Burundi, should be stopped, so Ireland helped fund the International Tribunal for Rwanda, which was to ensure that the ringleaders of the genocide were brought to justice.

Mary Robinson has mixed feelings about Rwanda (as have most of the people involved that I spoke to).[12] She was warmly welcomed each time she went there as President but got a cold, even hostile reception from Kagame when she returned in 1997 as UN High Commissioner for Human Rights. He saw her as representing the UN and was almost insulting. She raised the growing concerns about his army's actions in Zaire and the treatment of prisoners who, however heinous their crimes, were entitled to a fair trial. Kagame denied that his people were doing anything at all in Zaire and brushed aside complaints of harsh treatment of what he called the *genocidaires*. She told me that she understood Kagame's bitterness towards the UN whose mistakes in Rwanda were glaring. And she feels his attitude was partly understandable in that he was trying to protect his people against the return of those who attempted to wipe out all of their opponents. But she also saw a control urge at play, which has strengthened over the years and has brought about a decline in Rwanda's reputation for justice and the rule of law.[13]

There could have been an argument for making Rwanda a priority country for Irish Aid. But the challenges were formidable and I wonder if we would have been able to cope with the serious governance issues, which still exist there. I visited Kigali in 2008 and found a country which is prospering economically and enjoying stability of a kind. But the human rights concerns have not gone away and, although Paul Kagame is a charismatic and thoughtful leader, his authoritarian approach is still a cause of worry. The future of both Rwanda and Burundi is far from certain.

Two postscripts: the year after the genocide I met the UN Special Representative Shaharyar Khan at a round table conference on Rwanda and he gave me a copy of a diary he kept during his time there. He asked me to forward it to President Robinson, which I did. It is a searing document, all the more powerful for being just one man's personal account.[14]

And secondly, since the Government's response to emergencies is often the target of criticism for being too little or too late, or to the wrong people, I quote from a letter the Chief Executive of Concern, the late Fr. Aengus Finucane, wrote to the Tanaiste in October 1994 and which he copied to the newspapers:

> I want to say thank you to the many TDs and to Government. Generous grants were made to Concern and to other organisations. Critically valuable people were released from their posts

to help in refugee camps. A special Government scheme released personnel on fully paid leave to volunteer their services
working with Concern and other NGOs. This was one of the
finest hours for official Irish foreign aid.[15]

As if the world had not supped full of sorrows, terrible things
were happening in the first half of the 1990s closer to home. Yugoslavia was falling apart as the constituent parts of the Communist-
era state threw off the yoke of Serbian control. The Serb leader,
Slobadan Milosevic, had no intention of letting his neighbours go
their separate ways. Lesser conflicts that pitched Serbia against
Croatia and Slovenia were followed by a much bloodier war in Bosnia. Every night television showed the suffering of the people of
Sarajevo as their city was bombarded and the citizens starved and
shot by snipers. The term 'ethnic cleansing' entered the language,
as did the name 'Srebrenica'.

The conflict went from one atrocity to another with the international community seemingly unable to stop the killing. The UN
tried and failed to force Milosevic to the negotiating table. Only
when NATO upped the military stakes was a peace deal reached.

If Rwanda was primarily dealt with by Development Cooperation Division, the crisis in the former Yugoslavia was primarily seen
as a political problem and in the Department of Foreign Affairs it
was Political Division which took the lead.[16] Ted Barrington was the
Political Director and his views are worth recording in detail:

> I never felt the pressure of organised public opinion in the way
> that we had on apartheid, East Timor or Somalia for instance.
>
> I think there were several reasons for this. One was the absence
> of long standing links to the area. I am not aware of historic
> ties, and in the post-World War II period Yugoslavia was an-
> other member of the Communist bloc, albeit with an independ-
> ent stance under Tito. Another reason was the complexity of
> the conflict, especially in Bosnia where the Muslim, Croat and
> Serb ethnic composition of the area was quite complicated and

alliances were frequently shifting. A third was the fear of being dragged militarily into the imbroglio, which involved the major countries in Europe as well as Russia and the US. And there was also, I think, a religious element. Once the northern Catholic territories of Slovenia and Croatia achieved independence the war was essentially between the Muslim Bosniaks and the Orthodox Serbs (although with a considerable Catholic Croatian front around Mostar also). Finally, I think insofar as there was a public opinion it supported the main planks of the EU and UN efforts to recognise the independence of Slovenia, Croatia and Bosnia; to bring about a negotiated settlement through an International Conference; to achieve a ceasefire (indeed a series of ceasefires) and monitor them; to implement and patrol an arms embargo; and to provide aid.

Almost all of these planks had their critics. Some felt that greater effort should have been made at an earlier stage to keep Yugoslavia together and that the EU capitulated too easily to the German pressure to recognise Croatia. But in reality by 1991 there was no way that Yugoslavia could have been held together. Recognition faced this reality and in fact allowed the international community to intervene by transforming the conflict from being a civil war to an inter-State conflict. The arms embargo was also controversial because it disadvantaged the Bosniaks who had no substantial army (unlike the Serbs) and could not import arms easily (as the Croats, with their long coastline, could). But there was no way the UN Security Council could have achieved agreement on a partial embargo – Russia would have vetoed any attempt to impose an embargo on Serbia only.

There was considerable criticism of this in the US where there were strong voices in Congress for a policy of 'lift and strike' – lift the embargo and carry out more intensive air strikes. In practice the arms embargo was not strictly enforced when it came to the Bosnians – they got arms from Iran and the Middle East and there is evidence that the US itself was involved as well.

The one element in international policy that I think is justly criticised is the creation of safe areas. The idea was good but the UN (and the EU) failed to back up the policy with sufficient force. There was always a difficulty with the idea of more ground troops, with the British in particular opposed, mainly because they would have been the main European component. The Dutch troops could not protect the safe area of Srebrenica and, when it fell, so did the policy. After Srebrenica the US and NATO decided to step up the military response by intensifying air strikes against Serb forces in Bosnia. Some argue that if the policy of lift and strike had been adopted earlier the war would have been brought to an earlier end. I think there is something in this and the sad thing is that it took a massacre to convince people of it.

Maybe the EU could have argued more forcefully for a military response but it was divided internally on the matter and we were certainly in no position to take an advanced posture. On the other hand, the EU can, I think, argue that the eventual agreement did correspond in almost all points to EU policy as it evolved over the four years of the conflict.[18]

Ireland provided humanitarian assistance, mainly through UN-HCR and the Red Cross. Money was also given to the few Irish NGOs working with the victims – Refugee Trust and Cradle – and to the Dublin Rape Crisis Centre which provided counselling services for Bosnian women and girls who were deliberately targeted by the Serbs. After the Dayton Accords, which ended the fighting, Dick Spring announced a further £1 million package for urgent humanitarian and rehabilitation needs in Bosnia. The purpose of the money was to restore gas and electricity to the ravaged city and to support UNHCR's work of rebuilding people's homes. Barbara Jones got a sense of the people's plight when she went to Mostar and Sarajevo with Eugene Hutchinson of Political Division in 1995, and later to Goradze. The young people who were able to had fled, leaving the unfortunate older ones in the ruins, often in flats on high floors of buildings where the lifts no longer worked and there was no water. They were literally starving to death.[19]

I attended several meetings of the Oireachtas Foreign Affairs Committee where the war was discussed, together with colleagues from Political Division. Members of the Committee would express their frustration at what they saw as the ineffective response which the EU, and hence Ireland, were making to resolving the conflict. You could sense their relief when they turned to me and I was able to inform them that the Minister was authorising a new tranche of funding for humanitarian assistance.

Fergus Finlay told me that, while he valued the fact that Ireland could give relief aid, he regarded what we did as 'the soft side' of foreign policy compared to the harder options involving military or police action which political intervention entailed.[20] I was surprised at this as I found the work of identifying how to disburse funding responsibly and in an accountable way far from soft. But, thinking about it, I suppose he had a point. It is easier to announce a package of relief (especially when the aid budget is growing) than to find a way of agreeing on an EU approach to such a difficult problem as the former Yugoslavia. Even worse: relief could be turned to as an alternative to actually solving the political problem. Humanitarian assistance could create an illusion of action.

At least the Yugoslav crisis meant that there were frequent contacts between Political and Development Cooperation Divisions. I had very good relations with Ted Barrington, who played a central role in the drafting of the White Paper on Foreign Policy, on this issue and on all the other areas where the two Divisions' interests coincided.

Proposals have been made to strengthen the day-to-day links in the Department of Foreign Affairs between Political and Development Cooperation. A radical approach would be to merge them completely with a single unit in the Department dealing with Africa for example, or one dealing with all aspects of the UN. This would not, however, resolve the problem that the issues are dealt with separately by different experts and different working groups in Brussels and New York.

A decade after the Yugoslav experience I and my deputy Brendan Rogers arranged with the then Political Director Rory Montgomery to place cooperation on a more formal basis by having quarterly inter-divisional meetings. These proved very helpful to both sides with a full agenda of topics and a good flow of information. I will show later that the issue of closer interaction between the two divisions continues to be very much on the agenda.[21]

There was one other area where Irish Aid had an input to the war in the former Yugoslavia and that was in regard to refugees.

Oddly enough, in my time, responsibility for resettling refugees in Ireland was the responsibility of the Department of Foreign Affairs and not, as it is today, the Department of Justice. Until the 1980s it had been overseen by the Civil Defence branch of the Department of Defence; then, in 1985, the Government set up a policy advisory committee and transferred the Refugee Resettlement Committee to the Minister for Foreign Affairs. The person in charge was the late Michael Stone, formerly of the Department of Defence. Michael was old school and his approach would probably be seen today as paternalistic. But he took a personal interest in his charges and made himself available 24/7, and I would say that many a refugee was thankful that Michael was around in those days to help.

The refugees in question were those who the Government sanctioned for entry to Ireland – 'programme refugees' as they came to be called. They were groups of people escaping from persecution in their own country: Hungarians in 1956, Chileans in 1974, Vietnamese boat people in 1979/81 and Bahais from Iran in the 1980s. In 1991, as the pace of refugees coming to Ireland began to increase, the Refugee Agency was set up to oversee the practical arrangements for the programme refugees. Irish Aid provided the funding.

The Yugoslav war resulted in hundreds of thousands of people – mainly Bosnians – losing their homes and in urgent need of resettlement. Every EU country was expected to do their bit. A first

Patrick Keating of Bord na Mona, Burundi, late 1970s – an early Irish Aid-funded project

*Minister of State Jim O'Keeffe with Dr. Jonathan Lebua at the official opening
of the marketing centre of the Lesotho pony project.*

APSO seminar to mark International Volunteers Day, 5 December 1988: from left, Bill Jackson Chief Executive; the Rev. Father Bede McGregor; H.E. Dasho Jigme Thinley, then Ambassador of Bhutan to the United Nations; Doireann Ni Bhriain of RTE, who chaired the seminar; and Sean Calleary TD, then Minister of State for Development Co-operation

Professor George Dawson, TCD – he advocated the setting up of a Government aid programme

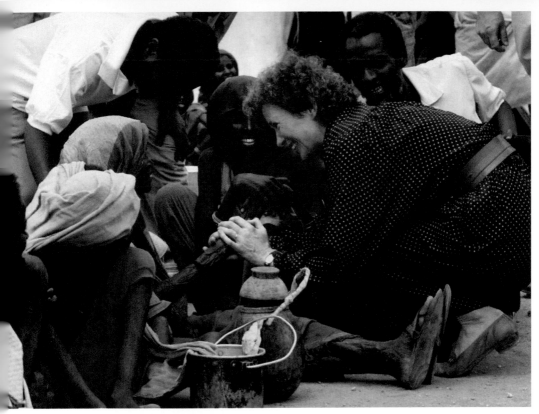

Mary Robinson, Somalia, 1992

The author and Tom Kitt speaking to a UN official at the Tanzania/Rwanda border, 1994

Garret FitzGerald paying a return visit to Lesotho in 2006 with his grandson, also Garret

Launch of the first ever White Paper on Irish Aid, 2006

Some of the leading figures in development in Ireland gathering in Iveagh House, 2006. Included Michael Kitt, Aengus and Jack Finucane, John and Kay O'Loughlin Kennedy, Dermot Ahern, Tom Arnold, Liz O'Donnell, Joan Burton, Michael O'Kennedy, Brendan Rogers, the author

Bertie Ahern in Tanzania, 2006

Plaque at the Mikumi Vocational School, Kilosa, Tanzania

Ireland's Ambassador to Uganda, Kevin Kelly, with specialst staff, Kampala, 2010

Peter Power, Haiti, 2010

Banda Aceh, Indonesia, after the 2004 tsunami

Mary McAleese in a hospice in Liberia

group of 200 Bosnian refugees came to Ireland in July 1992 and a further 200 a year later. Although the numbers were small compared to the thousands of asylum seekers who would make their way to Ireland during the Celtic Tiger years, they were the largest group so far admitted, reaching 800 by 1996. We worked closely with the Office of the High Commissioner for Refugees whose London chief, Diane Grammer, served on the board of Refugee Agency.

The arrangements for transportation were made through the International Organisation for Migration, a low key Swiss-based organisation which hired passenger jets and got the people on board and off with the minimum of fuss. The first groups of Bosnians to come to Ireland caused something of a shock because they were so different from the refugees we were accustomed to. These bewildered looking families of men, women and children were *Europeans*; interviews with them showed that many were highly educated, middle class people caught up in a nightmare. I think this brought home to people the enormity of what was being done to the Bosnians more graphically than TV coverage of atrocities.

One of the refugee experiences which almost went wrong was called Operation Irma. It arose from a UK initiative in 1993 during the siege of Sarajevo and was named after a young girl who was injured in one of the worst incidents of the war, the bombing of a Sarajevo marketplace. The objective was good – to evacuate seriously wounded Bosnians – but the whole thing was media driven and hastily put together. I remember getting the phone call from London on a Friday with the request that Ireland and Sweden join with the UK and feeling some doubts but I went ahead and got ministerial approval.

We sent out two officers who discovered that there were considerable doubts about the project locally on many grounds, not least the wisdom of taking casualties so far from their relatives for treatment, which was still in many cases available nearby. And it turned out that the number of evacuees suitable for treatment was much fewer than anticipated. It began to look as if we were only brought in so that the initiative would not be seen as solely British. What started out as a worthy cause saw the atmosphere between the different nationalities turn sour.

As it happened, our people were able to identify a dozen patients who needed treatment urgently and, with the help of the International Organisation of Migration, we got them to Dublin in a plane that was specially adapted for stretchers. I went to the airport to see their arrival, preoccupied by the wrangling of the previous weeks and unsure what reception the 'medivacs' (as they were called) would get.

I needn't have worried. As the plane released its cargo of casualties on stretchers or limping with the support of nurses, the journalists fell silent. The only sound to be heard was the clicking of cameras.

Endnotes

1. 'Development Cooperation: Ireland's Bilateral Programme' DFA, 1979, p. 7.

2. Fergus Finlay interview.

3. 'White Paper Foreign Policy Challenges and Opportunities', Government Publications, Dublin, 1996.

4. Op cit pp. 16, 42. See also p. 7: 'Ireland's foreign policy is about much more than self interest. For many of us it is a statement about the kind of people we are.'

5. Irish Aid has been separately located from the rest of the Department from its earliest days. The Assistant Secretary in charge (now Director General) sometimes had an office in Iveagh House – as I did briefly – but this was the exception. Most of the time, the entire Division has been located in 72 St. Stephens Green, then in Harcourt Street and later in Bishop's Square.

6. Like Somalia, the Rwanda genocide has produced a vast literature. Human Rights Watch published a detailed and much praised account *Leave None to Tell the Story: Genocide in Rwanda*, Alison Des Forges, Human Rights Watch publication New York 1999. Philip Gourevich's *We Wish to Inform You that Tomorrow We Will Be Killed with Our Families*, Farrar, Strauss and Giroux, 1998, is also required reading. The accounts of Romeo Dallaire and Shaharyar Khan are referred to below. But there is an immense range of publications, from UN reports to academic studies. Browsing in a bookstore at Dar es Salam airport recently I saw a whole shelf of books on the subject. For the Irish perspective see the article in Annual Report 1994, pp. 21-23, chapter on Rwanda in

Tony Farmar's history of Concern, Brian Mayes' history of Trocaire and O'Leary and Burke's biography of Mary Robinson, pp. 255-58.

7.   Anne Clery, formerly of GOAL, now head of Aidlink, interview.

8.   Lt General Romeo Dallaire *Shake Hands with the Devil: The Failure of Humanity in Rwanda*, Random House, Canada, 2003.

9.   David Andrews, *Kingstown Republican*, pp. 224, 237-8.

10. Barbara Jones interview.

11. Barbara Jones interview.

12. Mary Robinson interview. See also O'Leary and Burke, pp. 257-8.

13. By chance I was working for Mary Robinson in Geneva in 1999 when a report was published which was highly critical of the UN's human rights monitoring mission in Rwanda. Although the report referred to events that pre-dated her term as High Commissioner, Mary Robinson called in the donors, said she accepted the findings and pledged to learn the lessons – rightly in my view as the Office's reputation was at stake, although one old UN hand told me he saw no reason for the UN to explain itself to anyone!

14. It was later published as *The Shallow Graves of Rwanda*. Romeo Dallaire called it 'the most complete account of how the international community failed to help the survivors of the genocide'.

15. Letter in *Sunday Tribune* October 1994. A longer letter on the same lines was sent by Aengus Finucane to Tanaiste Dick Spring on 3 October 1994.

16. Reflecting the 'political' nature of the Balkan wars, there is less coverage in the Irish Aid Annual Reports than of crises such as Somalia and Rwanda with only brief mentions of the aid/refugee dimension, e.g. p. 18 of the Annual Report 1992 and references to the work of the Refugee Agency which appear from 1995 on.

17. Ted Barrington interview.

18. Barbara Jones interview.

19. Fergus Finlay interview.

20. A Management Review conducted by Farrell Grant Sparks in 2008 focused on this aspect in some detail. This is discussed further below in Chapter 16.

10

A CHANGE OF DIRECTION

The most significant change since Irish Aid was established began in the late 1990s. It happened without fanfare but it has
had a greater impact on the way the programme operates than any
other decision. And it has caused more controversy than any other
aspect of Irish Aid's work. I am referring to the move away from
funding individual projects to supporting governments in partner
countries.

The change in direction did not come out of the blue. International thinking on development policy had evolved as the evidence
mounted that the ways of doing it had not been effective and were
not achieving the core aim of bringing poor people out of poverty.
There was a second major reason for the change in the case of Irish
Aid: while the budget was rising significantly and would continue
to do so for another decade, personnel resources remained very
modest, in spite of constant appeals for more staff.

By this time I had moved on and would not return to the aid
programme until 2004.

It is worth mentioning one change which Irish Aid did not
make but which many of our fellow donors did around that time.
The collapse of Communism caused European donors to look to
the newly independent Eastern European countries and Russia as
suitable recipients of aid and many of them diverted considerable
chunks of their aid budget eastwards.

I saw this myself when I was appointed ambassador to Russia in
1995, with secondary accreditation to six countries of the former

Soviet Union. I visited projects funded with the generous money available from the EU and the member states, the World Bank and the newly created European Bank for Reconstruction and Development. What struck me straightaway was that the situation in these countries was completely different from Africa. Certainly many people were poor, especially in countries like Belarus, Armenia and Kazakhstan, but the countries of the former Soviet Union had well developed infrastructure, high levels of education and some had vast energy and natural resources. Their challenge was to replace the failed Communist economic model with a system which would produce growth and wealth for their people.

Irish Aid did commit to giving some assistance to Eastern Europe.[1] It is mentioned in the Strategy Plan and the Ireland Aid Review of 2002 would make a specific commitment to spend 2 per cent of the overall budget to Eastern Europe, Russia the Balkans and the countries of the former Soviet Union. In the event, the programme contributed comparatively little to Eastern Europe, rightly so in my opinion, as we had scant expertise and the situation was far from what people thought. The experience of other donors is salutary, too, as the approach of trying to turn the region into a replica of Western Europe fell at the first fence. The Big Bang approach to the Russian economy resulted in millions losing their savings overnight. Today, Russia and the countries of the former Soviet Union are finding their own solutions – and, some might say, making their own mistakes. But what is clear is that a great deal of the money which went into the region from donors in the 1990s went down the drain.

Where Ireland did play a role was through transfer of technical expertise, which our consultants provided under the EU's PHARE and TACIS programmes. Irish consultants displayed the same qualities which suited them to development work in Africa: they did not talk down to people, they were able to put themselves in the position of those they were helping and they did not have a particular agenda.

An even more practical contribution came when Irish entrepreneurs demonstrated through their own example the way to do business and make a profit. They were pioneers in that they went out ahead of others to Russia and neighbouring states when they were still largely unknown territory. And they were successful: all sorts of Irish-run businesses were thriving in Moscow when I arrived, including the first Western style supermarket on Novy Arbat and the profitable Aer Rianta duty free shops at Sheremetyevo and St Petersburg airports.

My 'aid' work in Russia was confined to securing funding for a project to help prisoners suffering from TB. Conditions in the prisons were appalling. A prison sentence could be the equivalent of a death sentence due to the prevalence of illnesses such as TB and malnutrition. The project was run by Medecins sans Frontieres. I was brought on a tour of the mobile health clinics MSF operated in the Moscow streets by an Irish doctor who showed me that frostbite was one of the biggest problems, especially for drunks who fell asleep outdoors in the freezing winters. When she saw me wince as she lanced the swollen fingers of one man she commented: 'This is all right. It's when the fingers and toes turn black that there is a problem.'

Meanwhile, back in Harcourt Street, my successor, Margaret Hennessy, had a baptism of fire when she had to arrange President Robinson's second visit to Rwanda just weeks after taking up duty.[2]

Margaret found, as I had, that the lack of sufficient staff made implementation of the ever-increasing funds a serious problem. There were constant crises, which prevented you from having time to think and plan. Margaret reminded me that I had described being in charge as trying to stay in the saddle of a bucking bronco! Later she wrote a dissertation for her Master's Degree in Trinity describing the management challenges of running the aid programme at a time of rapid and substantial increases of funding. Her analysis of the administrative constraints and the trade offs that had to be made to keep the ship afloat struck me as spot on.[3]

There was some good news on the staffing front. This period saw the recruitment to Irish Aid of more development specialists. Dr. Vincent O'Neill came on board as Health Adviser, Liz Higgins as Education Policy Analyst and William Carlos, a specialist in emergency assistance. Later Finbar O'Brien, who had been in charge of Irish Aid's programme in Zambia's Northern Province, came home and headed a new Audit and Evaluation Unit. What the newcomers had in common was field experience and a background of working for the Agency for Personal Service Overseas (Vinnie) and NGOs such as Concern (William) and Trocaire (Liz).

The strengthening of Irish Aid's specialist expertise, a process that would grow over the years, filled a gap in the programme's capacity which had been there from the outset. Development specialists were assigned to the missions in the priority countries to work with the diplomatic officers and this, too, was a good step forward. There was a downside in that the only way to get sanction to recruit these experts was by giving the specialists limited contracts. This was a ticking bomb which would cause a lot of trouble in time.

Margaret Hennessy had been Ambassador to India, which gave her a firsthand sense of the developing world. Her deputy, Martin Greene, who would succeed her in 2001 as Director General, was the first officer to take charge with the experience of working in the field for Irish Aid. Brendan Rogers, another future Director General, returned from being head of mission in Zambia as did two other highly experienced Africa hands, Pauline Conway and Frank Sheridan.

The Minister of State who succeeded Tom Kitt was Joan Burton, the first Minister with direct experience of working in Africa. She was delighted to get the job; she believed that aid is a long-term game and was proud of overseeing the change from short-term grants to the NGOs to longer term block grants.[4]

The 1990s were a time of change in international thinking about aid. The most significant change of policy was the movement away from funding projects to working through governments, first through support for individual sectors such as health and education and later through general budget support.

The reason why so many donors changed their basic approach in this way is down to a host of factors, but the fundamental rationale is the flaws in the model of funding individual projects, which became apparent over time.

To recap on the project format: donors such as Irish Aid would identify areas where the partner country lacked expertise; they would make an evaluation as to whether they could assist, estimate what funding would be needed and establish whether the necessary expertise was available; they would deliver these inputs in the form of Technical Assistance on the ground (agricultural experts, doctors and nurses, teacher trainers, mechanics, engineers) together with funding for equipment, buildings, transport etc; and they would train personnel from the partner country, the aim being for the trainees to eventually take over the jobs held by the expatriates. At the end of the process the partner country would take over the running of the operation, which would then continue without external support.

That was the theory. But the model often failed to deliver what it promised. Donors could fall into the trap of over resourcing a particular project, achieving what looked like impressive results but in reality following an approach that was neither replicable nor sustainable. Martin Greene carried out a study of Irish Aid's early projects in Lesotho. Out of 16 projects he concluded that only three had the essential quality of sustainability after the training and funding were withdrawn.[5]

There were flaws in the project approach:

- Projects often took place outside the system and plans of the partner government. Government ministries and regional authorities of the partner countries were often unaware of what donors were doing.

- There was duplication as a plethora of donors, both bilateral and multilateral, got involved in the same sorts of projects. Sometimes the number of different donors and projects in a given country was bewilderingly large.

- Donors had different accounting systems, different project cycles, different budget years which the partner countries had to adapt to. The jargon-filled paperwork placed a big administrative burden on partner governments' weak systems.

- Many projects were supply-driven. Spare capacity in the donor country did not necessarily coincide with the partner's needs. Ireland is justifiably proud that we have never tied our aid to purchase of our products in the way that some big donors do. But, in the early years of the programme especially, the availability of Irish expertise played a big part in the choice of projects.

- Projects, once started, were hard to bring to an end, even when they were not producing results. Heads of Mission complained that they inherited projects from their predecessors (some personality-driven), which were often past their sell-by date.

- Stakeholders had a vested interest in the continuation of a project – and not just the local people. Institutions and colleges in the donor country valued the funding from consultancy work. This could lead to institutional resistance to ending an unsuccessful project.

There were unintended consequences, too, in the project approach. Some technical consultants who went to partner countries found the life congenial and were in no hurry to leave. The administrative side of looking after large numbers of expatriate technical staff and their families took up a great deal of the Head of Mission's attention.

The training of personnel in Ireland also carried risks. It is not hard to see how some of those who travelled to Ireland might be seduced by the higher living standards they encountered and be reluctant to return home. The head of the Swiss development programme told me how his Government had identified forestry as an important skill that could benefit Rwanda, a country rich in forests. They funded Rwandan trainees to come to learn skills in Switzerland with a view to putting these skills to good use back home. But when they carried out an assessment they found that there was no great increase in forestry expertise in Rwanda but that there was a growing community of Rwandan foresters living in Switzerland!

Above all, the figures showed that, after decades of aid, countries targeted for assistance were not emerging from poverty. The key indicators – access to clean water, health and education, economic growth and jobs – showed few improvements and in some cases were worse than at the outset. This bleak picture is not meant to belittle the work done by those engaged in development assistance in the early days or to imply that the project approach does not have its advantages.

A project's outcomes may also be more beneficial than appears at first sight. The former Lesotho Ambassador to Ireland, Manette Ramilli, worked for UNICEF and then Irish Aid before being appointed her country's representative here.[6] She told me about a health project which aimed to encourage women living in remote villages to dispense medicines so as to avoid people having to travel long distances. The money collected was not sufficient for the dispensing scheme to continue and a review concluded that the project was not a success. But Manette thought that this bald conclusion did not take account of the impact the project had on the lives of the women involved. For them it was the first time they had worked together to gather money for a joint cause, and the first time they had a bank account and the experience of access to – albeit small – amounts of money to help their community. She feels that these kinds of outcomes, while they might not feature in a report, are no small achievement and can make a lasting difference.

A similar point was made to me about the knitting project in Lesotho. While the involvement of Irish Aid came to an end, the tradition of knitting and tapestry is still alive. There are many other examples of the lasting effects of projects, which on the face of it did not fully achieve their stated objectives.

What cannot be in dispute is that donors often sought to impose their ideas and plans on partner countries rather than listening to what local people had to say. The guiding principle behind the new approach to development that gathered strength in the 1990s was that, whether projects or programmes were used, the partners should be in the driving seat. The key objective was to enable partner governments to strengthen their own financial and accounting systems so that they could provide their people with essential services such as health and education themselves.

The funding of particular sectors of government activity such as health and education was known as sector support or SWAPs (sector-wide approaches). Donors would put money into a fund or 'basket' which the partner government would use to further its own plans, for example, the building of schools and training of teachers; or, in the health area, the building and equipment of hospitals and providing a full range of medical services. By earmarking funds for a particular sector, the money would be ring-fenced by donors so that it could only be used for the intended purpose.

Budget support takes it a step further: it consists of funding that goes straight into the partner government's budget. It is usually aligned with a poverty reduction strategy adopted by the government concerned whose progress can be monitored.[7]

Just as the drawbacks of the project approach look convincing, so the arguments in favour of sector and budget support look persuasive:

- Instead of bypassing governments, sector and budget support seeks to engage and increases a country's own capacity to deliver essential services.

- It strengthens country ownership of the process rather than operating a parallel system.

- It leads to better coordination among donors and hence more coherent delivery of assistance and less duplication of effort.

- It gives the partner country more predictability as to the funding that will be made available by the donors.

- It allows for greater scrutiny of budgets and spending by governments.

So why have sector and budget support sparked controversy?

The strongest criticism is that money could be diverted as a result of corruption or, instead of going towards poverty reduction, could be wasted on vanity schemes or the purchase of arms. Sector support would appear to offer better protection against this risk than budget support in that the funds are earmarked. But critics say there is still the risk that, by funding sectors such as health and education, donors may free up other funds for governments to spend on unproductive items. Obviously, the risk of such a development is even greater if general budget support is given.

There is a word for this – 'fungibility' – which means the ability to substitute one kind of expenditure for another. (Though it must be said that fungibility applies to projects also: for example, during the Idi Amin era in Uganda donors' support for health and education projects allowed the regime to allocate national resources to the military. And in Nyerere's Tanzania massive donor support for projects facilitated the spending of national resources on unproductive activities.)

John O'Shea of GOAL has argued against working with governments in the developing world, stating that they have a bad track record for corruption and for spending money on arms when their people are starving.

It would be foolish to argue that corruption does not exist in partner countries, or that diversion of funds has never happened, but there are ways of reducing the risk.

A crucial element is the role played by donors on the ground in tracking what happens to money going through government channels. A big advantage of sector and budget support is that it provides the opportunity of applying conditionality at the level of the national budget. To be effective, this must be accompanied by a strengthening of the local systems and watchdogs which monitor government expenditure. Bodies equivalent to our Public Accounts Committee and Ombudsman's offices need proper funding so that they can scrutinise the government's accounts and draw attention to any abuses. Parliamentary committees need to be assisted to build up their role as scrutineers of government policy. Irish Aid is engaged in this type of work in all of the priority countries – assisting the Lesotho Ombudsman and Auditor General and the Zambian Public Accounts Committee, for example.[8]

Just as important is the partner country's civil society – the media, private organisations, trade unions – in whose interest it is to ensure that their government does spend sector and budget support on poverty reduction. Civil society in many poor countries is weak so much effort has been put into helping them to develop the skills they need to make their voices heard.

Irish Aid came to sector and budget support slowly. By the time the issues were examined in the Ireland Aid Review of 2002, total budget support (to Uganda and Mozambique) came to just €7.6 million. The volume of aid being channelled through these mechanisms has increased very substantially since then. The Review endorsed sector support as a valid mechanism but was more cautious about budget support. It pointed out that:

> A balance must be struck between the need for prudence with donor taxpayers' money and fostering the desired sense of responsibility on the part of a partner government for its own economic and social development.

And it concluded that:

> The rewards offered by budget support in terms of poverty re-
> duction and overall development are likely to outweigh the
> risks involved. However, (the Committee) underlines the need
> for prudence and for careful and continuing risk assessment
> and management.[9]

Two further drawbacks associated with sector and budget support deserve mention.

The first is the loss of profile for the work being done. The removal of 'national flags' is an inevitable element in moving away from projects. Supporters argue that it sums up the change from solutions imposed by outsiders to ownership by the partners. This is a valid point but what about the donors? Public support for helping the developing countries is essential; what happens when there is little for them to see in terms of results of Ireland's funding?

The second, more serious question around direct support to governments is whether donors would really be prepared to suspend funding in the event that diversion or mismanagement of funds come to light, or serious human rights abuses were carried out by the partner government. Donors on the ground, who have invested their time and energy in working with a partner government, are unlikely to recommend putting an end to the partnership if at all possible. They are also at a remove from the criticism that can blow up at headquarters.

Irish Aid has taken action on budget support on several occasions: in Uganda we changed from budget support to a Poverty Action Fund which meant that the money was ring-fenced after evidence emerged that the Ugandan government was sending troops to the Democratic Republic of Congo. In 2006, €3 million of funding to Uganda was suspended because the government there had failed to meet a series of governance targets that the donors had set. In another priority country, Ethiopia, Irish Aid decided not to go down the road of budget support due to concerns about human rights abuses. Instead, it was decided to put funds into a safety nets programme to help very poor people. More recently, in Mozambique, the donors put pressure on the government to reverse measures they had taken, with the threat that budget support would be cut. The government backed down.

Interestingly, during a visit I made to Kampala shortly after we froze the €3 million, I was upbraided by several EU heads of mission who said that Ireland ought not to have cut funding to Uganda! And the European Commission – one of the strongest supporters of budget support – is quite vague about the action that should be taken in the event of things going wrong.

Funding governments directly has increased exponentially since the 1990s and today it is the preferred mechanism of many donors. But it can only work if the conditions are right. For the reasons mentioned above, it has to be approached with caution and must be accompanied by strengthening national and local institutions and civil society.

The replies I got from those I interviewed for this book ranged from the zealous to the sceptical, but the large majority felt the jury is still out on sector and budget support. Most favoured a mix of different forms of aid, including projects and programme support. This is the trend that Irish Aid has broadly followed.

The move away from projects radically changed the way Irish Aid worked. The number of Irish Technical Assistants in the field – at the height of the project phase, Irish Aid had more than 70 – was reduced drastically until hardly any remained. For example, when Fintan Farrelly arrived as Head of Mission in Lesotho in 1993 there were sixteen TAs and when he left in 1997 only seven remained, three of whom were finishing out their contracts.[10]

The move away from expatriate technical assistance was also seen in the design of new Area Based Programmes, which continued to be an important feature of the programme. Lessons were learned from the experience of Kilosa in Tanzania, where large numbers of TAs had been engaged in a wide variety of activities. The new Area Based Programmes were designed in very close liaison with the governments and the regional authorities. An example was the work carried out in the Kibaale district of Uganda. A remote and neglected area in the west of the country, Kibaale's partnership with Irish Aid started in 1994 and within a few years it had turned into one of the fastest growing districts in the region. The areas focused on – the building of roads, health and education – were no different from those assisted elsewhere. The difference was the emphasis on local ownership. The local administration was encouraged to raise revenue and administer its own affairs. A similar approach was followed in other Area Based Programmes begun in the 1990s, such as Sidama and Tigray in Ethiopia.

This period also saw a move away from the sending of volunteers to the field. The Agency for Personnel Overseas (APSO) was faced with a shift internationally away from the model of sending out young Westerners to change the world. The organisation had broadened its scope to include new activities such as monitoring elections, but there was no denying that as economic growth in Ireland brought more wealth and opportunities the numbers volunteering were falling.

Aidan Eames was the last chair of APSO, succeeding Dr. Anthony Clare; he also served as acting CEO during its final two years. When he arrived, APSO was 30 years old, founded in the context of a belief in technical assistance and north-south knowledge transfer comprised of both technical and development people. It still had the same model as when it was founded. The budget had risen to almost €30 million. Eames asked himself whether this was the correct strategic direction for APSO.[11] He commissioned professionals to study the situation and says that, to the credit of the APSO board, they rowed in. The verdict was that there was a large question mark over whether APSO's approach was sustainable and needs based. The end came when the Ireland Aid Review, commissioned by Liz O'Donnell, recommended that APSO be closed and the staff absorbed into the Department of Foreign Affairs.

It would be wrong to leave the volunteers' story untold as it is such a central part of the development story and so many of those who went on to be leaders in development started off as volunteers of one form or another.

Living in modest surroundings, and for very little pay, volunteers gave dedicated service, often under difficult and hazardous conditions, to the NGOs, international organisations and other donors. In many ways they were the successors of the missionaries, the difference being that theirs was not meant to be a lifelong commitment. Though for many, that is what it turned into.

Rosemary McCreery, who reached the top of her profession as an Assistant Secretary-General rank in the UN secretariat, began her career as an APSO volunteer.[12] She says she felt at a dead end in her job as Third Secretary in the Department of Foreign Affairs where her work in Anglo-Irish Division consisted largely of updating the lists of those killed in the North. She took the initiative to call in one day to APSO. There she met Bill Jackson whom she found contagiously enthusiastic. APSO sent her name to UN Volunteers where an Irishman, Sean Finn, was number two at the time.

UN Volunteers told her about a vacancy with UNICEF in Togo. She did not have proper qualifications and knew nothing about UNICEF or Togo but she got the job. Her title was Programme Associate but when she got to Togo she found that she would be working there on her own.

Rosemary based herself in the offices of the UN Development Programme where she had to start from scratch, buying the basic equipment she needed. She had a choice between hiring a driver or a secretary, as there was only money for one. She chose a driver as she could type better than she could drive. Communications were very difficult. The pouch took three weeks to get from UNICEF headquarters to Togo and phoning her boss in Abijdan was rarely possible. She found that she had to be almost totally self-reliant.

UNICEF was supplying health kits, nutrition and training and the programme budget was about $400,000 a year. She had a difficult moment when she discovered that some of UNICEF's money was being diverted to people in government and her Irish passport was taken away. She had a worrying few months wondering when she would get it back.

Her contacts with APSO were few once she got to Togo. Although she was required to send regular reports to APSO via UNV, she never knew if they were read or even forwarded to APSO.

After two years in Togo, Rosemary went to Madagascar. It was a time when UNICEF was in full expansionist mode under the leadership of Jim Grant. Up till then they had been assisting by remote control; now they wanted representatives in every country. From being a volunteer she now became a UNICEF staffer. The Madagascar office was just starting and again she was on her own. She marvels at the amount of work that the five staff in the office achieved. UNICEF offices have grown a great deal since. Recently she was talking to a UNICEF person from the Madagascar office who remarked: 'It's a small office, just 90 people.'

Rosemary McCreery says that APSO changed her life. If APSO had not been willing to take a chance on her she would never have had her UN career. 'Bill Jackson was a convincing advocate for development work. APSO's great strength was that people were given a chance.'

One initiative which was not abandoned was the funding of fellowships for postgraduate studies in Ireland. This is one of Irish Aid's oldest programmes. The story of Professor Yunus Mgaya, currently Deputy Vice Chancellor of the University of Dar es Salaam responsible for administration, is typical.[3]

He describes how a telex came in to his university in 1990 from Dr. John Mercer of University College Galway. He had met a Tanzanian Professor and was contacting him to say that he could get one fellowship for a candidate to work in his laboratory; he asked that a candidate be selected meritoriously to study for a PhD. Professor Mgaya was the only person eligible and aquaculture was the area he was interested in.

He already had offers of scholarships from Sweden and Germany and was faced with something of a dilemma as to which one to take. These were tough economic times in Tanzania with empty shelves in the shops so money was a consideration. Ireland offered lower money than the other two. Germany offered the most but he did not know the language and would have had to spend time learning it. He could have got by in Sweden as many Swedes speak English but it would have been difficult. Also, the Germans and the Swedes wanted him to further his studies under a sandwich arrangement whereby research work was to be conducted in Arusha and Zanzibar respectively, whereas the Irish did not specify a location. Another consideration was that he would be free to follow his specialty, which was mariculture, in Ireland. So he chose Ireland.

He spent 3½ years in Ireland between 1991-95. There was no funding available for his family and he had only one trip home during that time. He had to pay for his family to visit him. But he enjoyed Ireland. He was the only African in Connemara at the time, which made him something of a star. He lodged with an elderly lady together with two other students, one Irish, one Chinese. He made lots of friends and liked the pubs.

He has found that people often struggle with doctorates and have difficulty finishing them. But he saw light at the end of the tunnel half way into the programme and finished his within the allocated time. The only problem he faced in Ireland was loneliness and separation from his family, which was hard. His son was 10 months old when he left for Ireland and he did not see him again until he was 2½. When he first saw this strange man returning he ran out of the room!

In recent years Professor Mgaya has been active in the Tanzania-Ireland Alumni Association which he hopes will foster relations between the two countries. At the first meeting 150 people came . . .[14]

Endnotes

1. Strategy Plan, p. 27: '. . . assistance to Eastern Europe (will be) further developed.' *Report of the Ireland Aid Review Committee*, DFA publication, 2002; 'To tackle the real poverty in parts of Eastern Europe, the Balkans, the Russian Federation and the CIS and to assist in the transition of those states to democracy, the Committee recommends that an amount of about 20 per cent of Ireland Aid's budget be devoted to projects in that region', p. 9. See also pp. 60-61. My successor in charge of the programme, Margaret Hennessy, felt that Ireland could have been more visionary about Eastern Europe, 'not in regard to major infrastructural expenditure but in regard to governance and the rule of law. More could have been done to try to stem corruption, trafficking, crooked police forces and judicial services . . .'

2. Margaret Hennessy interview.

3. 'Efforts to build a Quality Overseas Aid Programme', Margaret Hennessy, Dissertation submitted for MSc degree, UCD, 2000.

4. Joan Burton, interview. Both Joan Burton and Margaret Hennessy singled out the move from individual NGO grants to longer term funding as an achievement they were particularly proud of.

5. Martin Greene interview.

6. HE Manette Ramilli was Lesotho's Ambassador to Ireland; she is now Minister for Tourism in the Lesotho Government. Interview.

7. From the growing literature about sector and budget support I would recommend a major study carried out by a consortium of donors and chaired by the Development Assistance Committee of the OECD in 2004 called *Joint Evaluation of General Budget Support 1994-2004*, Paris, 2006, OECD publication. The World Bank and the European Commission also have a lot of interesting material on their websites. I am grateful to William Carlos, head of Audit and Evaluation at Irish Aid, for sending me a recent Joint Irish Aid/UK Department for International Development evaluation of budget support in Tanzania, and to Liz Higgins for further background material.

8. The *Annual Report 2007* describes initiatives aimed at strengthening scrutiny of budgets and spending on the ground (pp. 42-3) and notes that 15 per cent of Irish Aid's expenditure goes towards support for governance.

9. *Ireland Aid Review*, pp. 73-5.

10. Fintan Farrelly interview.

11. Aidan Eames interview. I am grateful also to John Daly and Bridget Mayes of APSO for sharing their experiences with me, and to Donal McDonald for letting me see his work on the history of APSO.

12. Rosemary McCreery interview.

13. Professor Yunus Mgaya interview.

14. Training of personnel in Ireland has been a central feature of the aid programme from the start. Michael O'Hea, who has worked for Irish Aid in various capacities over the years, recalled an ambitious programme which the Institute of Public Administration carried out with Irish Aid funding in the 1990s whereby 25 Regional Commissioners from Tanzania came to Ireland for training in management and local government. Many went on to hold ministerial and other high offices in Tanzania. Interview.

11

KILOSA'S STORY

The move away from projects to sector and budget support saw the end of some of the older activities carried out by Irish Aid. The most ambitious project of the early years was in Kilosa, Tanzania. In its day the Kilosa District programme was regarded as the flagship of Irish Aid, not only in Tanzania but in the whole programme. In 2010 I returned to Kilosa to see what impact Irish Aid had had and what became of the district after the programme ended.[1]

Kilosa is one of six districts, which make up the Morogoro Region in central Tanzania. It is roughly the size of Munster and has a population of around half a million people. Irish Aid began to work there in 1979 and continued until the early 2000s.

The choice of Kilosa came about through Irish Aid's interest in building up its activities in Tanzania after it was designated a priority country. At the same time, the Tanzanian government had an interest in spreading donors around to different parts of the country and other donors were scarce in Kilosa. Ireland was not in a position to take on a whole region so we opted for a district.

It helped that a link with Ireland already existed. The Newbridge-based Irish Ropes factory had sisal interests in the district, which pre-dated the aid programme. This part of Tanzania is sisal-growing country and in the colonial days there was a flourishing industry. The sisal plant grows from the ground like a giant pineapple with big spiky leaves at the top. These leaves are the source of the fibre, which goes into the making of ropes and other sisal-based products. But with the arrival of synthetic materials the demand for sisal fell and the local economy suffered badly as a result. It did not help that the Tanzanian Government had nationalised the industry in the 1960s and thrown out many of the expatriates – Greeks, British and Germans – who used to run the industry.

Irish Ropes made Tintawn carpets out of sisal, a brand that was popular and a household name Ireland in the 1960s and 70s.

A feasibility study was carried out to see how Ireland could help Kilosa.[2] Agriculture was the mainstay of the people. The roads were washed away in the rainy season, which made travel and the transport of goods difficult for months at a time. Not surprisingly, given the link with Irish Ropes, a carpet factory was the first project to be funded, along with a dairy farm.

Benny Maxwell of Irish Ropes was project manager of the carpet factory.[3] The Tanzanians made a deal whereby they would guarantee supplies of sisal in return for Irish Ropes supplying expertise in the setting up of the Kilosa factory. Austria had shipped out equipment and machinery but this was still packed up in boxes; Benny Maxwell's job was to get the plant going. He went to Kilosa in 1977 and stayed until 1980. Basically, his job was to advise the government, his main contact being the Tanzanian Sisal Authority. He pulled back from involvement after a while and had more of a supervisory role, travelling to Tanzania twice a year. He also oversaw the training of Tanzanian operatives who came over to Newbridge. He recalls the dairy farm, which was the next project to get funding from Irish Aid.

Agriculture was the focus of a lot of Irish Aid's efforts. Jim Phelan, Professor of Agricultural Science in UCD, began travelling to Tanzania in the early stages and was particularly involved in setting up an agricultural extension programme, that is, a service to help farmers improve their production.[4] He found a lack of everything when he got there – education, inputs, proper storage. He saw close similarities with the Ireland he grew up in. Brought up on a farm where water was drawn from a well and horses did the pulling

work, agriculture was a way of life rather than a job, with farms
passed from father to son. The big difference was the shocking poverty in Tanzania. People had so little yet were friendly and welcoming. He was also shocked by the waste: fruit trodden underfoot,
barns full of rotting cotton, the destruction wrought by the nomad-
ic Masai pastoralists with their cattle.

Jim Phelan's aim was to train agricultural extension personnel,
to develop planning, fertiliser use and storage for crops such as rice
and maize. He established a baseline and database to calculate the
impact of the training and other inputs on specific villages in the
district, and to compare these with villages outside the test sample.
He showed that crop yields went up 20 per cent after extension services were put in place.

After the initial carpet and dairy projects, Irish Aid extended its
activities. Kilosa became a fully-fledged area-based programme for
Irish Aid with many different activities including water, health, education, forestry, technical training, infrastructure and cooperatives. A central feature was close cooperation with the District
Council. There was heavy dependence on Irish technical assistance
to deliver the programme.

When I visited Kilosa in the early 1990s the Irish presence was
highly visible. By that stage a dozen Irish technical assistants were
working there on as many projects in Kilosa. The expatriate staff
lived with their families in a series of houses built for that purpose.
It looked like a pleasant enough way of life: the Tanzanian people
were nice, they take things slowly (a bit too slowly?) and I could see
why some would find it hard to leave. The downside was obvious
too. The relatively comfortable life of the adviser contrasted strongly with the desperate poverty of those they served.

A decade later the Kilosa programme was closed down. Evaluation studies concluded that the area-based approach did not work,
creating at best pockets of development in poor countries and not
holding out the hope of the ultimate goal – sustainability. The studies were critical of the scatter-fire approach of trying to achieve a

lot of different things at once, often in an unconnected manner. There was an audit which showed up overcharging for some of the supplies and a number of district officials were sacked.

But the main reason for moving away from Kilosa was that the development model had shifted. The move was towards supporting governments to help their own people. Tanzania has had a good record, both politically where elections have seen peaceful change-overs of power and economically after it abandoned an early disastrous experiment in radical socialism. It belongs to the group of countries known as 'donor darlings' which benefit from aid and where progress can be shown (the opposite category is 'aid orphans' – countries which donors prefer to avoid because of poor performance and collapsed systems).

I was accompanied on my return visit to Kilosa in December 2010 by Vincent Akulumuka, the agriculture advisor at the Embassy in Dar es Salaam, who spent ten years working in agriculture in the district. I met the Kilosa officials who had worked with Irish Aid, former and present District Council members, agricultural and education experts as well as Irish Aid staff familiar with the programme. I had breakfast in Morogoro with the longest serving expert in the Tanzanian programme, Sizya Lugeye.

My impression over the years has been that there was little to show for all the effort put in to Kilosa. The visit showed me that there is more evidence of the impact of Irish Aid's engagement with Kilosa than I had thought.

The lasting impacts can be summarised as follows:

- **The roads**. Everyone mentioned these. Irish Aid upgraded three feeder roads, which made a big difference in linking the town with the main road to Dar. I travelled on two of them, from the main road to Kilosa and from Kilosa to Mikumi, and found them in good condition. Before they were upgraded, they were invariably washed out in the rainy season. They are gravel roads and so better suited to 4-wheel drives but on my drive they were being used by all sorts of vehicles including ordinary cars, trucks, buses and bicycles. The decision not to go one better and put in tarmac roads was based on the view that the council would be more likely to repair and maintain the gravel than tarmac for cost reasons. This approach may have been justified but the fact remains that the roads are still sometimes washed out. Nevertheless, I had the impression that these roads have made a positive contribution to communications between Kilosa and the capital, and are likely to have improved the local economy and people's lives.

- **Numerous buildings, bridges, schools and clinics** were built during Irish Aid's involvement. These appear to have been well built and many are still in use. I called into one of the primary schools at Mbwade and met the headmaster, Omari Sizya, who told me that enrolment has gone up from 120 in Irish Aid's time to 340 pupils today. The school is now part of the State system. I visited Irish Aid's former coordination building, which now forms part of Kilosa District Council and is in good condition. The staff houses have been converted to various uses, one being the home of the Finance Minister! I was told that the clinics and dispensaries built by Irish Aid are also still in use.

- **Mikumi Vocational School**. This was the big surprise. During my research I was told by colleagues who were around at the time that getting it up and running had been a huge challenge. Fr. Padraig Flanagan was the force behind it, securing equipment and materials from Ireland and making it a reality against the odds. Getting the Tanzanian Government to take it over when Ireland stopped funding was very difficult. Cost overruns were a big issue. Yet today, whatever the problems, it is a success story. Known as VETA (the Vocational Education and Training Authority), it has become a national vocational training centre and is a fine series of buildings, well maintained and with tarmac roads. Kilosa District Council was supposed to run it and to contribute 10 per cent of the costs, but this did not work out and the State eventually took it over. There were complaints that a promise to include a fixed quota of Kilosa students had not been honoured – the 360 co-ed students come from all over the country. Nevertheless it is a thriving establishment. Eleven trades are now taught at the college, up from four in Irish Aid's time. A large plaque on the main building records that the foundation stone was laid by Julius Nyerere and pays tribute to the assistance Ireland gave in making it happen.

- **Agriculture**. It would need an expert to quantify the impact of Irish Aid's contribution. It is clear that some interventions such as support for the co-ops did not get anywhere but other projects, and in particular the agricultural extension system, are seen as having made a lasting impression. One of the academics I met from Sokoine University said that the Kilosa agricultural extension model was taken up by the government and used throughout the country. A report commissioned by Irish Aid on conflicts between farmers and pastoralists was referred to by several as a useful contribution, though this thorny problem remains. The agro-forestry project in Ngeira was singled out as having made a significant impact. It was the first such initiative in the country and I was told that it still exists. Jim Phelan thought that Irish Aid should have made a longer commitment to improving the agricultural side; he thinks they left too early and that progress was being made and could have been built on.

- **Health**. The training given to nurses was mentioned as valuable though this of course would be hard to quantify. Several people mentioned the natural childbirth aspect as one which has had a long-term impact.

It must be said that Kilosa still does not have the appearance of a prosperous town. Many buildings, some dating back to the heyday of the sisal industry, are dilapidated. The railway bridge was washed out for months so that trains could not get through. The former carpet factory – much bigger than I thought it would be – has long since stopped being a factory; today it is being used to house people displaced by recent floods.[5] But Vincent Akulumuka, who worked for 10 years in the Ilanga agricultural research centre, said he saw a lot of improvements, for example in the number of houses made of brick and in the growth in local entrepeneurship. Jim Phelan goes back regularly to Kilosa and says that many people are better off today but there is a big divide between the well off and those who are not. He remains committed to Tanzania and leads groups of UCD volunteers out to the country every year.

The attitude of the Kilosa people I spoke to was one of regret at Irish Aid's departure but there was no expectation that we would come back. There was a sense that Kilosa was a favoured area in Irish Aid's time there, and that money was more plentiful, but that under the new budget and sector support system run by the government Kilosa had to compete for funds: 'every part of the country is getting funding'. Some District Council people were a bit reserved, perhaps having memories of the audit that led to sackings. Some had expected another donor to step in when Irish Aid left but none came forward.

I heard the usual reservations about the funding they get through the government and claims that Kilosa did not see much funding actually reaching them. As against that, I saw a compound of new health clinics outside the town and the acting head of the District Council told me that six new secondary schools were opened last year. This indicates that central funding is getting through at least in some areas. A complaint that is more justified is late disbursement. In agriculture this is a big problem as money can arrive too late in the season to be of any use.

Ironically, today sisal is making a comeback as customers see the value of natural rather than synthetic products. Freshly sown fields of sisal were all around and there is a market for by-products of the plant as well as its use in shipping ropes and carpets. The Chinese are taking an interest. They are the biggest customers in the world for sisal and are building a tarmac road to improve transportation, which could change the dynamic of the whole region.

To sum up: Irish Aid's work in Kilosa did have impacts across a number of areas and, while nobody would advocate returning to the days of lots of Irish advisers engaged in such a wide range of activities, the part that Kilosa played in the evolution of the aid programme should not be forgotten. Back in Dar es Salaam, I met the Minister for Justice, Celina Kambari, at the residence of Ambassador Lorcan Fullam. She praised Ireland's contribution in Kilosa warmly, even though she favoured budget and basket support. Anthony Fuime, former chair of Kilosa District Council, said that Ireland's role in Kilosa was worth remembering, as it was probably the longest engagement the programme undertook and because of the many benefits it brought.

Monica Gorman, who lived and worked in Kilosa and is now head of Oxfam Ireland in Tanzania, believes the programme did help the local economy and got people going, especially women. She pointed out that when assessing the impact it is important to bear in mind that the sums spent were not very large. She questioned the parallel approach whereby Irish Aid controlled the purse strings – something which may have constrained the council's scope to act on their own. She also asked the question: did Irish Aid know what it was seeking to accomplish?[6]

A similar line was taken by Liberaty Macha, an agricultural expert who knew the programme well. He said that, looking back, it was clear that both sides were learning. Kilosa District Council was struggling to find out how to work with a major donor. At the same time, Irish Aid was learning how to do development.[7]

Endnotes

1. Lorcan Fullam and his colleagues at the Irish Embassy in Dar es Salaam assisted me with this visit, in particular Vincent Akulumuka and Sisye Lugeye.

2. Progress on the Kilosa projects can be traced in the *Annual Reports*, starting with the 1979 booklet. In the mid-1980s in particular the programme attracts a lot of attention, for example, pp. 18-19 of the 1985 report. There are also files in the National Archive, for example, 2009/120/1599 on the carpet factory.

3. Benny Maxwell conversation.

4.   Professor Jim Phelan interview.

5.   There is a fascinating account of life in pre-independence Tanzania and of the role played by sisal in the economy in E K Lumley's *Forgotten Mandate: A British District Officer in Tanganyika*, London, 1976. Like many colonial officials, Lumley was Irish and he has left a vivid picture of the tough life of the sisal workers.

6.   Monica Gorman interview.

7.   Liberaty Macha interview.

12

CELTIC TIGER YEARS

Liz O'Donnell of the Progressive Democrats replaced Joan Burton as Minister of State for Overseas Development in 1997, just as Ireland's economic boom was really getting into its stride. She would hold the position for five years, joining the ranks of other long serving Ministers Jim O'Keeffe, Sean Calleary and Tom Kitt. David Andrews returned to his old position as senior Minister in Iveagh House.

The PDs supported helping the poor in the developing world. The coalition agreement between the PDs and Fianna Fáil reaffirmed the 0.7 per cent target and set an interim goal of reaching 0.45 per cent by 2002. The pace at which Irish Aid expanded during this time was faster than it had ever been. But it did not happen without a fight.

Liz O'Donnell recalls that she asked for the ODA portfolio, seeing it as one of two substantive Junior Minister briefs, the other being the Office of Public Works.[1] The PDs were a small party of four in 1997 so she wanted a significant portfolio. It helped that she was interested in the subject and was a lawyer. She had worked on Mary Robinson's election campaign and admired the stands David Andrews took on behalf of the poor.

David Andrews gave her the freedom to do the ODA job. She felt that he was someone who had confidence in women and in her. But, soon after the government was formed, the second IRA ceasefire was declared and she was thrown into the whole Northern Ireland issue. Mary Harney told her that Northern Ireland would be 'her other job' and it proved to be very time consuming, so much so that for the first year she was away a lot from Development Cooperation Division attending meetings in Northern Ireland.

The aid budget when she started was £110 million. Both the Fianna Fáil and PD manifestos contained commitments to increase it so she was very disappointed when she learned that the only increase envisaged for 1998 was £15 million for debt relief. She felt that more should have been sought from the Department of Finance and sensed a departmental wariness and resistance to the increases being espoused by politicians and concern about how the money would be spent.

There was a row with the Minister for Finance over the money at the end of her first year. She found herself at odds with Charlie McCreevy who was against increasing ODA. The Finance argument was that economic growth was so strong that reaching the 0.7 target would be extremely costly. She could understand their point of view but she strongly believed the GNP percentage was a fair barometer of a developed country's performance. She was adamant that she would not preside over a cutting back on aid at a time of unprecedented economic growth in Ireland. The row was serious and required the mediation of PD minister Bobby Molloy to broker a deal as O'Donnell threatened to resign if the commitment in the programme for Government on aid was not honoured. She got no significant increase that year but she did secure a commitment for the first time to a three-year package of increases for the period 1999-2001.

Despite the truce, Charlie McCreevy remained sceptical on aid so she persuaded him to go to Tanzania. He could only stay for a weekend but, however brief, the visit impressed McCreevy and she got the budget increase. She feels that two factors helped her to get the three-year commitment: that the PDs were a minority party – had she been a Fianna Fáil Junior Minister it would have been difficult to fight with the Minister for Finance. Secondly, Bertie Ahern backed her. And the fact that there was cross party support for

ODA in the Oireachtas helped. She believes that aid will always be a vulnerable budget line, competing as it does with domestic demands. But it was a time of prosperity and, in her view, the aid budget should be going up in line with that wealth. She was not about to be the one to drop the ball.

The period from 1999 saw big jumps in the aid budget. By 2002 the allocation amounted to €422 million.

Once the money was secure and cabinet approval given for Ireland to reach the UN target in a specified time frame, Liz O'Donnell felt the need to bring in outsiders to review all aspects of the programme. The 0.7 per cent target implied a possible eventual budget of €1.7 billion, more than the combined votes of the Departments of Defence and the Marine. So she set up the Ireland Aid Review Committee (the name of the programme had been changed from Irish Aid to Ireland Aid) and included business and public relations people as well as international development experts and two former secretaries general of Government departments.[2]

The time was appropriate to take stock: 1999 saw the 25th anniversary of the establishment of the aid programme. Professor Helen O'Neill of UCD, who publishes an annual report on the state of the programme, included a look at the first 25 years of Irish Aid in her 1999 review.[3] She concluded:

> Looking back over 25 years of Irish Aid, one sees a programme that has evolved from a rather *ad hoc* collections of projects managed by expatriates into one that has a coherence in terms of objectives and approach and is much more strongly linked into the structures of partner countries. While poverty alleviation has always been a declared objective of Irish Aid, all projects, as long as they were located in the poorest countries were assumed to be making a contribution, however indirect, toward this goal. This is no longer considered sufficient. Activities being supported by Irish Aid in the priority countries today are focusing directly on poverty. And the concept of poverty that underlies this more direct approach has itself undergone a fundamental reinterpretation – as has the concept of partnership.

These ideas are not unique to Irish Aid; they are part of the current orthodoxy in development thinking. What is remarkable is that they are now finding practical expression in Irish Aid in line with best practice among other donors . . .

Irish Aid's programme has grown significantly in terms of size since 1974. Despite occasional blips, it has grown fairly steadily over the years both in nominal terms and as a percent of GNP. On the latter measure, it now occupies a respectable position in the donor 'league table' although it will remain a small player in absolute money terms. As regards substance and approach, it now compares favourably with the other small EU donors . . .

Ireland's aid programme now forms a significant as well as an integral part of its overall foreign policy. It reflects well on the country. Looking back over 25 years of Irish Aid, Irish people can take justifiable pride in it.[4]

This was welcome encouragement and, as Professor O'Neill noted, the programme was looking beyond its traditional scope of activity at new areas such as debt relief and the role of trade and the private sector. Human rights was another area where the programme was strengthening its role. Liz O'Donnell was the first Minister of State to have Human Rights as part of her title. She saw this as appropriate as she believes that ODA is a real demonstration of our human rights commitment. (It also had a practical effect in that she worked with Political as well as Development Cooperation Divisions in Foreign Affairs.) The fund to support human rights and democratisation was increased and its remit extended.

The Ireland Aid Review confirmed many of the existing policies such as keeping the focus on Africa, addressing basic needs of poor people and working through governments. There were also some innovations.

One example was the recommendation to extend the programme's geographic range by considering a new priority country in Asia. This would eventually lead to the designation of Vietnam as a priority country for Irish Aid. Membership of the Asian and

African Development Banks was also recommended – Ireland had not joined either bank although the issue had arisen from time to time. (In the event, Ireland would join the Asian bank reflecting the considerable interest among the private sector.) The Review recommended that the fledgling programme of support for East Timor be increased. And, as already mentioned, the recommendation that APSO be closed down was implemented.

The Review revisited the old chestnut of who should be running the programme. It concluded that management should remain with Development Cooperation Division of the Department of Foreign Affairs. But Liz O'Donnell felt that the expanding programme needed strategic oversight and it was decided to replace the Advisory Committee with a board, to be known as the Advisory Board on Irish Aid. The difference between the Advisory Board and its predecessor was that the Board was given a broad remit including 'general oversight and the provision of advice to the Minister on the strategic direction of the Ireland Aid programme'. It was also given a substantial research role and budget. The Board's first chair was a senior political figure, Des O'Malley, who had served as chair of the Joint Oireachtas Committee on Foreign Affairs.

Two areas which the Ireland Aid Review focused on were:

- The importance of strengthening links with the NGOs
- The role of the missionaries.

That the non-governmental organisations play a major role in the aid programme goes without saying. Cooperation with NGOs in both emergencies and long-term development work has been a feature of the programme since its beginnings. What happened after the Ireland Aid Review was to raise that cooperation to an entirely new level through a programme known as MAPS – the Multi Annual Programme Scheme, to give it its full title.

Negotiations were begun with five NGOs – Concern, GOAL, Trocaire, Christian Aid and Self Help – on this scheme, which had as its aim to give more flexibility to the NGOs concerned and more predictability about the amount of funding they would be getting from Irish Aid over a multi-year period.

MAPS built on the block grant approach but was much more far reaching in its objectives. It is not an exaggeration to say that it has transformed relations between Irish Aid and the NGOs into a much closer partnership.[5]

Irish Aid's relations with the NGOs have improved a lot in recent times but they have not always been close.[6] The relationship, in fact, is complex and multi-faceted. The head of one of our NGOs told me that many of his staff remain uneasy about 'getting too close to Government'. They fear a loss of independence if they have to rely on the State for a large part of their funding. On the other hand, one Minister of State I worked for felt that Irish Aid had become too close to the NGOs. He said it was a trend observed in many organisations which become prisoners of their clients and were more concerned about keeping them happy than pursuing their proper objectives.

In the early years the NGOs, as well as building their individual competency and experience, devoted a lot of time to pressing the Government to establish an official aid programme and, once Irish Aid was established, to monitoring progress towards the 0.7 per cent target. The perception of many in the NGO community during the 1970s and 1980s, and even later, was that the Government was lagging behind in its responsibilities towards the developing world.

Governments, for their part, had suspicions about the NGOs' status and intentions. The concept of NGOs was not at all as rooted then as it is today. Before the aid programme got under way, the official line in the Department of Foreign Affairs was that such funds as were available should be channelled through the UN and the Red Cross. The argument was made that the NGOs should do their own fundraising and not be looking to the State. This position was probably influenced by the small amount of funding that was available. But there were concerns, too, in official circles that the

NGOs were pursuing objectives, which did not necessarily coincide with the Government's.[7]

A case in point was the Biafra experience where the newly formed Africa Concern and many of the missionaries supported the separatist cause, whereas in foreign policy terms the Government felt it had to take an even-handed approach. Nigeria was an important trading partner for Ireland, a senior player at the UN and the only African country where Ireland had a resident embassy. The Biafra experience left some bad memories in the Department of Foreign Affairs.

The trend whereby the NGOs were critical of the Government's bona fides on aid continued through the first decade of the programme, even though it was a period of growth and Garret FitzGerald as Taoiseach protected the budget during tight financial times. The budget cuts of the late 1980s soured relations badly, as I found when I took up duty in 1991. It required outreach on Irish Aid's part to get the message across that we genuinely wanted a cooperative relationship.[8]

A move that helped was the inclusion of NGO representatives in official delegations to major conferences. The issue came up before the Rio Earth Summit – I think for the first time – when NGOs, both on the development and the environmental side, asked to be included. I wondered if it would be feasible to conduct confidential business with NGOs around. But it worked well on the ground: the NGOs did not intrude when we needed to discuss things privately, their main aim being to have access to the conference hall which required membership of the delegation. And they brought a lot to the process through their own contacts and positions. (Though sometimes it led to strange combinations: at the Cairo Population Conference the Irish Family Planning Association and the Right to Life movement were both on the official delegation!) In time a Code of Practice was developed which set out the ground rules for NGO involvement on official delegations.

The MAPS programme was carefully designed to ensure a balance between the NGOs' freedom to spend the money on their own priorities and the need for Irish Aid to account for the funding which was substantial (the MAPS budget would eventually run into hundreds of millions of euros). The discussions with the NGOs on establishing the ground rules for the MAPS programme were long and detailed but they were mostly conducted in a positive atmosphere.

Relations with four of the five MAPS partners – Concern, Trocaire, Self Help and Christian Aid – were good. The organisation that Irish Aid has had its most difficult relationship with was GOAL. In the 1990s, relations were especially strained and they have never been close, even at the best of times. Critical letters from John O'Shea to the Minister, the Minister of State, the Taoiseach, TDs and Senators landed on my desk for attention, as they did on the desks of my predecessors and successors. Dozens of letters and articles appeared in the media. Responding to these – sometimes two or three letters a week – took up so much time that I recommended only responding when a new issue was raised.

The MAPS discussions with GOAL were difficult in part because of this constant correspondence, but also because MAPS required that participants meet high organisational and administrative standards. While GOAL has attracted able and committed staff at home and in the field, it had to meet the MAPS requirements on the organisational front. The problem for Irish Aid was that, however much we delegated responsibility to partners, public monies were involved and appropriate systems had to be in place.[9]

In the event, an agreement was worked out to enable GOAL to be part of MAPS, just as it was with the other MAPS partners. The contacts at working level have been good and I think that GOAL's participation in MAPS has helped both sides, though John O'Shea might not agree.

In spite of all the problems we have had over the years, nobody can doubt John O'Shea's commitment to the poor or his passion at the repeated failures of the international community to step up to the plate when emergencies happen. I disagree with his views on working with Governments as I think that, problematic and risky though it can be, it is a path that has to be gone down to see if it will deliver long term development where other approaches have failed.

Giving increased support to the missionaries out of the growing budget was a popular decision. The work of missionaries had always been supported by Irish Aid but somehow it had gone off the radar a bit over the years for reasons that I am not sure of – perhaps the declining number of Irish-born missionaries had an effect.

Someone who was a strong supporter of the missionaries was President McAleese. She made sure that their work was highlighted during her visits to Africa. Micheal Kitt, who served as Minister of State at a later stage, was also very supportive of missionaries. While some of the programmes Irish Aid spent money on kept me awake at night, the funding that went through missionaries never did.

I decided to put this to the test by checking back on one of the projects we funded. A modest grant is mentioned in the Annual Report for 1996 – £12,922 for 'Benedictines – water extension scheme'.[10] The reason this project stuck in my mind, out of the thousands that have received financing from Irish Aid, was that the person who put in the application had been a fellow student of mine at UCD, Christopher Dillon, who went on to serve as Abbot of Glenstal for 16 years. Before that, he spent two years at the Benedictine monastery in Ewu-Ishan in Brendel state in Nigeria and it was then that he approached Irish Aid about the water project.

I called down to Glenstal in 2010 and met Christopher and his colleague Fr. Andrew Nugent, who also served at the Ewu-Ishan monastery, to find out more about the story behind the project.[11] They told me that the Benedictine monastery is situated about 60 miles from Benin city in the south of the country. It is a place where the Igbo tribe are numerous but many others are too. Christianity, Islam and traditional African religions are all strong. The monastery, built in the mid-seventies, is seen as a neutral place and the novices come from as many as 15 tribes. Christopher and Andrew were novice masters there.

Both Christopher and Andrew stressed the vital role that water plays in the life of the villagers. The only water available to the five villages scattered around the site came from two streams that were several miles away, down a steep route. The villagers had to trek to the two streams: as Andrew put it, 'women and children spent their life fetching water'. They took basins, buckets and any available utensil to the streams.

The monastery leases land from the local king to farm and they have a pump which brings water from one of the streams. The monks installed an overflow pipe to help the villagers and hundreds would come to use it. But this was only a temporary solution.

Plans to improve the water situation in the villages go back to the 1970s. Achieving the goal required several attempts. The project to bring water up from the two streams was begun with funding, not only from Irish Aid, but from several different sources including a German priest who donated money. The plan involved a diesel-operated pump to drive the water up from the stream. The piping for the project came from Ireland and an APSO volunteer came out to help with the installation.

At the first time of trying, the piping was assembled the wrong way around and it blew the pump engine! They had to disassemble the whole apparatus and get a new pump. There was a lot of trial and error and problems with friction and the project went through several phases. It was only in 2006 that the new system was officially commissioned.

Andrew concluded: 'Warts and all, it was a success story and has given real assistance to the villagers.' (Strangely, it was the village men who had reservations about putting in the pump. They said, 'what will our wives be doing then? They will be idle!' But then they were not the ones doing the heavy lifting . . .)

The good news that I heard from Christopher and Andrew was that the area where the Benedictine monastery is located is doing quite well. The monastery has gone into the herb business; it employs 150 people in its clinic and laboratory and distributes herbal medicines to some 50 centres around the country.

Looking at Irish Aid's annual reports, what impresses is the sheer number of development projects of this kind run by missionaries that are assisted every year (development is key: Irish Aid only funds missionaries' projects such as schools, wells and health facilities – the funding of the church side is a matter for the orders). And each has its story like the well at Ewu-Ishan.

It was necessary to put order on the funding arrangements. The bigger NGOs had block grants and now were getting the MAPS programme. But for two decades the missionaries, like the smaller NGOs, got their funding through the NGO Co-Financing Scheme. This meant that individual nuns, priests and brothers applied to Irish Aid for grants, often through the local embassy if there was one, or through their order or just by sending forms in directly. This led to a great deal of paperwork and often to frustration on the part of those in the field who could find a worthwhile project left out because they could not put their case effectively.

It was imperative that a better system be put in place to allocate funding. The outcome was the establishment of the Irish Missionary Resource Service, later renamed Misean Cara, which now has 82 missionary orders on its books. Irish Aid gives funding to Misean Cara (substantial funding – in 2008 it amounted to €20 million), which it, in turn, disburses.[12]

Less visible than the work of missionaries but no less essential to the root causes of poverty were the issues of debt and trade, which Irish Aid sought to address.[13]

The debt burden on poor countries became a very live issue during the 1990s. Many African countries face crippling payments to service debts, in some cases having to spend as much as 40 per cent of government revenue that could have gone to health and education and other vital services. Some of the debts dated back to colonial times when newly independent states had to take on the debts left behind by their departing rulers. Some were the result of reckless borrowing but a large percentage of the debt resulted from loans given by donors such as the World Bank. The scale of the debt reached such a level that it was a grave threat to any prospect of economic growth in many countries and would have meant that they were condemned to permanent abject poverty.

The campaign to address the debt problem was particularly strong in Britain with the emphasis on pressurising the G7 richest countries. The Jubilee 2000 movement attracted widespread support. Later the Make Poverty History campaign, supported by Bono and Bob Geldof, and helped by the positive stance of Tony Blair and Gordon Brown, succeeded in achieving a landmark promise to cancel much of the debt of the poorest countries at the G8 Summit in Gleneagles in 2005.

In Ireland, support for debt relief also grew in strength from the 1990s on. The Debt and Development Coalition, a consortium of organisations, was formed in 1993 and eventually attracted over 70 bodies. They had an uphill task at first – it is easy to forget after an issue has become mainstream that it was once a novel idea greeted with suspicion – but they persisted in a campaign of letter writing and awareness raising.

Central to their argument was the principle that organisations such as the World Bank and IMF should be more accountable for their actions, which often had very damaging economic side effects. The Bretton Woods institutions had to respond to what was clearly a justified case. I remember attending a meeting where the head of the IMF, Michel Camdessus, came to Dublin to defend his organisation's position and received a stormy reception.

The strategy the World Bank and the IMF came up with in 1996 was to target the heavily indebted poor countries, or HIPC. It offered the 42 countries worst hit by the debt crisis relief subject to conditions. HIPC's aim was not to cancel debt but to reduce it and the pace of progress was slow. The same could be said of the successor initiative, HIPC 2, but Ireland decided to play its part. In 1998 a package of debt relief totalling £31.5 million was announced jointly by the Ministers for Finance and Foreign Affairs (as the funding came from both departments). The money took the form of contributions to World Bank and IMF funds for relieving debt in two of Irish Aid's priority countries, Tanzania and Mozambique. In 2001 an additional €4.5 million was given to the World Bank for debt relief in another priority country, Ethiopia.

The record is the more praiseworthy in that Ireland has never given development assistance in the form of loans. Irish Aid only gives grants. Most donors give some of their aid in the form of loans and, even though these are on favourable terms, this can result in the recipients being caught up in a spiral of debt, which, far from helping them, may end up worsening their condition.

Ireland also led the way in calling for the *total* cancellation of the debts of the poorest countries long before it became the generally accepted position. Developing and promoting the debt strategy saw the Departments of Finance and Foreign Affairs working together. Such was the opposition within the Bretton Woods institutions to our support for total debt cancellation that the then President of the World Bank, James Wolfensohn, visited Dublin to try to persuade us to desist from the policy. But Ireland stuck to its guns.

Trade is a difficult issue for any country, and especially for Ireland, with our strong agricultural base and high dependence on exports. Yet trade is arguably even more important than aid as a means of enabling countries to emerge from poverty.

Just as debt relief became the focus of attention in the 1990s so did the need to improve poor countries' access to world markets gather momentum. The main theatre was the talks led by the

World Trade Organisation, the body where the conditions of international trade and tariffs are thrashed out. A new round of talks began in 2001, known as the Doha Round, with the stated aim of improving the conditions for poor countries to sell their goods in the developed world's markets.

Trade seems to be a subject that tests the donors' determination to help poor countries to the limit. National interests are at stake in the WTO. Ireland, like every other country, fights its corner to defend jobs and prosperity at home. Standing up for the developing countries' right of access to European markets is all very well, but what if their exports undercut ours? This is not just theoretical – it can be a very real possibility where agricultural products are concerned.

In practice, what happens at the WTO talks is that the Minister of State for Overseas Development attends along with the Ministers for Agriculture and Trade. Tom Kitt and his successor Conor Lenihan both went to sessions of the Doha Round talks. Their role was to ensure that the concerns of the developing countries were kept to the fore. The WTO talks are unusual in that it is the Commission that speaks on behalf of the EU member states. Ireland has to make sure that Commissioners such as Peter Mandelson protect our interests – and those of the poorest countries – in the negotiations.

It is probably too much to say that trade puts us on a collision course with the developing countries. In fact, the EU has done a lot to open its markets through initiatives including Everything But Arms. And the biggest players among the developing countries tend not to be the poorest ones but the so-called middle income countries such as Brazil. But hard choices sometimes have to be made.

One thing that donors can do is to help developing countries to strengthen their capacity to export and to fight their corner in the international fora; this is known as aid for trade. Irish Aid has a good record on aid for trade and has given this practical expression by looking at ways of helping the private sector in partner countries. A private sector forum hosted by Tom Kitt in 2004 led to the establishment of Traidlinks, an organisation which aims to support enterprise in developing countries. Its board has representatives from most of the major Irish companies doing business with Africa. Irish Aid also supports the Fairtrade movement, especially in Central America, and gives funding to the World Trade Organisation to support the training of trade negotiators from the poorest countries.

Ireland's reputation in the aid field was well established at the start of the new millennium. The country had a big success in securing a seat on the UN Security Council, topping the poll against strong candidates Norway and Italy. Opinions differ as to whether the strength of our aid programme was a factor: Mary Whelan, who was the main organiser of the campaign, says it did not play a part and points out that Norway had a better aid record than us but still came behind us.[14] However, Bertie Ahern and others say that the image of Ireland as a small country doing a lot to help the developing world was instrumental in Ireland's successful campaign.

When Bertie Ahern addressed the Millennium Summit in New York in 2000 he made an ambitious pledge: that Ireland would reach the 0.7 per cent target by 2007. Liz O'Donnell was centrally involved in securing this commitment, a much more explicit one than previous promises and one which Finance did not favour. In retrospect, it could be said to have symbolised the state of mind of the country at the height of prosperity in the Celtic Tiger Years.[15]

The context for the promise was the hope that the new millennium could see a better and fairer world. This was summed up by the adoption at the UN of the Millennium Development Goals, a set of targets endorsed by the member states, the boldest of which was to halve the number of people living on less than a dollar a day by the year 2015.

The message from the Taoiseach's speech was that, as far as Ireland was concerned, we would play our part in achieving the Millennium Development Goals by raising our game. No more shilly-shallying. This time we would put ourselves up among the elite handful of countries that had achieved 0.7 per cent.

But that was not how things turned out.

Endnotes

1. Liz O'Donnell interview.

2. *Report of the Ireland Aid Review Committee*. The full list of members of the Committee is at p. 125.

3. Professor Helen O'Neill, review of the first 25 years of the programme in the *Annual Report 1998*, pp. 4-11.

4. Op cit, p. 10-11.

5. After discussions with the candidates for MAPS the programme was launched in 2003. See *Annual Report 2003*, p. 70.

6. DFA National Archive file 2004/7/57 contains the advice to the Minister that 'Government practice has been, and continues to be, to channel state aid through UN agencies and the Red Cross. The Government's view is that campaigns undertaken by Irish voluntary organisations under their own initiative and responsibility are more appropriately financed by subscriptions from their members and from the general public.'

7. See, for example, Brendan Nolan's note in DFA National Archive file 2004/7: 'The proposals by Concern must be treated with the greatest reserve and the Department of Agriculture are very aware of the embarrassment which this organisation have caused and could again cause to the government.'

8. Hugh Swift and I called to see each of the main NGOs personally.

9. Some NGOs see a danger of becoming merely delivery agents for the Government and over dependent on Government for funding. These issues are explored in an article by Mary Sutton and Tony Fahey in the Annual Report 2001 'An Abundance of Aid – Some Challenges facing the Irish Government and NGOs', pp. 7-10.

10. *Annual Report 1996*, p. 17.

11. Interviews with Christopher Dillon and Andrew Nugent. *Glenstal Abbey: A Historical Guide*, Mark Tierney OSB, 2009, tells the story of Glenstal's activities in Africa including the Ewu-Ishan project, pp. 89-96.

12. Mike Greally, CEO, Misean Cara, interview.

13. I am grateful to Tom Hanney for his assistance with the following pages on trade and debt. Articles on debt have appeared in several issues of the *Annual*

Report 1998, pp. 18-19; 2000, p. 11; 2002, pp. 70-72 – article by Tom Hanney). Trade is the subject of articles in the *Annual Report 1999*, pp. 12-13; 2006, pp.41-42).

14. Mary Whelan message, 6/10/10, Bertie Ahern interview.

15. Taoiseach's statement at the opening session of the Millennium Summit, New York, 6 September 2000: 'Today, in this public forum, Ireland commits to meeting the 0.7 per cent target by the end of 2007, with an interim target to increase its share to 0.45 per cent by the end of 2000.' UN press release, 7 September 2000. See 'An Historic Commitment', Annual Report 2000, p. 8.

13

MORE TROUBLE WITH TARGETS

I returned to take charge of Irish Aid for the second time in the autumn of 2004. I found a much bigger, more professional operation than when I left, with an atmosphere of confidence about the place, symbolised by the new premises Irish Aid had recently moved to in Bishop's Square, near what had been Jacobs factory and was now the Dublin Institute of Technology.

The programme even had a new name – Development Cooperation Ireland – which was felt to be more politically correct than to be referring to 'aid'.

There were two clouds on the horizon, however, and they lost no time in making their presence felt. One was the fact that progress on the target set by Bertie Ahern at the UN in 2000 of reaching 0.7 per cent by 2007 was faltering.[1] The other was the Government decision of December 2003 that the staff of Development Co-operation Division should move to Limerick.

It took some adjusting to get used to life at home after nine years away. I had the same sensation I always had after I returned from a posting: pleasure at being back in the old familiar places with people I knew, working in an area I liked, but a sense of strangeness too, surrounded by changes of all sorts which I had to get used to.

After Moscow I had worked for two and a half years in Geneva as adviser to Mary Robinson during her term as UN High Commissioner for Human Rights. My time there was frustrating in many ways because the UN, despite having decided to create the position of High Commissioner for Human Rights, did not follow up with the necessary staff and funding to do the job properly. The Commission on Human Rights and the General Assembly had no compunction about assigning new tasks to the Office and then voting down the provision of the necessary resources. Much time and effort had to be spent seeking funding and staff when there were all too many examples of human rights abuses to highlight. On the positive side, it was a pleasure to work for a remarkable person who refused to let a lack of support limit her work in homing in on human rights abuses and pressing countries large and small to remedy them. There was also the advantage of becoming familiar with the human rights agenda, including the right to development, which goes to the heart of the development debate.

After Geneva I served for three years as Ambassador in Vienna. Vienna was a great city to live in but, had I been solely accredited to Austria, I would have been underemployed. The Austrians love Ireland for a variety of reasons and I never had to do the hard sell with them. Luckily, Vienna is one of the UN's capitals and houses UNIDO, the UN Office on Drugs and Crime, the International Atomic Energy Agency and a group of smaller organisations dealing with disarmament, and part of my job was to represent Ireland at these bodies. The IAEA was particularly interesting. It was the time of the build up to the Iraq war, the saga of the weapons of mass destruction and the pressure on Iran to allow inspections of its nuclear facilities. The UN Office on Drugs and Crime was an interesting organisation too and during Ireland's EU Presidency I chaired the negotiations towards a new UN Convention on Corruption.

My return in 2004 came as Ireland's EU Presidency drew to a close. Once again Ireland carried off the six months of stewardship of the EU extremely well; in fact, it could be said that this was one of Ireland's finest hours as we succeeded in steering the EU Treaty negotiations to a conclusion and overseeing the entry of the ten new member states into the Union. It was fitting that a small member state should be the one to welcome in the ten mostly small new entrants and I watched the ceremony at Áras an Uachtaráin on the first of May on television in Vienna with pride.

On the development side, the 2004 Presidency was also a great success. A highlight was a major conference on HIV/AIDS in Europe and Central Asia, which was held in Dublin Castle in February 2004. The idea for the conference came about when Minister of State Tom Kitt visited Geneva before Ireland assumed the Presidency.[2] There he met a familiar face – Philip O'Brien of UNICEF – who had successfully led Operation Lifeline Sudan and who was so helpful to us on our visit to southern Sudan. Philip pointed out to the Minister that Eastern Europe and Central Asia were experiencing the greatest growth in cases of HIV in the world but that many countries were in denial about its existence. The World Health Organisation held a similar view. Just organising the participation of over sixty ministers, mostly of health, was a logistical nightmare for David Donoghue who replaced Martin Greene as Director General in 2001. But the conference brought kudos to Ireland and was still often mentioned to me in glowing terms long after I replaced David. Philip O'Brien says that the conference made a real difference in raising awareness of a neglected problem.

It was good to see the multilateral side of the programme getting credit.[3] The multilateral work is less popular and less visible than the bilateral work. Why this should be I am not sure. Perhaps it is because the results are less tangible and because it is regarded as less hands-on. But the European Commission has a huge aid programme to which Ireland makes a substantial annual contribution. When combined with the programmes of the member states, the EU is the largest donor in the world so servicing the complex Brussels-based machinery through which it delivers aid is an important task.

Ireland played a central role in the early years of our EU membership in shaping the Union's development policy, in particular through our chairing of the Presidency negotiations on the various Lomé Conventions. There were fewer opportunities to make that kind of impact in later times. The former Ministers of State I interviewed had different opinions about the EU aid work, some relishing the cut and thrust at the Brussels meetings, others feeling that the decisions were pre-cooked and that ministers from the member states had little say when it actually came to ministerial councils.[4]

One problem is that there is an ongoing struggle between the Commission and the member states over who should be in charge of development with many suspecting that the Commission would like to have more control while donors with long experience see no reason to cede more power to Brussels. In addition, Ministers found it hard to defend some of the Commission's positions – for example, its championing of Economic Partnership Agreements, the successors to the Lomé and Cotonou Agreements, which many saw as less favourable than the earlier agreements with the developing countries – but EU solidarity required that they present a united front.

Among the Ministers at Development and General Affairs and External Relations Councils have been some impressive figures: Jan Pronk of the Netherlands and Bernard Kouchner of France, for example. The British have fielded heavyweights including Lynda Chalker and Clare Short. And Ministers from the Nordic countries are always listened to with respect because their countries have such a strong record on aid. Ireland belongs to a like-minded group which seeks to ensure that EU aid was delivered as effectively as possible – and that all of the allocated monies were spent.

One thing is certain: the EU development responsibilities add a heavy burden of work during a country's Presidency.

In her review of Irish Aid's programme for 2004, Helen O'Neill lists a formidable catalogue of activities which had to be carried out during the first six months of that year, beginning with a presentation in January by Minister of State Tom Kitt of the programme for the Irish Presidency to the European Parliament, including views on the role which development could play in the new constitution for Europe; chairing the meeting of the EU/ACP parliamentary assembly in Addis Ababa; chairing the HIV/AIDS conference and producing a plan of action and 'the Dublin Declaration' which included specific targets and timeframes for fighting HIV/AIDS in Eastern Europe and Central Asia; hosting an Informal Meeting of development ministers at Kilmainham with Bono as a guest; leading the EU's contribution to the World Information Society Summit in Tunis; advancing work on the Green Diplomacy Network; and co-chairing talks with Japan on aid for the Balkans and the former Soviet Union.[5]

At the orientation debate under the auspices of the General Affairs and External Relations Council (GAERC) Ireland succeeded in securing the first ever Council conclusions that agreed on the need to move development policy closer to the heart of the EU's external policy. The Minister for Foreign Affairs Brian Cowen hosted delegations from the EU and the African Union in Dublin, one outcome of which was the announcement of an EU Peace Facility of €250 million to support African peacekeeping and strengthen the African Union. Brian Cowen also visited Ethiopia and Eritrea during the Presidency.

During our Presidency Irish Aid also coordinated the EU input into the UN Conference on Trade and Development in Sao Paolo and the sensitive work of the Commission on Population and Development in New York.

The EU work was for a long time combined with servicing the UN agenda and both areas were ably carried out by the Counsellor in charge, Tom Hanney.[6] But he found the two areas a heavy burden and was relieved when more staff were allocated and the responsibilities for EU and UN funding were separated. Assistance to the UN bodies was a substantial body of work in itself. By 2004 voluntary contributions to the UN bodies totalled €43 million. The range of organisations receiving assistance was very broad – over a dozen in number – and in its 2003 review the OECD's Development Assistance Committee recommended that Irish Aid reduce the number of recipients and take a more strategic approach. This made sense as the capacity to track donations and contribute to these bodies' policies was crucial.

Handing over large sums to UN bodies might seem like an easy way to spend money when budgets are expanding and some donors have resorted to this. But there is no guarantee that money channelled through multilateral organisations will be well spent. Big multilateral donors such as Norway and Spain have found it essential to keep a close watch on what actually happens to their donations. I had my own reason for favouring extra scrutiny, having seen what can happen to donors' contributions during the period I worked for the UN.

Tom Hanney set about streamlining Ireland's approach to the UN organisations. As well as reducing the number of bodies assisted, Irish Aid for the first time entered into multiannual agreements with some of the bigger UN bodies including UNDP, UNICEF and UNHCR. This followed a joint review, which Ireland carried out with Denmark, on the capacities and systems of the UN bodies. The increase in funding gave Ireland more clout. We were able to insist on greater accountability for our donations and tighter financial controls. We actively sought – and secured – seats on the boards of the UN bodies.

In 2003, reflecting Ireland's increased standing in development circles, the influential UNDP Human Development Report was launched by the Taoiseach in Dublin in the presence of the UNDP Administrator, Mark Malloch Brown, Bono and Tom Kitt.

In its interactions with the UN Funds and Programmes, Irish Aid adopted a constructive but critical approach, holding the UN agencies to account for money given, supporting cooperation between the members of the UN family and pressing for more local ownership of UN programmes. Ireland also made a significant input into a series of important UN conferences including the Millennium Summit and the Conference on Financing for Development.

The 2003 DAC report was very positive about Ireland's aid effort and this, together with the presence in the Division of colleagues such as Brendan Rogers and Frank Sheridan who had long experience of the programme and had served several tours of duty in the field, the increasing number of seasoned personnel heading up our programmes in the field, and the wealth of specialist expertise in the technical section, all augured well for the programme's well-being.[7] But controversy over the budget target blew up quickly.

I thought that I would be working for Tom Kitt when I returned but September 2004 brought a cabinet re-shuffle. Bertie Ahern moved Tom Kitt to the Chief Whip job and replaced him with Conor Lenihan. Dermot Ahern replaced Brian Cowen as the senior Minister, with Brian Cowen going to Finance.

At my first meeting with Conor Lenihan, the Minister of State asked me what was the biggest challenge the programme faced. The answer was obvious: we were not going to reach the 0.7 per cent target by 2007 as promised by the Taoiseach. The only thing that surprised me when I looked at the figures was that the development community – usually eagle-eyed about the budget – had not spotted this. The problem dated back to 2002 when the shock-waves of 9/11 jolted the international economy. Government spending was reduced. Liz O'Donnell's three-year package of increases was not renewed; in fact, the aid budget was cut (though not by as much as Charlie McCreevy would have liked).

One of the features of targets is that when they falter it is extremely hard to make up the ground. This is especially true when the economy is experiencing strong growth. I knew once I saw the figures that, even though funding was due to be increased again in 2005, there was no way that the 2007 deadline could be met.

I discussed the figures with the new Minister of State and he saw it was true and said so publicly. The storm of criticism which followed took me by surprise.[8] I expected disappointment but the public reaction went deeper: there was a sense of betrayal, accusations that the government had reneged on a solemn promise. The pledge made in 2000 was public and specific; it was made at the UN and repeated in the Programme for Government.

The months that followed were uncomfortable to say the least. It was useless to point out that the budget was sizeable by any standards – €489 million in 2004 representing 0.4 per cent of GNP, or that Vietnam was about to become a new priority country, or that an office was to be opened in Sierra Leone to help that country, and neighbouring Liberia, to emerge from terrible civil wars. Dochas, the umbrella group representing most of the NGOs, was scathing. At the Oireachtas Foreign Affairs Committee we got a roasting, as we did in the media. It was not just the development community – all sorts of people complained. They simply could not accept that at a time of great prosperity, Ireland would go back on its promise to help the world's poorest. I think also that it did not gel with the Celtic Tiger-era image which we had of ourselves; I would hear people say that Ireland should not just reach 0.7 per cent but that we should be the biggest donor in the world without stopping to reflect that this would require annual funding in the billions.

Brian Cowen was in his new role as Minister for Finance for the budget negotiations that autumn. His Department proposed a new three-year package of annual increases totalling €195 million. Finance also offered twenty additional staff, to be assigned to monitoring expenditure and auditing. (This showed that some of the warnings which my predecessors and I had sounded about the risks of not having sufficient staff to keep track of the money were getting through.) The staffing offer was welcome and we accepted it but the three-year package, which in other circumstances would have seemed generous, was just not enough. Both Conor Lenihan and the senior minister, Dermot Ahern, knew that the 0.7 per cent target had to be got back on track and that much bigger increases would have to be put in place to achieve it.

Dermot Ahern took a greater interest in the development cause than some of his predecessors. In his very first interview after being appointed he spoke of the scourge of HIV/AIDS and said he wanted to do something about it.

We let the dust settle but it was obvious soon enough that all the good work being done in the programme was at risk of being overshadowed by the row over the target. Gradually the shape of a strategy emerged: Government approval for a new target date would be sought and, for the first time, a White Paper on Irish Aid would be published.

Negotiations towards re-setting the target date took up much of my time over the following year. A UN conference was scheduled for September 2005 when progress on the Millennium Development Goals would be reviewed in New York – though we could not be sure that the Taoiseach would go to the summit as he had taken a lot of bruises over the missed target. The ground was prepared in talks with the Department of the Taoiseach.[9] The most difficult part was getting the Department of Finance on side as they were being asked to commit large sums of money over a multiyear period.

The Taoiseach instructed the Ministers for Finance and Foreign Affairs to get together and come up with a proposal which they did in May 2005. Finance held to their position that the increases already on the table were the most that could be offered. But the atmosphere at the meeting was amicable and I came away feeling that we stood a good chance of success. More exchanges and projections followed and soon it became clear that the Taoiseach was prepared to set a new target date and to raise the ODA funding beyond what Finance had offered. The target date issue was tossed back and forth. One factor was that the EU was putting pressure on member states to increase their national spending to reach the 0.7 per cent target by 2015. Dermot Ahern and Conor Lenihan felt that Ireland could do better. So the date of 2012 was agreed – three years earlier than the EU target.

As well as setting the 2012 date, interim targets were decided: 0.5 per cent was to be reached by 2007 and 0.6 per cent by 2010. The final decision to go ahead on that basis was only reached at the eleventh hour, just as happened with the earlier target in 2000. In fact, the Informal Government Decision recording the 2012 target was only issued after the Taoiseach had addressed the UN Summit.

Once the target date was settled, work on preparing a White Paper began. Written suggestions were invited (around 150 were received) and a series of town hall-style meetings were held at venues around the country. Conor Brady, the former editor of *The Irish Times*, chaired the meetings. The largest event was a forum held in Dublin Castle in October 2005, which saw a strong turnout of NGOs and people interested in development. It was harder to get the crowds in at the regional venues – even with the bribe of free tea and biscuits! – though some of the bigger cities such as Cork and Galway saw high turnouts. Colleagues in the EU Division, who had organised countrywide consultations on Europe after the Nice Referendum, had warned me that people were slow to leave their TV and fireside and so it proved. But there were some lively meetings. A phenomenon that showed the changing nature of Irish society was the number of people from the developing world who came along to express their views. We also consulted our partner countries and major players such as the OECD and the UN.

Gathering opinions was one thing but writing the text – which had to be authoritative and accurate – was a big challenge. My colleague Brendan Rogers and I did what is usually done in these situations – we assigned two staff members to work fulltime on the draft and to keep us informed of progress. Rory Coveney and Ciaran Madden, two very able young colleagues in Irish Aid, took on the difficult task and they did a terrific job.

The first White Paper on Irish Aid was published in September 2006.[10] I look back at the launch, which took place in the Mansion House in Dublin, as one of the highlights of my time with Irish Aid. Bertie Ahern, Dermot Ahern and Conor Lenihan spoke. The event was attended by the leading figures who have contributed to development over the years. It was a landmark occasion in that the calls for a comprehensive statement on Irish Aid's objectives, calls that went back to the first days of the aid programme in the 1970s, were finally answered. And all of us involved in preparing the White Paper felt that we had got it right, a view that was endorsed by the very warm reception the White Paper received.

New initiatives in the White Paper inevitably received the most attention:

- The decision to designate Malawi as Ireland's ninth programme country and programmes of assistance to fragile states with the focus on Sierra Leone and Liberia

- The establishment of a Rapid Response Initiative to respond more effectively to sudden-onset emergencies

- Support for the new UN Central Emergency Response Fund to improve the response to emergencies

- The setting up of a Hunger Task Force to examine the particular contribution Ireland could make to tackling the root causes of food insecurity, particularly in Africa.

But the main aim of the White Paper was not to seek to break fresh ground. Rather it was to make a public statement of the pillars and goals of Irish Aid's work in a coherent way. (A good start was the decision to rename the programme Irish Aid. Changing to Development Cooperation Ireland was a brave attempt to adopt a more politically sensitive name but it never caught on and the abbreviation, DCI, was described as sounding like a business conglomerate! Use of the word 'aid' still offends some but I think that Irish Aid is the title which people can most identify with.)

Important principles were confirmed in the White Paper: the chief geographic focus confirmed as being on Africa; the new emphasis on regional approaches in Africa – and in South East Asia – based on the embassy that was opening in Vietnam; the inclusion of such 'political' aspects as the promotion of human rights and the fight against corruption as well as support for the African Union and other regional organisations; the move to five-year funding cycles across the range of Irish Aid's partners; and new efforts to help fragile states.

One principle that I especially welcomed was the decision to maintain a mix of aid delivery methods in our partner countries. By this time the lion's share of Irish Aid was going through sector or budget support, or through schemes run by governments or regional authorities in our partner countries. This was in line with best practice internationally for the reasons mentioned in an earlier chapter. But the White Paper spelled out that each aid modality has its own advantages and disadvantages and that 'no single approach can meet all of the needs of Ireland as a donor, or of the partner governments as recipients'. The White Paper concluded:

> We will maintain a mix of complementary modalities in each of our programme countries. In each case, the mix will be determined taking into account the particular circumstances of each country in line with international best practice.[11]

As well as the content, the design and format of the White Paper was of a very high standard. The company Red Dog, who did a lot of work for Irish Aid, excelled themselves. Whenever I gave out copies to partners and development figures at the OECD or in Brussels they commented favourably on the format: a red slipcover with a removable holder that carried the words 'Why Give Aid?' To which the answer could be read on the cover of the White Paper itself:

> First and foremost we give aid because it is right to help those in greatest need. We are bound together by more than globalisation. We are bound together by a shared humanity. The fate of others is a matter of concern to us. From this shared humanity comes a responsibility to those in great need beyond the borders of our own state. For some, political and strategic motives may influence decisions on the allocation of development assistance. That is not the case for Ireland. For Ireland, the provision of assistance and our cooperation with developing countries is a reflection of our responsibility to others and of our vision of a fair global society.[12]

That seems to me as succinct a description as you could get of what Irish Aid is all about.

We arranged for a million copies of the summary version to be posted through every letter box in the country, a logistical ordeal which ran into such thorny problems as the fact that we did not produce enough Irish language versions as we should have. But the importance of informing the public was essential, especially now that the amount of public funds going to aid would increase even further. Two other information initiatives were the commissioning of a six-part TV series on RTE called *Far Away Up Close* which was very professionally done, and an annual award for journalists writing about development topics, named after the journalist Simon Cumbers who was murdered in Saudi Arabia in 2004 while working as a freelance for the BBC.

Minister of State Conor Lenihan had a background in journalism which he brought to bear on publicising the programme. He believed that, rather than paying attention to the broadsheets – which were largely in favour of aid anyway – we should reach out more to readers of the tabloids. Short, newsy articles were what would attract people's attention. He even wrote some of these himself, such as when he happened to be in Sierra Leone at the very time when the warlord Charles Taylor was transferred to the International Criminal Court in The Hague to stand trial for war crimes. I remember him bashing away on a word processor in his hotel room in Freetown to get his story back to Dublin!

Malawi was identified in the White Paper as a new programme country (the term 'priority' had been dropped in favour of 'programme'). Malawi was a good fit for Irish Aid. A decade earlier Malawi was under consideration and I travelled to Lilongwe and had talks there on the margins of a conference of the Southern African Development Community (SADC). (One of my memories of that visit is that the hotel where delegates were staying had lost all the booking information and had no idea who did or did not have a reservation. The sight of hundreds of sweaty delegates in the lobby desperate to get a room had its amusing side!) The conclusion we reached then was that Malawi could enter the priority category but in the event we decided that three new ones were enough and we did not go ahead.

To recap on the programme countries:

- Five were chosen in the first phase in the 1970s: India, Lesotho, Sudan, Tanzania and Zambia.

- India never got off the ground and Sudan was dropped in the mid-90s when it became too difficult to work with the Government there.

- Three new countries were added in 1993: Ethiopia, Mozambique and Uganda.

- East Timor became the seventh programme country in 1998.

- Vietnam was designated a programme country after the Ireland Aid Review of 2002 and an embassy was put in place in 2006.

- Now Malawi was to be the ninth programme country.

I was in favour of increasing the number further to ten or even twelve as I felt the size of the programme justified it. In the light of the economic downturn I am glad in retrospect that the number was kept to nine however, as it is unfair to raise expectations of assistance and then be unable to deliver.

The choice of Vietnam as a programme country was a new step. All of the others were in Africa, with the exception of East Timor where the moving force was the fact that that very poor country's plight was the subject of such concern in Ireland – thanks to the determination of Tom Hyland, who almost single-handedly kept East Timor in the public eye, and to David Andrews for his persistence in seeking international help for the country.

Vietnam had experienced enormous destruction and loss of life in the war with the United States. A Vietnamese delegation came to Ireland in the 1990s and I remember thinking how poor they looked in every respect – their clothes, the cardboard cases they brought. But they also had a single-minded approach that impressed everyone they met. Their interest then was the restoration of the country's electricity system and their target was to get the ESB, which had a strong international arm, to help them do that. Vietnam had already begun its drive to emerge from poverty and reach middle-income status, which it has successfully continued.

Another argument was that Vietnam's neighbours Cambodia and Laos were very poor countries and that a regional strategy could be put in place, based in Hanoi. But experts warned that the three countries were very different and that each required its own approach; this proved to be accurate. There was also a sense that it would serve Ireland's economic interests to open an embassy in Vietnam. Some of the more purist development people were suspicious of this and I often had to defend the choice of Vietnam at meetings with the NGOs – something I rarely had to do with other programme countries.

Whatever the reasons, the decision was in place when I took over and it was a case of making it happen. Sean Hoy, a seasoned development specialist with long experience in the field, was the first head of development in Vietnam.[13] It was his toughest assignment for Irish Aid, not because of the country or the people whom he found interesting and resourceful, but because of the assumption at headquarters that the African model which worked for most of the programme countries would also work here. This was not the case and a specific approach had to be designed for Vietnam with the focus on strengthening the private sector and protecting vulnerable minorities.

There was detailed discussion of this and all aspects of the programme at meetings held after the White Paper was published, which were referred to as the Farmleigh Meetings because most were held in Farmleigh House in the Phoenix Park. The thinking behind holding the talks there was to get away from distractions of the daily challenges facing the Department – though mobile phones often went off and people had to hurry away to deal with some crisis. They were attended by the Minister and Minister of State and their advisers as well as the Secretary General Dermot Gallagher and the Political Director Rory Montgomery.

Brendan Rogers and I represented Irish Aid. A second Assistant Secretary post had been created for the programme – not before time given the amount of money and the many complex issues we were dealing with – and Brendan was the obvious choice to fill the position. An organisation with two chiefs of equal rank could have spelled trouble but Brendan and I divided the work into operations and policy with him taking the former. We made sure that the new system worked well by meeting every morning and I believe that people saw that we were determined to make an unusual set-up work.

There was plenty to discuss at Farmleigh. The White Paper had laid the foundations but there were all sorts of aspects that had to be fleshed out. An example was the Rapid Response Initiative. Brendan made the running on this, drawing up a plan at short notice which found immediate support and which has stood the test of time. He proposed three elements:

- The prepositioning of supplies for use in emergency situations in a number of locations and their transportation to disaster sites. The idea was that these supplies – tents, food and water etc – would be ready to be drawn on when an emergency occurred rather than having to start from scratch each time.

- Setting up a roster of highly skilled individuals, from the public and private sectors, including from the Defence Forces, for deployment at short notice to emergency situations.

- Ireland to contribute to improving the capacity of international agencies involved in humanitarian response.

Staffing was another constant topic. As the programme approached a billion euros the need to be able to account for all that money was becoming acute. Finance's twenty, Liz O'Donnell's extra staff and the second Assistant Secretary post all helped but they were not enough to run a programme of that size. The reputational damage that could arise from fraud or diversion of funds was acute. As usual, there were difficulties in persuading the Department of Finance so it was decided to carry out a comprehensive management review. Farrell Grant Sparks were the consultants who won the contract and they spent many months examining all aspects of the programme. A steering group was chaired by Frank Murray, the former Secretary to the Government and, importantly, the Department of Finance was represented.

At the same time as this longer-term planning was being carried out, challenges such as the long-running abuses by the Sudanese government and their allies in Darfur had to be faced. Darfur was one of those situations where the killings and rape were plain for all to see and the plight of the terrorised communities wrung people's hearts. But no amount of external pressure, not even the threat of trial for war crimes by the International Criminal Court, could move the government in Khartoum. At least the Irish people contributed generously, as they always did, to helping relieve the situation of the refugees, and the Defence Forces again stepped up to the plate by serving in an arduous and demanding peacekeeping tour in neighbouring Chad.[14]

I mentioned at the start of this chapter that two issues overshadowed Irish Aid at a time when so many positive things were happening and that the missed 0.7 per cent target date was one of them. The target issue was eventually resolved and the row over the first missed target actually helped to focus attention on the implications of the big budget increases.

The other problem, the decision to decentralise most of the staff of Irish Aid to Limerick, was not so easily resolved. It was the elephant in the room at the discussions, both at Farmleigh and back in Bishops Square, and a particularly large elephant it was too. I first heard the news when I was still in Vienna and it came as a shock, as it did for most people. The Secretary General asked me if I was still prepared to come back as Director General in the changed circumstances. I thought hard about it but in the end I decided to go ahead, my main motivation being that I valued the development work very much. The question also occurred to me, would decentralisation actually happen? It would not have been the first decision to begin with fanfare only to fade away once the obstacles appeared. Some decentralisation of Government departments had taken place in the past but the announcement of December 2003 was a radical one, affecting not one or two but all Government departments.

However, my discussions on the phone with David Donoghue, whom I was to replace as Director General, convinced me that the Government was determined to press ahead with the plan. Even before I returned, a site had been identified for the Irish Aid building in Limerick, close to King John's Castle. (In the event, the search for suitable premises took ages and the Irish Aid offices in Limerick were only officially opened in 2009, a year after I left.)

The more I thought about it, the stranger the decision to move Irish Aid seemed. All the programme's 'clients' – NGOs, Dochas, the Oireachtas committees, the other Government departments – were in Dublin. Visiting dignitaries, too, would have their main business in Dublin and were unlikely to make their way to Limerick. How would it work?

I spoke to the head of the Revenue Commissioners branch which had moved to Limerick and it became clear that senior management would have to spend a lot of time on the road between Dublin and Limerick. I also visited the decentralised part of the UK's Department of International Development. It had moved staff to East Kilbride in Scotland and the people there showed me around and spoke frankly about the issues that arose for them. I came away with the impression that it was the support side of DFID that had moved and that attempts to add on policy sections were not very successful. In any event, our situation differed greatly in that almost all of Irish Aid was earmarked to move to Limerick whereas most of the DFID staff complement stayed in London.[15]

The decision to decentralise was unpopular with most of the staff of Irish Aid. I chaired one large meeting which was dominated by those opposed and it was such a stormy session that I decided not to use that method of communication again. Instead, we instituted an information update process, which informed everyone of the state of progress. The message I sought to convey was that, whatever anyone thought of the decision, we had to behave professionally and carry it out as best we could. This was the same approach that I found when I met Assistant Secretaries in other Government departments. What was striking was that none of the officials I spoke to actually favoured the plan. Even odder was the fact that the politicians I came into contact with, while determined that Government policy must be implemented, privately showed no enthusiasm for decentralisation.

The principle behind the decentralisation project was that it was voluntary, with the added carrot (or stick, depending on how you saw it) that promotions would be based on a willingness to move to the decentralised location. When the figures came out in 2005 it was clear to me that the move to Limerick would go ahead because in all ranks, including the most senior levels, there were sufficient volunteers from the wider civil service to make up the numbers. In some Departments, and especially in the semi-state bodies, much smaller numbers came forward but Limerick was a popular destination, usually because people had family connections to the city. The numbers applying from within Irish Aid were small so the spectre loomed of a huge turnover of staff.[16]

It was in vain that the risks and problems arising from this scenario were pointed out, or the particular difficulties presented by the fact that diplomatic staff rotate between postings at home and abroad and that, if they went to Limerick on promotion or otherwise, there was no guarantee that they would be assigned there on their return. The Department of Finance was tasked with making the Government decision on decentralisation happen. As far as they were concerned, the numbers for Limerick stacked up. Lengthy negotiations in Finance's personnel offices in Mount Street did not produce any concessions.

There were some compensations in what was overall a gruelling experience. People in the Department working on decentralisation were unfailingly supportive and patient (often more patient than I was!). Marie Cross and her successor as Head of Management Services, Adrian O'Neill, were terrific colleagues and sympathetic to our plight, and Gerry Gervin, who was in charge of Support Services in Irish Aid and had to do most of the legwork, was a rock of sense in a very difficult situation.

Another positive side was the welcome we got from everyone we had contact with in Limerick. The city was in the news for all the wrong reasons at the time with gangland killings having reached new heights. What I found on the ground was that Limerick was a fine city with a lot to offer. All of the people in the Council and the various authorities we met went out of their way to be helpful.[7]

One consolation was that the status of the development specialists in Irish Aid was resolved. The specialists had never been given permanent contracts, a situation which led to a longstanding grievance. As part of the discussions on the move, the status of the specialists was regularised and they, in turn, agreed to the move to Limerick on the same conditions as the rest of the staff.

The move to Limerick has become a reality and must be made to work as many people who faithfully followed the Government's decision made life-changing decisions to move themselves and their families there. But the problems foreseen, in particular those arising from the rotating conditions for Foreign Affairs staff, have already loomed and will not go away.

When I think back on decentralisation, and on my own role in it, I am reminded of what somebody once said: that the worst thing you can do when confronted with a plan you feel is wrong is to go along with it in the hope of making it better.

Endnotes

1. The interim target of 0.45 per cent for 2002 was not reached (0.41 per cent was the figure achieved) and the percentage actually fell in 2003 to 0.40 per cent.

2. Tom Kitt interview.

3. Thanks to John Morahan, then head of EU section in Irish Aid, and Tom Hanney, for providing information about the 2004 EU Presidency.

4. Interviews with Tom Kitt, Liz O'Donnell, Jim O'Keeffe.

5. Helen O'Neill, 'Ireland's Foreign Aid in 2004', *Irish Studies in International Affairs*, Vol. 16 (2005), pp. 281-5.

6. Tom Hanney provided material about the approach to the UN bodies.

7. *DAC Peer Review Ireland 2003*, OECD publication.

8. 'Coalition broke Third World Aid Pledge – Dochas' *The Irish Times*, 11 November 2004, is a typical example of the very negative reaction which greeted the failure to meet the target.

9. Michael Collins who was on secondment from DFA to the Dept of the Taoiseach was sympathetic to the argument that the target needed to be reinstated.

10. *White Paper on Irish Aid*, DFA publication, September 2006.

11. *White Paper*, p. 72.

12. Cover of the White Paper. On the slip cover were the words, 'Every Day you are helping the World's poorest people', a slogan which has been widely used to promote the programme.

13. Sean Hoy interview.

14. Brendan Rogers devoted much time and energy to Darfur and later played a central role in helping to resolve the Sharon Cummins kidnapping case.

15. Mark Lowcock, Director General in the UK's Department of International Development, facilitated the visit and was a helpful colleague during my time as Director General.

16. In some Departments there was a preponderance of junior staff among the applicants – this was not the case for Limerick. We had more applicants than there were positions at the Counsellor/Principal Officer grade (the most senior after Assistant Secretary).

17. Len Dineen, the developer of the premises in Henry Street, eventually chosen for Irish Aid's headquarters, was also easy to work with.

14

HAND OF GOD

Christmas 2004 will stay in many people's memory for the Asian tsunami, which struck on St. Stephen's Day. It was a time when families in Ireland were enjoying the holiday season. The disaster happened in parts of the world well known to Irish people – beautiful beaches and countryside in countries like Thailand and Sri Lanka, which many Irish people had visited. Many of those who died were foreign holidaymakers which brought the tragedy home even more than most.

The facts are well known: a huge earthquake took place under the Indian Ocean off Sumatra, measuring 8.7 on the Richter Scale, causing a giant wave that spread across the entire region, extending as far north as India and Burma and as far west as the Maldive Islands and even to Somalia on the east coast of Africa, causing death and destruction in these countries and, most of all, in Thailand, Sri Lanka and Indonesia. In all, some 228,000 people died.

Pat Bourne, First Secretary at the embassy in New Delhi, was in Sri Lanka when the tsunami struck.[1] He was in Galle on the southern coast of the island for a Christmas holiday with his Sri Lankan born wife Sonali, his children and other family members on 26 December. They were actually on the beach when it happened. Pat recalls that his daughter and her cousin were briefly swept away but a local boatman managed to rescue them. The word tsunami has entered the language now but at the time they had no idea what was happening or what a tsunami was – they thought it was just a freak wave.

Pat and his family went back to their hotel and found that it was inundated. There was a scene of total panic. All their possessions – money, passports, clothes, and Christmas presents – had been washed away. The phone lines were down. The trip back to Colombo took several hours on smaller inland roads but they got there. It was only as news filtered through on the car radio that they learned how bad things were and how close they had come to disaster. They were lucky to have gotten out alive.

As Pat began to understand the nature and extent of the disaster his attention turned to the fate of other Irish citizens on the island. As soon as he could get to a working phone line, he rang John Neary, the head of Consular Section in Foreign Affairs in Dublin to let him know that he was available and on the spot, and he immediately established an Emergency Response Centre for Ireland on the ground. Pat stayed for the next four weeks in Sri Lanka helping Irish citizens who had been affected by the disaster, and then assisting Irish NGOs. In the immediate aftermath of the tsunami, Pat worked through lists of Irish citizens to track their whereabouts. Working with the Irish Honorary Consul in Colombo and EU colleagues including the local German embassy (Germany held the EU Presidency), he issued temporary passports and gave consular assistance to those who needed it. There were no Irish deaths on Sri Lanka, but several injuries and many lost passports and possessions.

Meanwhile Dan Mulhall, Ireland's Ambassador to Malaysia, who was also accredited to Thailand, was spending Christmas with his family at the embassy residence in Kuala Lumpur when he received a call from the duty officer at Foreign Affairs in Dublin.[2] The duty officer asked for information about the wave, which had struck the region a few hours before. There had been nothing on Malaysian TV at that stage so Dan switched over to CNN and that was how he found out about the tsunami. He went in to the embassy office straightaway and started calling Irish citizens in Thailand to check on the situation. Many were away from home because of the holidays, but he did manage to piece together enough information to know that this was a major disaster. He remembers ring-ing a friend on a yacht off the Thai coast who gave him a terrible account of bodies and debris in the water.

The following day he flew to Phuket. As it is a major tourist re-sort, there are regular flights there. He found the Thai authorities well organised – they provided food and drink to the survivors and were already arranging flights home for foreigner on Thai Airways, even providing makeshift travel documents for people who had lost their possessions.

Dan spent the next days trying to trace Irish people who had been reported missing. Every year as many as 45,000 Irish people came to Thailand for holidays so he knew the chances were that Irish people would be among the casualties. He received help from members of the Irish community, including the Honorary Consul in Bangkok, Gary Biesty, and an Irishwoman living in Phuket, Hel-en Fallon Wood, who would later be appointed Honorary Consul in the town.

Amid chaotic scenes he used a megaphone to let Irish people know of his presence. He was assisted by Kyle O'Sullivan who came out from Dublin. One of the biggest difficulties was to establish those who were genuinely missing as opposed to merely reported as having been in the general area of the tsunami. A crisis centre had been set up in Dublin and he worked closely with it and with relatives and friends of those missing. He heard many stories of close shaves. Low-lying hotels were a big source of the deaths; those fortunate to be in hotels with higher floors had a good chance of survival.

A great help to him was a local Thai man, a golf professional, who volunteered to drive Dan and act as his interpreter. He did this for two weeks and refused to take any payment.

In contrast with Sri Lanka, there were Irish fatalities in Thai-land, four in all, though it would take many weeks before all of the identifications took place. The body of Eilis Finnegan was found during the first week and Dan helped to organise the repatriation to Ireland. During that week (he would spend three weeks in all in the country and would return numerous times after that during the continuing identification efforts) he paid visits to hospitals and morgues in Phuket and Krabbi island. The most poignant sight for him was the rows of photographs everywhere, mainly of young people, smiling in their holiday gear, and the knowledge that after a few days the chances of them being found alive were almost nil. The four Irish citizens who died in the tsunami were Eilis Finnegan, Lucy Coyle, Conor Keightley and Michael Murphy.

Just as the consular dimension of the disaster required an immediate response, so too did the humanitarian crisis which the tsunami unleashed. The needs of the affected countries were apparent from the start. Áine Hearns, who worked in the Emergency and Recovery Unit in Irish Aid, was spending Christmas with her family in Abbeyleix when she heard about the tragedy. She spoke on the phone to Brendan Rogers, the head of the unit, and came into the Irish Aid offices in Bishop's Square on the 27th.[3] Áine had long experience of working for Irish Aid and would be appointed Ambassador to Uganda the following year. Brendan Rogers assembled a team to respond to the calls from NGOs and international humanitarian organisations which were already pouring in. The public response, as always, was generous. In fact, it became clear that contributions from the Irish people would dwarf anything seen before: donations would finally total €80 million, more per head of population than in any other country. There was a clear expectation that the Government would also respond generously on behalf of the Irish people.

An initial pledge of €1 million was made on the evening of the disaster; this was doubled to €2 million the following day. By New Year's Eve the Government commitment had risen to €10 million, which was to come from additional funds over and above the allocation for ODA in 2005.

Organising such large amounts of expenditure is a tough task. It is not a case of simply handing over a cheque and hoping it will be well spent. The procedure is that the Emergency and Recovery Unit has to evaluate all applications for funding and make a recommendation to the Minister. Factors that have to be taken into account are the applicant organisation being up to the job, having a proven track record, a presence in the country and the capacity to account for the money. Contracts are then signed with the agency or NGO concerned which set out the conditions of the grant. Where pressing circumstances exist, as they certainly did in the aftermath of the tsunami, the procedure has to be carried out quickly so that funds can be disbursed. But public money is involved and Irish Aid has to be satisfied that the project in question is worth supporting and that the grant will be accounted for. The bigger NGOs and international agencies are familiar with the rules; troubles that arose usually came about where smaller organisations were concerned.

On 4 January, the Taoiseach and the Minister for Foreign Affairs met the heads of the NGOs to discuss Ireland's response. While a gathering of the NGOs to plan strategy was the normal thing after a disaster, the holding of the meeting in Government Buildings, chaired by the Taoiseach, demonstrated how public expectations had grown with the size of the economy during the Celtic Tiger period. The volume of monies being discussed was much larger than I was familiar with from my earlier time with the programme. I remembered the row over the £2 million for Rwanda in 1994 yet here we were thinking nothing of pledging €10 million for the tsunami. It demonstrated to me the extent to which there was no criticism of the scale of the response by the Government; on the contrary, if anything, the public feeling was that even more should be done.

Following the meeting, the Government announced that Dermot Ahern would visit the region hit by the tsunami. It was a tall order: a visit at short notice to unfamiliar parts of the world where we had few contacts and which were bound to be in a chaotic state. Yet the visit was pulled together within five days. The Air Corps in charge of flying the Government jet were magnificent and huge credit must be given to Áine Hearns for making it all happen.

At the same time as the ministerial visit, Brendan Rogers put together a technical team to prepare an analysis of the situation on the ground and to make recommendations. On Brendan's team were the head of Irish Aid's Technical Section, Dr. Vincent O'Neill, William Carlos and Bronagh Carr, also from Irish Aid, and Lt. Colonel Jim Foley from the Defence Forces.

The ministerial party was to fly to the three countries worst affected: Thailand, Indonesia and Sri Lanka. Accompanying the Minister on the Government jet were Dermot Gallagher, the head of Consular Division, John Neary, the press officer Orla O'Hanrahan, Áine Hearns and me. In addition, the Minister invited the CEOs of GOAL, Concern and Trocaire – John O'Shea, Tom Arnold and Justin Kilcullen respectively – as well as the General Secretary of the Irish Red Cross, Carmel Dunne, to accompany him.

The first country we visited was Thailand. The delegation arrived in Phuket on 9 January to be met by Dan Mulhall who gave a briefing on the situation, the first of many we received over the following days. We visited the Disaster Victim Identification Centre. I don't think anyone could have come away unmoved from that place or fail to reflect on our mortality in the face of so many deaths, many of them young holidaymakers. It was not just the scenes inside; outside people were scrutinising big boards in the street where photographs of thousands of missing people were posted. Even more poignant were the many handmade slips of paper with photos of missing people sellotaped onto every available surface.

At a meeting with the Thai Interior Minister Dermot Ahern offered Ireland's help but the response of the Thai Minister was that his country did not need foreign aid. His main interest was in technical forensic support in the identification of bodies. The Thai people faced shelter and housing problems, he said, and losses in the crucial tourism and fishing industries, but the Thai Government was tackling these problems. The UN Disaster Team confirmed to us that the Government was very much on top of the situation and had mobilised an effective response.

After meeting the Irish community, the delegation flew in a Thai Government plane to Krabi, the main centre for the retrieval of bodies. The devastation wrought by the tsunami was pointed out en route. Hotels and other tourism-related buildings along the coast had been demolished; palm trees were submerged up to their tops in water. The vastness of the land areas which had been inundated impressed most of all, the marks still clearly visible after the water's retreat. At Krabi the scenes were as distressing as might be expected, especially at the morgue, outside which the now familiar rows of photographs of the missing were lined up. Before leaving Dublin, the services of fingerprint experts from the Gardaí had been offered and taken up by the Thai authorities. This was badly needed as in many cases the authorities had only jewellery, fingerprints and tattoos to go on. Eventually they would have to take DNA samples from relatives. It was a relief to think that at least Ireland could contribute something that was needed in the form of the Garda expertise.

If the mood in Thailand was sombre and quiet, the scene in Indonesia was one of total destruction. Getting there proved harder than we expected. The government jet had to get permission to enter Indonesian airspace and this had not yet been given when we were airborne. Strict air traffic restrictions were in force because of the high volume of aircraft flying in and out to deliver humanitarian supplies. The Air Corps crew circled and waited in the hope that they would get clearance but eventually we had to divert to Kuala Lumpur. We sat on the runway there – and wondered if we would be able to continue as planned – until permission finally came through.

It was evening when we arrived in Medan, the military airfield close to Banda Aceh where the tsunami's effect had been particularly devastating. We were greeted at the airfield by Hugh Swift, the Ambassador to Singapore who was also accredited to Indonesia. The military were clearly not comfortable with the presence of foreigners at the military airfield and Áine Hearns and I had to stay behind after the ministerial party left to clear the luggage.

The scene in Banda Aceh, which we visited the following day, was truly appalling. Not even the fact that images of the destruction had appeared on television could prepare you for the sight of all the features associated with a busy town transformed into a twisted, mangled heap of wood and metal – cars, trucks, houses, public buildings, all smashed to pieces. The image that has become famous is of fishing boats flung up onto the roofs of houses – and there they were, some of them big trawlers, balancing on the tops of buildings. Under the wreckage were thousands of bodies, which had yet to be removed. Markers stood at the site where people lay under the ruins and every so often a shout would go up to signify that another body had been found. At that stage some 2,000 bodies were being collected every day.

The statistics for Aceh province tell the story: 167,800 dead, 127,000 houses destroyed, 500,000 made homeless.

Yet it is the individual pictures from the tsunami that stick in the memory: the prison which was engulfed, leaving the prisoners no chance; the smell of death and the body bags piled up ready for use; people's personal possessions among the debris – children's toys and photographs; the yellow single decker bus far out in the sea off the coast at Galle . . .

The presence of Irish NGOs in Banda Aceh was very evident. In fact, the number of NGOs, agencies and charities assembled was astonishing. As we drove to the centre of the humanitarian relief effort we passed hundreds of tents that displayed the logos of the different organisations. It should have been reassuring to see so many people eager to help but there was something unsettling about the scene too and it was no surprise to hear that coordination was a big problem.

The Irish NGOs were already stuck in and there was the familiar sense of pride at the practical work being done by the volunteers of Concern, Goal, Trocaire, the Red Cross and many other Irish bodies. It was reassuring to see the familiar face of Fr. Jack Finucane of Concern at the briefing. Minister Ahern was briefed by the Indone-

sian Minister for People's Welfare, who happened to be in Banda
Aceh. We were told that the biggest food shortages were in the out-
lying areas and that the Indonesian Government was trying to open
up roads to get to those in need. The US military was playing a key
role in lifting food supplies to remote areas.

Then it was on to Sri Lanka. Pat Bourne met us there, together
with the Ambassador to India, Kieran Dowling. After the first chaotic days, Pat's attention had turned to the development aspect as
NGOs such as Concern and Trocaire representatives arrived in the
country. He was on hand to meet the technical team from Irish Aid,
which had set out at the same time as Minister Ahern. He was also
able to set up meetings for Minister Ahern with top political figures
including the Prime Minister and Foreign Minister who briefed him
on the measures the Sri Lankan Government were taking to deal
with the crisis.

The party set off by road to Galle, one of the worst affected
towns. En route we stopped at what has become another iconic image of the tsunami – the passenger train swept sideways off the
tracks by the wave. This was a truly extraordinary sight: it looked as
if God had reached down his hand and simply pushed the red car-
riages over on their side and twisted the tracks into hoops to warn
mankind that it cannot always have its own way. Two of the car-
riages had been flung into a lagoon by the force of the wave. On
that crowded train alone, 800 passengers perished.

Galle was once an attractive port town but now the scene of destruction was on the same scale as we had seen at Banda Aceh. A feature of both disaster sites was the huge areas of waste ground where
buildings had not stood up to the shock of the water and everything
was reduced to wooden planks that looked like broken matchsticks.
Where the occasional sturdier building had survived it was just a
shattered hulk that looked as if it would give up the struggle any
moment and collapse down into the rest of the detritus.

The Minister and delegation met the Governor of the Southern
Province and the main relief agencies including the UN family and

the World Bank as well as Australian and US military personnel.
We were told that, in addition to the 4,300 people dead or missing
in the town, the main industries of Galle – fishing and tourism –
had been devastated. Some 23,000 families had lost their homes
and here, as everywhere hit by the tsunami, housing and shelter
were top priorities. The Minister met representatives of Concern
and Trocaire who were already looking ahead to assisting with
housing and rebuilding livelihoods, as well as trauma counselling.

Some of the party accompanied the Minister on a helicopter
journey to Hambantota to visit GOAL projects. We stopped on the
way back at the small fishing village of Paiyagala to attend the
launch of a project supported by the Sri Lankan community in Ireland aimed at helping the local community to restore their fishing
fleet.

Back in Colombo, the Minister was briefed by the technical
team on their findings to date and he held a wrap-up meeting with
the NGOs. One of the clear messages that came through was that,
while there had been a fantastic response to the immediate needs,
more funding would continue to be required in the medium to long
term. It was obvious, too, that the situations of the three countries
visited were different as were their needs. The Minister announced
that Ireland would make a further allocation to the region of €10
million from Irish Aid's Emergency Fund.

A point which Dermot Ahern made throughout the visit was
that Ireland should leave a footprint behind – both because of the
scale of the catastrophe and as a mark of gratitude for the help giv-
en by the authorities in the different countries to the many Irish
caught up in the tsunami, including the identification and repatriation of the four Irish victims. One project so funded was a hospice
for AIDS sufferers in Phuket. Many Thai women contracted AIDS
as a result of the sex tourism industry and the hospice at least provided dignity and care.

There was also a strong sense that lessons needed to be drawn.
As a practical follow-up, the Government decided later in January

to appoint a Special Envoy. Chris Flood, Chair of the Advisory Board on Irish Aid, was the person chosen. Over the following year Chris made three visits to the region, checking on progress in Irish Aid's assistance and identifying lessons to be learned. Uniquely among those who travelled to Sri Lanka at the time, he visited the area controlled by the Tamil Tigers, which had also suffered from the tsunami. He presented a series of reports to Government, the final one of which summarised his conclusions and recommendations.[4]

Chris Flood's reports placed particular emphasis on the need for better coordination in the face of disasters such as the tsunami. He recommended that Irish Aid should continue to support the UN as the main coordinator in such disasters. While praising the unprecedentedly generous public donations that poured into the disaster regions, he pointed out that the huge number of formal and informal actors who came on the scene with the best of intentions posed very big challenges. He drew attention to the lack of qualified, experienced personnel, which arises in disasters of this kind, and recommended that a register be drawn up of people with skills needed to respond to emergencies. And he praised Irish Aid's decision to channel funding for medium to longer-term assistance through Multi-Donor Trust Funds.

Good can come out of bad. Terrible though the tsunami was, it proved to be a catalyst in improving donors' approach to emergencies.

In 2006 Irish Aid proposed that the tsunami response be the subject of one of the Value for Money reports which every Government Department is required to make.[5] These reports go beyond the mere question of whether monies spent can be accounted for and seek to establish if expenditure represented the best value for the taxpayer. The process is coordinated by the Department of Finance and the reports are published and presented to the Oireachtas.

The Value for Money study was carried out by an international consulting firm, INTRAC, after a tender process. It concluded that Irish Aid made a prompt and appropriate response and that they found no evidence of funds being wasted. At the same time, the authors concluded that the tsunami had revealed areas where Irish Aid could improve its efficiency, effectiveness and 'value-added' when responding to emergencies. Concern was expressed, as it had been by Chris Flood, at the very large number of agencies and NGOs which Irish Aid funded. (In Banda Aceh alone 124 international NGOs and 430 local NGOs were registered as well as a plethora of national donors, UN and Government agencies.) It pointed out that €18 million of Irish Aid's total allocation of €20 million was disbursed through 34 organisations. The study warned that Irish Aid could become fragmented if a similar approach were adopted in the future.

The Value for Money report endorsed Chris Flood's proposal for a register of experts and for channelling funds through Multi-Donor Trust Funds and it advised that a range of procedural and staffing issues be addressed including improved monitoring and evaluation of grants.

The tsunami provoked considerable soul-searching in the international development community about the effectiveness of humanitarian response. A group of international donors decided to band together and examine the issue in depth to see what lessons could be drawn. They went under the name of the Tsunami Evaluation Coalition, or TEC for short.[6] Irish Aid was one of almost 30 donors which contributed funding to the exercise. This was more than just a routine evaluation: the outcome was a massive report, probably one of the most exhaustive examinations of a disaster ever carried out. Yet the conclusions, which are gathered in a shorter summary report, were in many ways quite simple.

One of the basic finding of the TEC report was that it was local people who provided almost all immediate lifesaving actions and most of the early emergency support. In this, as in other disasters, far more people were rescued by the local community than external agencies.

It might seem obvious that the local communities would be best placed to help but that did not prevent many of the organisations who rushed to help from seeking to impose their views on the people affected. Pat Bourne, who knows Sri Lanka well, saw arrogance in some of the agencies – treating the Government as if it were incompetent when it had a functioning administration, an army and other services which were in a position to help.

The report called for the local effort to be put in the driving seat in future disaster response. It found that international action was most effective when enabling, facilitating and supporting local response. The report also found examples of poor quality work in the response to the tsunami, and criticised the arbitrary nature of the funding system for humanitarian emergencies.

The TEC report had four main recommendations:

- The international humanitarian community needs a fundamental reorientation from supplying aid to supporting and facilitating communities' own relief and recovery priorities.

- All actors should strive to increase their disaster response capacities and to improve the linkages and coherence between themselves and other actors in the international disaster response system, including those from the affected countries themselves.

- The international relief system should establish an accreditation and certification system to distinguish agencies that work to a professional standard in a particular sector from the others.

- All actors need to make the current funding system impartial, more efficient, flexible and better aligned with principles of good donorship.

Drawing on the TEC report, the Value for Money report and the work done by Chris Flood as the Government's envoy, Irish Aid's approach to emergency response was reshaped in the years that followed. The White Paper of 2006 reflected the change of approach. The keynote was advance preparation and improved coordination.[7]

The White Paper initiatives were implemented. The Rapid Response Corps was established and by 2008 twenty-seven deployments had taken place to fourteen countries. Supplies prepositioned by Ireland at the UN base in Brindisi, Italy and at the Curragh had been dispatched to ten countries facing emergencies including Iraq, Mozambique, Togo, the Democratic Republic of the Congo and Zimbabwe. Irish Aid became a major contributor to the UN's Central Emergency Response Fund, contributing €22.6 million since its establishment in 2006. One of the advantages of the CERF is that it uses a third of its money for so-called 'forgotten emergencies' – the places which do not hit the headlines but where the need can be just as great.[8]

An important further development along the same lines was Irish Aid's entry into strategic partnerships with the key players in emergencies. Agreements were reached for multiannual funding with organisations such as the World Food Programme and the Red Cross to ensure greater predictability in their funding.

Lessons learned from the tsunami have enabled Irish Aid to react in a more coherent fashion to disasters such as the Haiti earthquake and the Pakistan floods. Members of the Rapid Response Corps were able to be put in the field right away and funds allocated to the CERF released. And on the strategic front, in line with the main finding of the TEC report, Irish Aid now places greater emphasis on using local systems to deliver aid.

For me, the most positive aspect of the tsunami response was the dedication of the staff of Irish Aid and the Department of Foreign Affairs. From the moment the Emergency and Recovery Unit and Brendan Rogers' technical team assembled during the holiday period through the months that followed they put in all the hours that were needed – and more – and at all times behaved with tremendous professionalism. The logistical difficulties of visits such as those to the tsunami region, by the Minister, by Chris Flood and by others, the quick decisions that have to be taken – these cannot be overstated. Nor can the risks, whether security-related, health risks or the trauma of coping with scenes most people happily never see. The Air Corps, the Army, the Garda technical experts all played a very positive role. The Department's consular job of assisting Irish citizens in distress was fully discharged both by staff at headquarters and by people in the field such as Pat Bourne and Dan Mulhall.

I have found that the spirit of those working for and with Irish Aid is terrific. It is one of the great positives about the programme. Nowhere was this more in evidence than after the tsunami.

Endnotes

1. Pat Bourne interview. I am grateful to Pat, to Dan Mulhall and to Áine Hearns for sharing their recollections of the tsunami with me.

2. Dan Mulhall, later head of EU Division in Dublin, Ambassador to Germany interview.

3. Áine Hearns interview.

4. 'The Tsunami: Ireland and the Recovery Effort, Final Report to the Minister for Foreign Affairs Mr. Dermot Ahern TD and the Minister of State Mr. Conor Lenihan TD'. Chris Flood, Government Special Envoy. DFA publication, 2005.

5. 'Support to Tsunami affected Countries, A Value for Money Review' DFA publication 2006.

6. John Cosgrave, 'Joint Evaluation of the International Response to the Indian Ocean Tsunami Synthesis Report Expanded Summary', publication of the Tsunami Evaluation Coalition (TEC). This summary appends a list of sub-thematic reports which fed into the main report pp. 39-40.

7. White Paper, pp. 34-38.

8. Diarmuid O'Leary updated me on emergency response initiatives. Interview.

15

FRAGILE STATES, HIV/AIDS, HUNGER

Increased spending during the first decade of the millennium enabled Irish Aid to expand and intensify its interventions in a lot of fields. Three areas of Irish Aid's work in this period call for special mention: a new focus on fragile states, the fight against HIV/AIDS and the campaign to combat hunger.

Tackling the aggravated problems that affect countries in a state of collapse poses special challenges. East Timor is an example of a country that Irish Aid helped in its transition to independence after years of struggle.

Two neighbouring countries which suffered greatly in the course of appalling civil wars were Sierra Leone and Liberia. Both fall into the category of fragile states, a loose term which has never been properly defined but is applied to countries that are in a particularly vulnerable condition, usually as a result of conflict, and in danger of turning into failed states as happened to Somalia. There was good reason for Ireland to take an interest in the two countries: missionary links go right back to the first half of the nineteenth century.

A more recent link was the peacekeeping role of our armed forces in Liberia. After two periods of civil war that lasted eleven years, the UN asked member states to provide peacekeeping troops for a major operation in Liberia, known as UNMIL, aimed at consolidating the peace and returning the country to normality. Ireland agreed to take part.

Ireland's involvement with UNMIL started in 2003 and ended in 2007. Colonel John O'Reilly described to me his experience serving in Liberia.[1] He was there from November 2005 to May 2006, the usual tour of duty being six months. Irish and Swedish troops combined to form a quick reaction force, with Ireland providing 420 troops at a time and Sweden contributing 250 to make a full battalion in strength. This was not the largest Irish peacekeeping operation – that record is held for Lebanon where 650 troops at a time were assigned.

The task of the Irish-Swedish quick reaction force in Liberia was to provide a mobile presence that could react to trouble anywhere in the country, and in the capital Monrovia especially. Their transport was MOWAG armoured personnel carriers and Panhard armoured cars. Their normal activities were to patrol the country showing the flag and reassuring the local population who were still very frightened after the civil war. The local people found these tours reassuring. The troops' presence served to defuse tensions which could flare up due to the large number of former combatants who had nothing to do and were poverty-stricken. The peacekeepers had to be available at all times in case of need. The overall commander was a Nigerian General, and Alan Doss, a Welshman, was Special Representative of the UN Secretary-General. The largest contingents in UNMIL were Nigerians, Ethiopians and Pakistanis.

It was also in UNMIL's mandate to provide supplementary security for the special court looking into the atrocities during the civil war in neighbouring Sierra Leone. There was a big security operation surrounding the transfer of Charles Taylor to the special court in The Hague. He had to be brought from Nigeria to Monrovia and was then escorted by Irish troops to Freetown. Alan Doss was concerned about security surrounding this transfer so it was high alert. The Irish soldiers stayed in Freetown as part of the defensive force until Taylor had been safely flown out.

Another occasion which called for high security was the inauguration of Mrs. Johnson Sirleaf as President of Liberia in January

2006. Before Colonel O'Reilly's tour of duty, the elections were a big focus of attention. The quick reaction force had to be on constant alert. There was a difficult moment after George Weah failed to win and his supporters were angry, but the elections passed off peacefully.

Colonel O'Reilly says that the climatic conditions in Liberia were not as difficult as those faced by the Irish troops in Chad where the tours were for four months at a time because of the hardship involved. Camp Clara, where they were deployed, was located near the sea in the grounds of what had once been a fine resort. The buildings had been destroyed in the fighting so that accommodation was mostly under canvass. Lessons have been learned over the years about the importance of providing decent facilities; the food is good and the troops get regular leave and have access to the Internet and Skype.

Service in Liberia opened the troops' eyes to the appalling poverty in the country and the destruction and brutality that had taken place. It showed them how a country could fail and the effect of tribal enmities. As in other countries where Irish troops have served as peacekeepers, support was given to good causes. In Liberia funding of $15,000 from Irish Aid was made available for projects including refurbishing an AIDS orphanage, an AIDS hospice run by nuns of Mother Teresa's congregation and the Agnes and Alfred Orphanage where orphans from the civil war were housed until they reached the age of sixteen. The soldiers also raised money separately at home at the different barracks and through fundraising events while on leave. After an RTÉ Nationwide team came out and made a programme on the Irish troops a lot of cash was raised, including a cheque for $2,000 from a lady in Dungannon and another $1,000 donated by a priest. Containers full of books and clothes were sent out. The army chaplain supervised the work, which included re-roofing and rebuilding accommodation for the orphans.

President Mary McAleese visited Liberia in 2004 for the inauguration of the country's first peacetime president. The visit was both in solidarity with the country as it struggled to rebuild itself and as a mark of support for the Irish peacekeeping presence. She saw the humanitarian work of the Irish troops and told me how proud she was of what the soldiers were doing:

> Everywhere the troops have gone – Lebanon, Kosovo, Liberia – you hear the same message from the local people. Of all the troops they encounter, the Irish are the ones who get out from their barracks and say, 'is there anything we can do to help around here?' They refurbish orphanages, they help kids, and at the end of each tour the progress on these projects is evaluated and a report sent to the next soldiers coming to take up duty. This ensures that the help is not a one-off affair but that progress is checked and that the work continues from one tour to the next.[2]

After a visit by Minister of State Tom Kitt to Liberia and Sierra Leone in 2004, it was announced that Irish Aid would open an office in Freetown with the aim of giving support to both countries.

Grainne O'Neill was the first person to take up duty for Irish Aid in Freetown in February, 2005.[3] Her status was not as defined as that of the personnel assigned to embassies in the programme countries; officially, accreditation to the two countries was from the embassy in Abuja and Grainne called herself Country Representative. Despite that, there was an openness and welcome for Irish Aid, influenced in part by the fact that many senior officials and ministers had been educated by missionaries. Liam Caniffe, the Ambassador to Nigeria, was very helpful and visited his two new countries of accreditation regularly, which helped to enhance the status of the new office. Others in Freetown were simply glad to see a new donor; the country truly deserved the title 'aid orphan' as few donors were prepared to take the risk of engaging.

Grainne arrived in Freetown with nothing but her suitcases and files. The head of Concern's country programme, Paula Connolly, met her at the airport, took her to the hotel and helped her to hire a car. Then she was on her own. But this did not bother her;

Grainne had worked her way up from the general service to qualify as a development specialist and had served already in Rwanda, the Balkans, East Timor and the DRC. She felt as if everything she had worked for was coming together and says she never thought of failure. The UNDP allowed her to use their IT facilities. She was fortunate to find a house which was near the UK High Commission and which she felt would be suitable. It had no roof but it was being restored and the location was good from a security perspective.

She organised to bring in all the equipment which was not available locally to set up a mission and functioning office. She believes that IT, computers, generators and, above all, reliable access to e-mail and phone communication in such a fragile state were key and that these have revolutionised aid work and brought the field closer to HQ.

Once she got herself set up, Grainne attended coordination meetings of the few donors in the country and the UN and made herself known. Following a pattern that has become regular for Irish Aid, the first interventions were made through UNDP and NGOs such as the Tear Fund, Trocaire and Concern. A two-year strategy was then drawn up in collaboration with HQ colleagues. The holding of credible national elections was seen as a critical benchmark in Sierra Leone's efforts to consolidate peace and democratic rule. Help was given to build up independent institutions from scratch and to work with civil society and the UN in ensuring that the 2007 elections were free and fair. The head of the National Electoral Commission, Christiana Thorpe, an ex-Cluny nun with links to Ireland, had a tough job and Grainne went out of her way to help her. The elections eventually went off successfully even though the situation was extremely tense as there was a risk that a change of power from the first elections would not go smoothly.

Irish Aid in its strategy focused on nutrition and agriculture.[4] Sierra Leone has great natural advantages (and mineral wealth including diamonds) but Grainne found it a difficult working environment with weak governance and leadership. The incentive was the huge needs that were apparent all around. An example is the slums in Freetown which had the same effect on me when I went there as they did on Rodney Rice: the only reaction that you could have is to be outraged that people have to live in such inhumane, disease-ridden conditions.[5]

As well as the challenges in Sierra Leone, there was scope for assisting Liberia which Grainne travelled to often – every month to begin with – by plane or by road. She found that Liberia was not a poor country in terms of resources, just poorly managed. It has huge iron ore deposits and, like Sierra Leone, diamonds. It has land ownership problems like so many African countries. And the trauma of the terrible civil war was still fresh there. But Liberia proved to be better than its neighbour at organising itself to receive vital aid and rebuilding roads and other critical infrastructure. The United States has a strong influence (just as the UK has in Sierra Leone). The country had a much needed stroke of good fortune when it elected Mrs Johnson Sirleaf as President in 2006. A former economist with the World Bank, she was able to use her expertise and contacts to lay out a path to recovery. It was almost a case of starting from scratch because of the destruction wrought during the fighting which featured child soldiers, maiming, rape and murder.

Irish Aid has helped Liberia to restore water, health and sanitation services and assisted the young government to combat gender-based violence. It is vital in fragile states that aid helps deliver a peace dividend for the population and that they begin to see a difference.

The amounts of money channelled to these fragile states are small compared to programmes in other countries – but Ireland's assistance is greatly appreciated and is making a difference.[6] I saw this for myself when I accompanied Minister of State Conor Lenihan to Liberia and Sierra Leone in 2006. At a meeting with the Minister of State, President Johnson Sirleaf was extremely positive about Ireland's help both through the peacekeeping presence and financial assistance. When Grainne O'Neill left Liberia in 2009 she was given the rare honour of a lengthy one-to-one meeting with President Johnson Sirleaf who was re-elected to a second term in 2011.

Grainne attributed Ireland's high standing in Liberia to the performance of the Irish troops and Irish Aid's assistance. She says that the Irish Army were terrific; their professionalism was still talked about long after they left:

> It was the first time the civilian population saw soldiers behaving as they should. They were so used to associating the military with abuses and repression. The Irish peacekeeping troops made a lasting impression.

Since its emergence in the early 1980s, HIV and AIDS have devastated families, communities and nations, killing many people in their most productive years and leaving countless of orphaned children to fend for themselves.[7] Sub-Saharan Africa has been the worst hit region in the world with 22 million adults and children living with HIV in 2009 out of an overall total of 33 million. Countries such as Botswana, Swaziland, Lesotho, Zambia and South Africa have seen some of the worst rates of infection, with as many as one in four adults living with HIV.

As well as bringing death and disease, the timing of the HIV/AIDS pandemic was particularly unfortunate for the African continent. Many countries were emerging from conflict and savouring their first taste of peace and freedom from colonial rule and apartheid. The prospects were good for real progress in bringing people out of poverty. Then along came AIDS, destroying hope for millions and setting back the economic potential of whole countries.

The devastating effects of AIDS are well known. Even if the rate of growth has fallen in recent years, the number of people newly infected in 2009 was still 2.6 million (down from a high of 3.2 million in 1997), and the number of AIDS-related deaths that year 1.8 million (from a high of 2.1 million in 2001). Frightening though these statistics are, it is the human detail that brings home the enormity of the problem. Here is Jeffrey Sachs's account of a visit to a village in Malawi where he saw crops withering in the fields:

> If the village were filled with able-bodied men who could have built small-scale water harvesting units on rooftops and in the fields to collect what little rain had fallen in the preceding months, the situation would not be as dire as it is this morning. But as we arrive in the village, we see no able-bodied young men at all. In fact, older women and dozens of children greet us, but there is not a young man or woman of working age in sight. Where, we ask, are the workers? Out in the fields? The aid worker who has led us to the village shakes his head and says no. They are nearly all dead. The village has been devastated by AIDS, which has ravaged this part of Malawi for several years now. There are just five men between twenty and forty years of age left in the village.[8]

I visited AIDS orphanages and treatment centres to see the work being funded by Irish Aid and again it is the detail that remains in my memory. Like being told, almost casually, when visiting schools in the Limpopo region of South Africa where Irish Aid was helping to refurbish classrooms, that the biggest problem they faced was not so much bricks and mortar as the fact that so many of their teachers were dying from AIDS. Or the scene at a clinic which Irish Aid co-funded with the Clinton Foundation in the highlands of Lesotho, where people queued to be tested and the young American doctor on duty told me that the positive rate among those tested there was one in three. It seemed so incongruous, up in that remote part of the world, accessible only by pony or by helicopter, that AIDS should have reached its tentacles even up there – and to such a devastating extent.

It took time before the international donors responded to the enormous scale of the pandemic. Those who had been working on the ground in the 1980s and 1990s said that there were alarming reports and anecdotal evidence long before the system swung into

action. When it did, however, it can be said to have acted effectively and taken a comprehensive approach to the different aspects of
the disease which needed to be addressed. The UN set up a Joint
Programme on HIV and AIDS, known as UNAIDS, in 1996 with the
aim of bringing greater coherence to the UN's activities in the area.
The Millennium Development Goals, adopted at the Millennium
Summit in 2000, included a specific target of halting and beginning
to reverse the spread of HIV/AIDS by 2015.[9]

Agreement was reached to establish a new body, the Global
Fund to fight AIDS, Tuberculosis and Malaria. The decision to set
up the Global Fund was backed by the G8 countries, which was essential as combating all three would require very significant funding. In this case, the expectations were met as donors pledged billions in the years after the Global Fund got off the ground in 2002.

Most of Ireland's programme countries were affected by the
pandemic, some to a terrible extent, which meant that it had a particular resonance.

Bertie Ahern told me about the impact a visit to Lesotho in
2000 made on him.[10] The visit was in many ways a joyous one, Ireland being seen as a country that had stood by Lesotho after most
other donors left. The whole cabinet turned out at the airport in
Maseru to greet him. But it was the way that AIDS was ravaging the
struggling Lesotho population which stayed with Bertie Ahern. He
visited the same remote clinics which I saw and was struck by the
extent of the problem.

His understanding of the threat posed by HIV and AIDS went
back further, however. He saw the disease developing in Ireland as
early as the mid-1980s, in our case mostly as a result of the drug
abuse problem. He managed to have it put on the EU's agenda as
Minister for Labour during Ireland's EU Presidency of 1990. He
agreed to attend the first UN Special Session on HIV/AIDS in 2001,
the only European head of government to do so.

Within Irish Aid two people stand out as having contributed
greatly to the programme's substantial role in the fight against HIV

and AIDS – Dr. Vincent O'Neill and Nicola Brennan. They spotted at an early stage that the pandemic was having a disastrous effect on many of the countries Irish Aid was striving to help, not only in terms of death and suffering but also in destroying hopes of economic development.[11]

Vinnie had worked as a medical doctor in Uganda before joining Irish Aid in 1995. He and his wife Bronagh were APSO volunteers in Rakai District, recognised as being the epicentre of the African AIDS epidemic. More and more patients were being diagnosed as HIV positive. At that time the only thing that could be done was to treat the symptoms to slow the progression. Many presented late, died and left young families behind them.

The first task he was given in Irish Aid was to develop the programme's health brief and it was natural that a response to HIV would form part of it.

Ireland's first major policy statement came during our term on the UN Security Council when there was a US-led discussion on HIV/AIDS and global security. Vinnie worked with Tom Hanney on Ireland's contribution to the debate. The Security Council became more engaged and in 2001 Kofi Annan convened a Special Session on HIV/AIDS. Ireland made a significant contribution to the Declaration at the Special Session with the issue.

Nicola Brennan returned to headquarters after postings in South Africa and Uganda. She remembers attending a presentation by a health expert in South Africa from the UK's Department for International Development in 1998, which highlighted the scale of the AIDS problem. Even at that late stage, it was still not a big story. But the problem in South Africa was becoming ever more obvious and was out in the open when she was transferred to Uganda in 1999. Infection rates in Uganda were among the highest in the world at that time – at one stage 30 per cent of those tested were positive. Unlike in some affected countries, the authorities in Uganda, led by President Museveni, made HIV/AIDS a public issue and vowed to tackle it seriously. In this they have had considerable success and have managed to reduce the rate of infection dramatically.

At headquarters Nicola worked with Vinnie O'Neill to shape Irish Aid's approach. A dedicated HIV/AIDS Unit was set up in Irish Aid. And Ireland put its money where its mouth was: in 2002 a pledge was made to increase spending on the fight against HIV/AIDS to €30 million per year. Not only was this promise kept, but in 2005 the commitment was raised to €100 million a year to combat AIDS and other communicable diseases.

Irish Aid was well ahead of other donors in publishing its strategy on HIV/AIDS in 2002.[12] The approach adopted by Irish Aid was multifaceted, as the pandemic required. Education, prevention, treatment and addressing the development implications all formed part of the response. The channels for delivering assistance were also numerous: partner government health systems, local AIDS organisations on the ground engaged in awareness raising, Irish and international NGOs, hospices and treatment centres and, above all, through the major funds and programmes which emerged once the scale of the pandemic was known. As well as UNAIDS and the Global Fund, where Ireland punched well above its weight, support was given to bodies engaged in research aimed at expanding the boundaries of what can be done to combat a disease for which there is no cure. The main targets for Irish Aid research funding were the International AIDS Vaccine Initiative and the International Partnership for Microbicides.

The economic impact was always high on Irish Aid's agenda. Not only was there a human tragedy in the huge loss of life and the thousands of children orphaned, but the impact on a country's economic well-being was seriously affected, as Jeffrey Sachs' account above shows.

Ireland was recognised as a leader in the fight against HIV/AIDS. Technical conferences were hosted in addition to the one held during our EU Presidency in 2004 where the focus was Eastern Europe and Asia. Leading figures such as Peter Piot, Executive Director of UNAIDS, and Michael Kazachine, the head of the Global Fund, came to Dublin for consultations. UNICEF – another major recipient of Irish Aid funding – chose Dublin as the location of its conference on HIV/AIDS and children in 2008.

One of the most significant partnerships for Irish Aid was with the Clinton Foundation. The former President identified the pandemic as a key target for the charitable work of his foundation and sought funding from Ireland. Bertie Ahern was in no doubt that he should be helped:

> Bill Clinton had proved himself to be a true friend of Ireland and I welcomed Irish Aid's cooperation with him in the fight against HIV/AIDS. Ireland was the first country to give money to the Foundation and this helped President Clinton to leverage funding from others and to persuade the drug companies to support the use of generic drugs.[13]

Not that it was all plain sailing. The Clinton Foundation had big figures in mind for Ireland's contribution, as my predecessor David Donoghue found, and no matter how worthy the cause, there could be no question of a blank cheque.[14] Also, the Foundation's approach was challenged by Irish Aid: they had planned to use funds to hire doctors and other staff to roll out their own anti-retroviral programme in developing countries. But Irish Aid argued strongly for the Foundation's work to be integrated into countries' national health plans to avoid setting up parallel service and instead to give the partner countries ownership of what was clearly going to be a long-term service. The Clinton Foundation adopted this approach in Mozambique and Frank Sheridan, who was ambassador there at the time, believes that it was a positive learning process for the foundation.

Bill Clinton, meanwhile, used his considerable skills to get the agreement of countries such as India and Brazil to provide generic versions of the vital antiretroviral drugs to developing countries. Bill Clinton came to Dublin to discuss the progress of the cooperation with Irish Aid. At the press conference in Farmleigh he gave one of the most eloquent speeches I have ever heard about what his Foundation was seeking to achieve. My only regret was that his words did not reach a wider audience that day – just a few dozen journalists and officials were privileged to be in the room.

HIV/AIDS became a mainstream activity throughout Irish Aid. A Technical Advisory Group was set up, drawn from some of the top medical experts in the country who gave their time freely to monitor and shape Irish Aid's policy. A particularly successful way of raising awareness was activities surrounding World AIDS Day, which is marked each year on 1 December. Nicola Brennan organised an annual lecture in the name of Father Michael Kelly, a renowned authority on AIDS in Zambia where he works.

Fighting HIV/AIDS needs big money. I was struck when attending meetings of the Global Fund how the figures discussed were in the billions rather than millions. Michael Sidibe, the current head of UNAIDS, said in his 2010 Report on the Global AIDS epidemic: 'We have halted and begun to reverse the epidemic. Fewer people are becoming infected with HIV and fewer people are dying from AIDS.'[15]

But the growth of funding flattened for the first time in 2009 and demand far outstrips supply. The Global Fund, which had such success in getting donors to put up big money, is experiencing serious funding difficulties for the first time and has had accountability issues in some partner countries. The problem is not about to go away; getting more and more sufferers onto cheap antiretroviral drugs is costly and is only part of the solution. At least it can be said that Ireland played its part. The 2009 OECD Review of Irish Aid concluded that 'Ireland leads the way in the EU in the proportion of overseas development assistance allocated to combating HIV/AIDS'.[16]

For the majority of people living in the developed world, chronic hunger is happily rarer today than it has ever been. Certainly, poor people in Western countries sometimes go hungry or are unable to afford nutritional food, but they are in a minority. In the developing world it is a very different story. Hunger there affects over a billion people. The typical image is of acute hunger caused by conflict or floods or drought. Far more common is chronic hunger where people's lives are dominated by the absence of the nutritious food necessary for growth and survival. It is not surprising that when the Millennium Development Goals were being drawn up the goal of eradicating extreme hunger and poverty became Goal Number 1.

On a visit to Northern Province in Zambia, I heard something that brought the issue home to me. The journey from Lusaka was long and bumpy and I was taking a rest in the Irish Aid compound before a meal which was to be served in the evening. There were good smells of cooking around. Two little local boys were outside the window, joking and playing around. Then one said to the other, who was being particularly jiggy, 'Why are you so happy?' To which the other boy replied, 'I am happy because today I will eat.'

Travelling with Vincent Akulumuka in the Tanzanian countryside – where Vincent engaged in agricultural research for a decade – he told me that chronic hunger and malnutrition was a major problem which showed itself in stunted growth and bodies weakened by lack of proper food.

> People around here only recognise hunger when people are visibly starving. When someone is too small for their age people will say it is because their parents were small. But in most such cases it is because the person is not getting enough food.

Hunger has always had a special resonance in Ireland because of our own experience of famine. Even in the early twentieth century nutrition in Ireland was far from adequate; people of my generation were familiar when growing up with illnesses associated with poor nutrition – rickets, anaemia and TB.

The search for ways through which Ireland could address the global problem goes back a long way. The first serious effort was the Freedom from Hunger Campaign of the 1960s. And the NGOs saw relieving hunger as a major goal from the start.

Throughout its history, there has been a strong agricultural focus in the aid programme. Early projects like support for cooperatives in Lesotho or for the dairy industry in Sudan and Zambia were examples of Irish Aid attempting to come to grips with this vital sector. Yet agriculture has not been as successful as other interventions. Irish Aid is far from being alone in this; most donors have little to show for their efforts in agriculture and some have given up on it altogether. There are many reasons. Ownership of land and tenancy arrangements are particularly fraught issues. Then there are the long-standing enmities between farmers and pastoralists, the cost of seeds and fertilisers, soil degradation etc. And, above all, climatic conditions. Drought and floods play havoc with the best-laid plans.

Yet, it is hard to think that more cannot be done to produce the food that will alleviate hunger, especially when you see the fertile soil of many of the countries of sub-Saharan Africa. How often do you hear that such and such a country – Uganda or Zimbabwe or Zambia – has the potential to become the breadbasket of Africa? So why has this not happened?

Peter Power, the last Minister of State I worked for, took on the hunger agenda and made it a central theme of his time in office. He raised it repeatedly with fellow EU Development Ministers. To look at all the questions relating to hunger, the Government set up a Hunger Taskforce in 2006. Fittingly, it was chaired by a former Minister for Agriculture, Joe Walsh – fitting because of his own background and expertise and because the Department of Agriculture has been the most involved of all departments in cooperating with Irish Aid. Responsibility for servicing the World Food Programme and the Food and Agriculture Organisation rests with the Department of Agriculture.

The Task Force had an impressive membership: among its number was Tom Arnold, the Chief Executive of Concern, who has a well earned reputation for his work on hunger both in Ireland and internationally, and who has served on the UN's task force on hunger. There were distinguished academics and experts from Ireland and abroad: Josette Sheeran and Sheila Sisulu of the World Food Programme, Bono, Jeffrey Sachs. Driving this project for Irish Aid was Brendan Rogers, who succeeded me as Director General in 2008. Brendan McMahon, an experienced Africa hand who had served in Kenya and as Ambassador to Nigeria, acted as Secretary.

The group's mandate was to identify the particular contribution that Ireland could make to tackling the root causes of hunger. The language of the Task Force's report is refreshingly direct.[17] It acknowledges that many studies have been done and that the issue is enormously complex, including new challenges such as climate change, depletion of natural resources and food price inflation. It notes that most of the promises and commitments made by donor and partner countries have not been implemented. And it draws a number of conclusions:

- Hunger is far from being accorded the degree of priority it deserves. Many donors have moved away from the sector – in the 1980s over 12 per cent of Official Development Assistance went on improving agricultural production in poor countries; today just over 6 per cent is spent on it.

- Governance of the fight against hunger, both in countries affected by it and in the international structures which seek to address it, is faulty and must be improved. Frequently there is no single Government Ministry dealing with hunger, in spite of the scale of the problem. And there is not enough coherence between the numerous different multilateral agencies trying to help.

- Special account needs to be taken of how women are affected: as much as 80 per cent of agricultural work is performed by women but women and female children have lower nutritional intake than men and boys.

The report looked at case studies of countries that have had success in combating hunger – countries as diverse as China, India and Ghana. It concluded that Ireland *can* make a pivotal contribution. It called for Irish Aid to make eradication of hunger a cornerstone of the aid programme and to work towards allocating 20 per cent of total funding to this by 2012. It called for action in three critical areas:

- Increasing agricultural productivity in Africa with a particular focus on women who account for up to 80 per cent of food production in most developing countries

- Targeting the prevention of maternal and infant undernutrition, the cause of 3.5 million child deaths annually and of irreversible damage for future physical and mental development in children

- Changes in governance and leadership priorities at both national and international levels to ensure that governments fulfil their commitments to reducing hunger and malnutrition. Regardless of the current international economic climate, without both developed and developing countries acting on their commitments, hunger will not be reduced.

An operational recommendation was for the appointment of a Special Envoy on Hunger. This has been implemented with the appointment of Kevin Farrell, formerly of the World Food Programme.[18] There is a renewed focus on hunger and improving agricultural production in Irish Aid since the Task Force report. In 2010, Minister for Foreign Affairs Micheál Martin joined the US Secretary of State Hillary Clinton for the launch of a new global forum on nutrition called the One Thousand Days Initiative. The one thousand days represents the period from conception to the child's second birthday. It has been identified as the crucial period for ensuring adequate nutritional intake if mental and physical stunting of the child is to be avoided. One of the speakers at the Forum was

Tom Arnold who is a leading advocate of the one thousand days approach.

The renewed focus on agriculture could be seen as the wheel having come full circle since many of the earliest interventions by Irish Aid were in this field. A practical example of the new approach is Malawi, the latest programme country for Irish Aid. Malawi is an extremely poor country, one of the world's poorest. Over 40 per cent of the population live in poverty and one in two children are undernourished. Eighty per cent of the people live in rural areas and rely on small-scale agriculture as a source of income and food. Maize, the staple food, is grown by 90 per cent of households. And Malawi is chronically vulnerable to droughts and flooding.

The Government of Malawi began a programme in 2005 to subsidise improved seed and fertiliser and to make them available to smallholder farmers who are least able to afford these essential farm inputs. Irish Aid supported the Government's subsidy scheme as part of its initial work after it was designated a programme country in 2006. It is an expensive operation, Vinnie O'Neill, head of development at our mission in Lilongwe, told me, but it is having impressive results.

The fight against hunger looms large in Irish Aid's Malawi Country Strategy Programme 2010-14, which has recently been adopted. Its central goal is 'To ensure households are better nourished, food secure and less vulnerable to poverty'.

Objectives aimed at achieving this include improving crop productivity and diversification adapted to climate change, strengthening the resilience of the poorest households and improving governance and service delivery.

Malawi will be a test case for putting Ireland's commitment on hunger into practice on the ground. Few countries are so badly in need of this help.[19]

Endnotes

1. Colonel John O'Reilly interview.

2. President Mary McAleese interview.

3. Grainne O'Neill interview.

4. The strategy of Irish Aid in regard to Sierra Leone, as with other major pro-grammes in recent years, has been published both in hard copy and on the Irish Aid website.

5. Conditions in the Freetown slums were among the worst I have seen; the only consolation was that Irish NGOs were present, providing basic services.

6. In 2006 €5 million was spent in Sierra Leone and €2.9 million in Liberia, com-pared to €29.9 million in Ethiopia and €32 million in Uganda.

7. My thanks to Vinnie O'Neill and Nicola Brennan for their assistance with this section on HIV/AIDS.

8. Jeffrey Sachs, *The End of Poverty*, Penguin UK, 2005, pp. 5-6.

9. MDG Goal No. 6.

10. Bertie Ahern interview.

11. Vinnie O'Neill interview; Nicola Brennan interview.

12. Irish Aid's approach to HIV/AIDS is well documented. A list of publications can be found on p. 71 of the report *Value for Money and Policy Review of Irish Aid Support to HIV and AIDS 2000-07*, DFA publication, 2008.

13. Bertie Ahern interview.

14. David Donoghue interview.

15. Michael Sidibe, UNAIDS Executive Director, in *UNAIDS Report on the Global AIDS Epidemic*, UN publication, 2010.

16. *OECD Development Assistance Peer Review Ireland 2009*, OECD publication, p. 25.

17. *Hunger Task Force: Report to the Government of Ireland*, DFA publication 2008. See also *Hunger Envoy Report to the Government of Ireland*, Kevin Far-rell, DFA publication, 2010.

18. Kevin Farrell had a long distinguished career with the World Food Pro-gramme over 27 years, most of it spent in field operations including Lesotho, Nepal and Ethiopia. Interview.

19. I am grateful to Vinnie O'Neill for assistance with the material on Malawi.

16

A SERIOUS PLAYER

The story of Irish Aid is a story of growth. In volume terms that is easy to demonstrate.[1] By the time I left in 2008 the budget had gone up from £1 million in 1973 to €920 million. That is a remarkable jump by any standards. It meant a rise from 0.03 per cent of GNP to 0.59 per cent, making Ireland the sixth biggest donor per head in the world. Even after recent cuts in the budget, the percentage figure, at 0.52 per cent in 2010, remains one of the highest in the world.

Irish Aid has also grown in quality and professionalism over the thirty-eight years of its existence. By the start of the millennium, Irish Aid had become a serious player on the development scene.

There is a much more thoughtful approach these days to issues such as HIV/AIDS, hunger and how best to deliver emergency humanitarian assistance. The size of the programme and its quality means that Ireland is respected as a donor, a member of the Nordics+ and other best practice donor groups, highly regarded in the OECD Development Assistance Committee, rated by organisations such as the Brookings Institute and the Centre for Global Development as among the best donors in the world. The DAC's 2009 Peer Review of Ireland said that 'Irish Aid is a strong, cutting edge development cooperation programme, highly regarded both nationally and internationally'.[2] And it noted that Ireland is 'a champion in making aid more effective'.

It is difficult for me to write about the programme's achievements – and shortcomings – as I have been so close to it over the years. But the record would be incomplete without a stocktaking so here goes.

To start with, Irish Aid has managed not to be diverted from its core principles: the focus on the poor, on local ownership, on meeting basic needs. Other donors have sometimes changed direction, usually in response to a political imperative such as in the 1990s when many countries moved funds to Eastern Europe or, more recently, to Iraq and Afghanistan. Ireland has put some funding into these regions but this has stayed a minor activity. Similarly, Irish Aid has not moved towards helping middle-income countries (with the possible exception of Vietnam which is heading towards this category) but has continued to place the greatest emphasis on least developed, very poor countries.

Second, Irish Aid has not experienced the scandals or misappropriations of funds that have hit some donors, including the best ones. Mistakes have been made and the programme has experienced diversions of funds from time to time as all donors do. But problems encountered have been of a minor nature. This is a considerable achievement since aid is essentially a risky business. Money is disbursed in countries where audit and monitoring may be weak or channelled through civil society organisations that lack the capacity to keep a proper track of spending. And corruption is a constant concern. But there is no such thing as a risk-free approach to development – the best you can do is to minimise the risks.

It may be that Irish Aid's relatively small size has protected it from the more egregious mistakes that bigger donors have sometimes made. It is important to acknowledge that Ireland is, in volume terms, still a relatively small donor. But that can have its advantages. When funds are modest, extra care has to be taken to ensure value for money. The biggest blunders have often occurred when donors were awash with money.

Third, the priority/programme countries have by and large turned out to be well chosen. India was an exception but this happened at the very first stages of the programme and those involved sensibly recognised that a wrong decision had been made. Sudan proved a difficult country to work in from the start but programmes might have continued had it not been for the difficulties of working with the government there. The number of programme countries has been kept manageable. Pressures have come from time to time, especially during periods of expansion, to extend the number, but I think that the current level of nine is about right.

Fourth, two basic approaches that were adopted from the start have been maintained: that aid would not be tied to the purchase of Irish goods or services, and that all funding would take the form of grants rather than loans. In the early days much of the programme was supply-driven, that is, the existence of certain types of expertise in Ireland influenced the choice of projects. My research showed me that this was more of a prevalent practice than I had realised – indeed, shaping projects to suit capacity available in Ireland was actually one of the principles behind the early programme. As against that, it can be said that in most cases the partner countries wanted to avail of the expertise concerned. And Ireland has never engaged in the pressure some donors put on their partner countries to purchase their goods and services in return for aid – an approach that amounts to blackmail since the recipients are not in a position to say no. The policy of only giving grants has meant that Ireland has not added to the already huge debt burden of the partner countries.

Fifth, Irish Aid's institutions have matured over time. The early days were very much a case of starting with a blank sheet and making things up as you went along. Some in the development community doubted that the Department of Foreign Affairs was capable of delivering an aid programme. But structures set in place in the 1970s like the Project Appraisal and Evaluation Group have proved their worth. The Interdepartmental Committee was an unwieldy body and its role is less important today. But it still meets to agree on the annual spending plan and this ensures Department of Finance involvement. Meanwhile, a different interdepartmental committee meets to discuss the crucial question of coherence on development policy.[3]

Systems for planning and assessment are much better today. Country strategy papers, which outline a comprehensive approach to relations with a priority country, take a lengthy period to be produced with input from all sides, especially from the partner country (some complain that the process is too lengthy!). Audits and evaluations are conducted by professional accountants and auditors, not just to check on whether money has been properly spent but to see if value for money was achieved. Policy papers have been produced for most areas of the programme.[4]

And oversight is of a high quality. The Department of Foreign Affairs has an independent Audit Committee, set up in 2005, which examines the aid programme, as well as the rest of the Department's work, and issues an annual report on its findings. The Oireachtas Foreign Affairs and Public Accounts Committees take a close interest in the programme. Shortly before I left Irish Aid I accompanied members of the Public Accounts Committee, led by their chair Bernard Allen, as they inspected projects on the ground in Zambia. I was very glad to see them taking such an interest in the programme – and reporting positively on its quality.[5]

Sixth, there is broad cross-party political support for development. This is one of the very few policy areas where such a consensus exists. It does not mean that all sides in the Dáil have identical views on what the focus should be or on the size of the budget,but it does represent wide agreement on the need for the programme and on its having an appropriate budget. The position of Minister of State for Overseas Development is regarded as one of the few junior ministries with substance. Ministers of State from Jim O'Keeffe to Jan O'Sullivan have told me how interesting and fulfilling they have found the development brief.

Seventh, the expertise available to Irish Aid has been built up over time. The programme now has a strong cadre of specialists. Just as important is the number of diplomats who have built up experience in the developing world – people like Brendan Rogers, who served in Zambia and Uganda and went on to be Director General; Frank Sheridan, who was Head of Mission in Zambia and Mozambique as well as spending six years playing a central role at headquarters; Pauline Conway, who served as head of mission in Tanzania and Uganda; Bill Nolan, who did four tours of duty in Irish Aid, ending up as Ambassador to Zambia; Brendan McMahon who has gone on to be Ambassador to South Africa and many more.

Irish Aid has also championed the use of expertise from the partner countries. In the 1990s the staff of a country programme who would assemble to meet me were predominantly Irish, reflecting the strong emphasis in those days on technical assistance. Now, apart from the Head of Mission and the Head of Development, almost all the people around the table are from the partner country. The calibre of local staff is usually very high and they have the enormous advantage of knowing their own country and how the system works in a way that a foreigner, even with the best intentions and long experience, will never have.

Eighth, the approach to development is more sophisticated as Irish Aid has learned from experience. Things have come a long way since the rather scatter-fire approach of the first years. Irish Aid has kept abreast of changes in international thinking on development and changed its approach where necessary, while maintaining core principles. The concerns of partners have always been to the fore in Irish Aid thinking. I have been somewhat surprised looking back at the extent to which the programme has adopted best practice. I rarely found time for reflection when I was in charge – it seemed like I was always trying to put out fires! I know that those who preceded or followed me – people like Margaret Hennessy, Martin Greene, David Donoghue and Brendan Rogers – felt the same. But recommendations from outside sources, such as evaluations and DAC Reviews, and conclusions from international findings on best practice, have greatly influenced the programme's development. The tsunami experience is a good example of how lessons were learned and recommendations were followed up to deliver emergency assistance better.

Finally, relations between Irish Aid and the NGOs are much closer today than thirty years ago. This is not solely due to the fact that Irish Aid has more funding to make available than in the early days, although that obviously does play a part. I have the sense that most NGOs realise that Irish Aid now has the expertise and the high quality personnel to do the job; in other words, that the programme has established its credentials.

In order to get a sense of our partners' views of Irish Aid I decided to go back again to one of the programme countries, Uganda, and to look for views on the ground.[6]

Uganda has experienced over twenty years of stability after the turmoil and abuses of the years of Idi Amin and Milton Obote. There has been criticism of the level of corruption in the country and of President Yowar Museveni's monopoly on power, but Uganda is making big economic strides. The discovery of oil in the west of the country – where an Irish company, Tullow Oil, has business interests – is a new development which could improve the country's chances of escaping from the poverty to which millions of its citizens are still condemned. Uganda became a programme country of Irish Aid in the mid-1990s; in the early years the main feature of the programme was area-based programmes in Kibaale and Kumi. Today, most assistance is channelled through sector or budget support, with a particular emphasis on the Karamoja region, and on the justice and law and order sector.

I went back in November 2010. With the help of the Ambassador in Kampala, Kevin Kelly, and his colleagues, I met a wide range of Ugandans either familiar with Irish Aid or having worked with the programme in the past. Some of the impressions I took away:

- High praise on all sides for Irish Aid's work in Uganda over the years. I thought it went beyond flattery or saying what they thought I wanted to hear – there is a genuine appreciation of Ireland's contribution.

- When I asked Ugandans what was distinctive about Ireland's approach the most frequent reply was the lack of baggage or a hidden agenda. 'The Irish genuinely want to help.' 'They are do-ers.' The warmth and friendliness of Irish people working in development were often mentioned.

- There was a sense that Ireland chose sectors and partners in Uganda well over the years. Flexibility was mentioned as a valuable asset for Irish Aid. A contrast was often made with big donors, which are regarded as having a rigid approach.

- I heard frequent references to the area-based programmes in Kibaale and Kumi, which Irish Aid used to help – even though it no longer focuses on these regions. Also praise for the current focus on the Karamoja region. It was interesting that interlocutors referred to specific examples that can be identified as having a recognisably Irish stamp. Some were less enthusiastic about budget support on the grounds both of the risk of corruption and because results were less visible.

- Ireland is seen as having blazed a trail with the extensive use of Ugandan advisers to carry out the aid programme. Other donors have followed the example.

- Uganda's record economic growth of 8 and 9 per cent in recent years was welcomed but 'there are still huge numbers of poor'. It will take three to four years for oil to make an impact on the economy and doubts were expressed as to how well its contribution to the economy will be managed. Aid will continue to be needed 'for a long time' even if it has fallen as a percentage of the overall budget and the economy is growing. Even sceptics about aid saw the need for it in the short term at least.

This was my fourth visit to Uganda and I came away with the feeling that the country is, as one speaker put it, 'on the cusp of economic success'. It remains a very poor country but the signs of entrepreneurship were everywhere. I drove back one evening to the capital from a meeting with Dr. Maura Lynch, a wonderful nun who runs a hospital for women with postnatal problems such as fistula, through a maze of little streets lit by fires and lamps where every sort of business was going on.

The overwhelming impression I had was that Irish Aid's contribution to the country was well focused and of practical use to ordinary people. Where a critical note was sounded it was in relation to the aid modalities, with a preference often expressed for an identifiably Irish input.

Shortcomings which I see in Irish Aid's record can be summed up as follows.

There is an information deficit about Irish Aid. Despite a lot of effort, people are still very much in the dark about the programme.[7] This is not for want of initiatives to get the message across and it is puzzling that all the activities – from attractively produced publications to a useful, high quality website, from events such as Africa Day to the Volunteering and Information Centre on O'Connell Street in Dublin and another information centre at Irish Aid's office in Limerick – have left many unaware of what Irish Aid is and does.

A number of reasons can be suggested. The change of name – from Irish Aid to Ireland Aid to Development Cooperation Ireland and then back to Irish Aid – has caused confusion. I hope that we have seen the end of uncertainty over the name. Another factor is resistance to the Government's programme being promoted under the heading of development education. This is a long running issue, perhaps dating back to the days when NGOs saw themselves as being in competition with the official programme.

A further problem is that some of those who work in development think the sector's importance is self-evident and that there is something not right about Irish Aid blowing its trumpet. I think this is a mistaken view. It is true that Irish Aid is not the same sort of fundraiser as GOAL or Gorta or Self Help, and that it should take care not to cut across those organisations that have to publicise their work to raise funds. But in a way Irish Aid *is* in the fundraising business in that it needs Government and public support to secure the annual budget.

I see a danger of development aid becoming over specialised, too far removed from people's understanding of what aid should be. The language of discussion about development can be dense and jargon-filled. This tendency has worsened as aid modalities have changed. The earlier projects were easy to understand – the Lesotho ponies and handweavers, the Lusaka maternity clinics – even if their drawbacks were easy to see. It is much harder to show what distinctive contribution Ireland makes when it channels funds through aid modalities like budget and sector support. The arguments in favour of these modalities are strong as long as the local conditions are right. But it will always be important to demonstrate that Ireland's contribution is making a real difference in bringing people out of poverty.

The second shortcoming is one that has bedevilled the aid programme since the outset – inadequate staffing levels. As mentioned above, the quality of those sent out to serve in the field has greatly improved and is matched by very able personnel from the partner countries. But the overall numbers have never been sufficient for the scale of the programme or the risks. To give an example: in 2009, Concern had 284 staff at headquarters, Trocaire had 138 and Irish Aid had 145. Yet the Irish Aid budget was four times the combined budgets of Concern and Trocaire. It must be recognised, however, that the chances of this situation improving soon, given Ireland's financial problems, are slim indeed.

Third, decentralisation will be seen as a decision that set the programme back.[8] Locating the programme far away from its clients and partners and the rest of the Department of Foreign Affairs made no objective sense. The risk of loss of institutional memory was ignored. No account was taken of the fact that Foreign Affairs staff rotate to posts in the field and may be assigned back to Irish Aid or to posts in Dublin and the impact that would have on families and their finances. Yet the decision was made and had to be implemented. It says a lot about the dedication of people in the department that so many staff worked to make the best of the situation. How the arrangement will work out is not clear yet.

Fourth, there is the issue of the relationship between Irish Aid and the rest of the Department of Foreign Affairs. As mentioned, various ad hoc arrangements helped to bridge the gap such as the regular contacts I had with Ted Barrington when he was Political Director in the 1990s, or the more structured meetings which Brendan Rogers and I held with Rory Montgomery ten years later when he was Political Director.

The Management Review carried out by Farrell Grant Sparks in 2008 called for a more integrated approach between Irish Aid and the rest of the Department, for example by having a single Africa Unit which would bring Development Cooperation Division and other parts of the department closer together, in particular Political Division. In recent times a high level Steering Group has been set up, chaired by the Secretary General, David Cooney. This meets quarterly and brings together the heads of Political Division, Irish Aid, Administration and the Promoting Ireland Abroad Division. An Africa strategy was published which embraces political, economic and development aspects of Ireland's relations with Africa, including issues such as trade and investment. Hopefully these arrangements will work as there is certainly a gap to be bridged.

The fifth area I would mention is the role of advisory bodies. Irish Aid has had a series of advisory bodies monitoring and giving views on the programme. First there was the Advisory Council on Development Cooperation, then the Irish Aid Advisory Committee, then the Advisory Board for Irish Aid.

The chairs and members of these bodies have been distinguished figures who did a lot of good work, and at certain points played an important role in the direction which the programme has taken. Yet I have the impression, having worked with all three, that these advisory bodies would have liked to make a greater impact

than they did and were somewhat frustrated by the role they were
expected to play. Procedurally, the lines of responsibility in Irish
Aid are the same as in all civil service operations: they go up from
the Director General to the Secretary General of the department
who is also the Accounting Officer who in turn is answerable to the
Minister and the Minister of State who are answerable to the Oireachtas. There is no scope, therefore, for an advisory body to do
anything other than advise, whereas some would like to have had a
say on issues such as the budget.

That said, the contribution made by the advisory bodies has
been valuable. The first one to be set up, the Advisory Council on
Development Cooperation, brought much needed expertise to bear
on the programme at a time when this was lacking. The Irish Aid
Advisory Committee did important work on areas such as
HIV/AIDS. The Advisory Board on Irish Aid, which was chaired by
Des O'Malley and then by Chris Flood, was the most high powered
of the three; I think that the most valuable work it did was research, for example into the issue of coherence between different
aspects of Government policy which affect development.

The latest manifestation is an Expert Advisory Group set up in
2010, a lighter model than what has gone before, reflecting the fact
that the expertise which now exists within the programme is con-
siderably stronger than it once was.

I could mention other areas where I feel in retrospect that
things could have been done differently or better. The fact that
Irish Aid has so little input into the activities of the World Bank
and the IMF is one example. The Department of Finance guards the
servicing of these institutions as their preserve with the result that
development aspects do not get as much of a look in as they
should.[9]

Or the area of volunteers. There must be a question mark over
whether closing the Agency for Personal Service Overseas was the
right decision, even if the closure reflected the fall in interest in
volunteering generally. There has since been a revival of interest in

volunteering and Irish Aid plays its part through the Volunteer and Information Centre and the Rapid Response Initiative but much of the work is now done by other bodies.

But the dominant feeling I had in researching this book was that the aid programme is a success story that everyone in Ireland can be proud of. Debate will continue as to how to deliver aid so as to get the best results and the best value for the taxpayer's money. But the feeling I have looking back on the programme's history is pride, pride that from such small, rough and ready beginnings a programme was grown and made professional so as to reflect Irish people's desire to help the poorest people on the planet. There can be no doubt that thousands of lives have been saved and hundreds of thousands of lives improved thanks to Ireland's actions.

A final thought: Ireland is passing through a very difficult phase in its financial and economic history, arguably the worst economic crisis the State has ever experienced. No area of spending will be unaffected by the cuts which have to be made to pay off the huge debts that have piled up and to restore the public finances to good health. Clearly, this has implications for the aid budget.

Money is only one aspect of the story of development aid but it is the basis on which a programme is built. Vote 29 (or Vote 27 as it now has been renamed) has always been a vulnerable budget line. If you look at Table 3 in the Appendix it quickly becomes clear that the aid budget follows the country's economic fortunes closely. That does not mean that prosperity guarantees a substantial aid budget; the struggle to get a sizeable allocation for official development assistance is constant, even in good times. But when budgets are being cut, the aid budget is at particular risk.

Some in the development community have argued that, even when the economy is doing badly, the aid budget should not be touched on the basis that, however bad things in Ireland may be, they are infinitely worse in the countries we seek to help. Personally, I have always felt that you have to take account of the full spending picture, first because the 'hands off' argument does not take account of the reality of discussion at the cabinet table where a host of worthwhile spending causes are under scrutiny and political choices have to be made. And second, because I think it is dangerous to pitch the argument for overseas aid against needs at home. In difficult times, the need to balance needs at home with needs in the developing world becomes more prominent. If the issue were to be engaged in in a serious way I could only see one winner.

What I think is a worthwhile objective is that the aid budget should be not be cut disproportionately in bad times, but should get treated as fairly as other budget lines. Vote 29 should not be seen as a soft target.

Obituaries are being written for the Celtic Tiger, which is characterised as a time of excess, reckless borrowing, and property speculation. All this may be true. But it is well to remember that it had its good features too. Even in a time of prosperity, the poorest were not forgotten. On the contrary, philanthropy in Ireland boomed during the Celtic Tiger years, just as Irish Aid's budget did.

It is heartening that in 2010 the plight of the people of Haiti led to tens of millions of euros being raised in Ireland – and this at a time when the scale of our economic difficulties was widely known.

The Irish impulse to help is too deeply rooted to fail. I believe it will continue, not just in the form of private donations to charities – where Ireland has an outstandingly generous record – but also in the public's support for the Government raising its game and ensuring that Ireland remains a serious long-term donor.

Endnotes

1. See tables in the Appendix showing growth in ODA in cash and percentage terms.

2. *DAC Peer Review 2009*, p. 24, *The Irish Times* report, 8/5/09.

3. Policy coherence is an issue close to the DAC's heart. It attaches particular importance to the new Interdepartmental Committee on Development set up in 2007 to strengthen coherence across Government Departments in the field of aid. See pp. 32-34 of the 2009 *DAC Peer Review*.

4. Examples of policy papers published by DFA and available on the Irish Aid website are those on Civil Society, Environment, Humanitarian Relief, Health, Development Education – to name just a few.

5. *Oireachtas Public Accounts Committee Interim Report on Irish Aid*, Oireachtas publication, July 2008.

6. My thanks to Kevin Kelly, Kevin Carroll and all of their colleagues in Uganda for their assistance with the visit.

7. A DCU study of student opinions about aid found that 'Irish development NGOs are seen as the public face of development assistance and there is little recognition of Irish Aid', Connolly, Doyle and Dwyer article in *Irish Studies in International Affairs*, Vol. 19, pp. 209-26.

8. It cannot be said that the drawbacks were not pointed out. Virtually every media and other public coverage of the decision was negative.

9. Towards the end of my time with Irish Aid I visited the World Bank in Washington and was told that Ireland could have a second person seconded to the bank, in addition to the Department of Finance representative who would cover development issues. For a time it seemed that Finance would agree to a DFA person being appointed but in the end they decided they should keep the post for themselves. Interestingly, Ronan Fanning's *History of the Department of Finance* (IPA, Dublin, 1978) shows they were not at all keen to join either the World Bank or the IMF when it was first proposed!

Afterword

Is Aid the Answer?

'How easy it is to do harm in seeking to do good!'
– *Jacques Turgot*

I hope I have shown that I admire the progress that Irish Aid has made in becoming a highly effective deliverer of aid and that it has stuck to fundamentally altruistic principles over the years.

But there are bigger questions that arise when it comes to development aid. Why is there not more to show for the decades of effort and the trillions spent? Why are some countries poorer today than they were when they achieved independence? Is aid the answer to poor countries' needs?

Posing these questions can be unwelcome in development circles. It throws the whole effort into doubt. It is like a person in church standing up and asking if God really exists.

But they are valid questions – and ones that are increasingly being asked. If we take the post-war period as the starting point for the major push to improve the lot of the developing countries, then the project has existed now for over sixty years. It is legitimate to ask why there is not more progress to report – why, for example, some of the countries being helped have actually fallen back in terms of poverty and disease.

During the period when I worked in Irish Aid, the topic would come up at social gatherings, especially in recent years when I detected a change of attitude towards the value of giving aid. Whereas in the days of Somalia and Rwanda there was pretty much universal approval of Ireland doing its bit, I found more scepticism a decade later. The type of question I was asked was: Are we getting value for money? Is this really the way to do it? Are administrative costs too high? Does aid not end up in the pockets of the rich because of corruption? Is it all not just a waste of money?

The fact that Irish people would still dip deeply into their pockets when asked to help victims of the earthquake in Haiti or the floods in Pakistan, or that opinion polls would show continuing strong support for the Government's funding of aid, does not take away the fact that there is a lot more scepticism around today about the effectiveness of aid.

I asked interviewees for this book what they saw as the reasons for Africa's continuing underdevelopment and got a range of answers. The main reasons given were:

- The time scale: it is only a few decades since most African countries emerged to independence. It took European countries hundreds of years to get to prosperity. Growth takes time.

- Conflicts: many countries have experienced or are still experiencing long, bitter conflicts, mostly internal, which have had a devastating effect on their economies. Mozambique lost 600,000 dead, Angola half a million, the DRC as many as 3 million.

- HIV/AIDS was a huge setback for many countries in sub-Saharan Africa. As well as the immense human cost, development was seriously affected.

- Climate: the challenges some sub-Saharan countries face, whether from drought or floods or both, make agricultural production highly unpredictable.

- Population growth poses enormous challenges, especially in the cities.

- The Brain Drain: sectors like heath and education lose thousands of their best and brightest to the West.

- Obstacles to trade: rich countries give aid but they subsidise and protect their industries and block imports from developing countries.

- Corruption, weak governance, poor leadership.

- Donors using the wrong aid models. Structural adjustment, tied aid, loans leading to debt were singled out for mention.

- The gap between words and deeds. Promises at G8 meetings and in Brussels and Paris don't always result in real increases. Taking down national flags in the interest of closer coordination between donors and hence better delivery of aid is slow to happen.

- Over-emphasis by donors on social sectors such as health and education instead of the private sector.

- The Big Man syndrome: allegiance to family and tribe rather than the State.[1]

All of these seem to me to be relevant but do they tell the whole story? A new school of thought says that aid itself is the problem.

There is no shortage of books and articles on the topic.[2] In fact, books criticising or sceptical about the value of aid have become an industry not unlike development itself which has produced so much literature. Books like William Easterly's *The White Man's Burden*, Robert Calderisi's *The Trouble with Africa: Why Foreign Aid Isn't Working* and Dambisa Moyo's *Dead Aid*, have been best sellers which shows that they strike a chord with the general public – and not just with right wing activists who would like to see an end to aid so that the money could be used for purposes closer to home. (A striking example of the latter was a column by Simon Heffer in the *Daily Telegraph*, 'Our Overseas Aid Bill could pay for Trident', which argued that the UK should cut off all aid and spend the money instead on nuclear missiles!)[3]

A feature of the revisionist writers on aid is that many have in-depth experience of working in development, through having worked for institutions like the World Bank or the IMF or through lengthy analytical study and years spent living in Africa. Their arguments cannot be shrugged off as uninformed.

Summarising their arguments would not do justice to their detailed critiques, but a flavour of their views of aid's shortcomings may be gained from the discussion below.

William Easterly: finds fault with most aspects of the aid industry from the slow international response to HIV/AIDS to the failure to face up to corruption at government level. The sub-title of his book, 'Why the West's efforts to aid the rest have done so much ill and so little good', gives a clue to his approach. He takes pot shots at some sacred cows:

> Even humanitarian aid can make political conflict worse rather than better. In the worst case scenario of Somalia in the early 1990s, food aid increased violence among rival clan militias who fought to steal the food. The warlords may even have provoked the violence to get more food relief . . .

> The big problem with foreign aid has been its aspiration to a utopian blueprint to fix the world's problems.

On UN peacekeeping efforts:

> Intervention suffers from the patronising assumption that only the West can keep the locals from killing each other.[4]

Robert Calderisi recommends a kind of tough love:

> Contrary to conventional recommendations, direct foreign aid to most African countries should be reduced, not increased. Out of necessity, leaner budgets would be better managed.[5]

Dambisa Moyo is scathing about what she sees as the corrosive effect of aid. After noting the number of conflicts on the continent she concludes:

Foreign aid foments conflict. . . . By lowering average incomes and slowing down economic growth . . . aid increases the risk of conflict . . .

Aid fosters a military culture . . .

The net result of aid dependency is that, instead of having a functioning Africa managed by Africans for Africans, what is left is one where outsiders attempt to map its destiny and call the shots.[6]

Dambisa Moyo has the advantage of writing from the point of view of an African whose country has been on the receiving end of aid. Her passionate resentment and rejection of the aid model probably reflects the frustrations felt by many African officials who have to deal with the donors. Her book highlights the strains and faultlines in the donor/partner relationship. Development experts are conscious of the problem and seek to even out the relationship by use of more sensitive language and talking of equals. But the inescapable fact is that it is not an equal relationship if one side has the power to switch off the money supply at any time.

I got a flavour of the anger which aid can provoke at a conference in Kigali in 2008. One of the last tasks I performed as Director General was to co-chair a session at the Accra Conference on Aid Effectiveness. The topic I had to deal with, together with my Tanzanian counterpart, Mugisha Kamugisha of the Finance Ministry, was mutual accountability. It is a fascinating subject, which goes to the heart of the aid debate, embracing the notions of accountability of donor and partner countries to each other and to their own citizens. We were fortunate to have Mary Robinson as our keynote speaker.

A series of regional meetings was held to prepare for Accra and, while my work prevented me from getting to any of the others, I was keen to attend the African regional meeting which was to be held in Kigali. The understanding was that I and the handful of other donor representatives who went to Kigali would be observers in every sense – we were there to learn and not to take part.

At some point a speaker made critical comments about the actions of donors. This suddenly opened a floodgate as other speakers took the floor and the air was filled with stories of the arrogance and insensitivity of the donors.

I suppose it was a tribute to donors present such as Ireland, the UK and the Nordics that the speakers were making these highly critical comments in our hearing. But the bitter intensity of the comments was striking.

It is unfortunately true that some of those involved in delivering aid can be insensitive to their surroundings and the people they are meant to be helping. The bad side of the aid industry is symbolised by the shiny four-wheel drive, a well fed, well clothed westerner at the wheel, sporting the all-important donor's logo. I have come upon many a donors' gathering where the four-wheel drives were clustered around and it always struck me as incongruous, especially in remote places. Granted, a four-wheel drive is necessary to cope with roads and weather but it can come across as a symbol of arrogance.

All that can be said is that aid attracts a wide range of people, a more mixed group perhaps than other professions, some driven by their own need to prove self-worth (underlining the suspicion that aid can sometimes be more about the giver than the receiver), others motivated by career, by personal enrichment even – happily not too often – some with messianic delusions. But in my experience the ones with suspect motives are very much in a minority. I have found the number of dedicated, selfless people, prepared to work in hardship and in some cases appalling conditions, to be the vast majority.

What the aid sceptics have in common is that they are stronger on analysis of what is wrong with aid than in prescribing what would work better. Some of their proposals are radical: Moyo suggests that all aid should be cut off and support for the developing countries left to China and the bond markets. The role of China as a major player in Africa is beyond doubt, as is the potential role of the other BRICs (Brazil, Russia and India). But the notion that their partners' welfare is high on their agenda would strike most people as pretty farfetched. China's support for the Sudanese government in its flagrant human rights abuses in Darfur is a case in point.

As for Moyo's belief in the bond markets, people in Ireland might have a view on whether it is wise to rely on them! [7]

Calderisi comes up with an old chestnut: focus on a handful of countries 'that are serious about reducing poverty'.[8] Deciding to ignore a large number of very poor countries to focus on the ones with better prospects raises quite a few issues, not least why donors should have the power to play God in this way. Interestingly, the five countries he suggests include three of Irish Aid's priority countries – Uganda, Tanzania and Mozambique – but what of the other countries Irish Aid is assisting – like Liberia, Sierra Leone and Malawi which face huge problems that they are trying to tackle?

An antidote to the sceptics can be found in Jeffrey Sachs' *The End of Poverty*. He places particular emphasis on the poverty trap into which many countries fall for a variety of reasons. But he remains optimistic about the West's capacity to help:

> The combination of Africa's adverse geography and its extreme poverty creates the worst poverty trap in the world. Yet the situation in Africa is not hopeless. Africa's problems, I have come to understand, are especially difficult but still solvable with practical and proven technologies. Disease can be controlled, crop yields sharply increased and basic infrastructure such as paved roads and electricity can be extended to the villages. A combination of investments well attuned to local needs and conditions can enable African economies to break out of the poverty trap.[9]

Yet, for all the eloquence of Sachs' arguments (and his writings reveal not only his deep understanding of the issues involved but an empathy with the ordinary people who are caught in the poverty trap) his advocacy of big increases in national aid budgets has been attacked by many. I remember reading his reports in the run up to the 2005 Millennium Development Goals review, when he was advising the UN Secretary-General, and having serious doubts about the idea that large increases in funding were the answer. Even though Ireland raised its budget substantially at that time, I was not persuaded that a massive stepping up of cash flows globally would alone produce the desired results.

Two books that seem to me to find a path between the two camps are Paul Collier's *The Bottom Billion* and Roger Riddell's *Does Foreign Aid Really Work?* Neither work is uncritical of what aid has achieved or can achieve – in fact there are some strong criticisms of the way aid is done. But they recognise the value of aid and pay fair tribute to the motives that guide most of those involved.[10]

Both make the point that aid is only one of many factors in the fight against poverty. Philip O'Brien, formerly of UNICEF and Operation Lifeline Sudan and now working for an American HIV/AIDS foundation, also stressed this:

> In a way, your question about why aid has not produced better results misses the point. Expectations that aid will solve poor countries' problems are too high. Official Development Assistance represents only a relatively small proportion of most (recipient) governments' finances and will never make a big difference to their economies. But it will always be necessary to address the issues that affect the poor and here ODA has had some extraordinary achievements – falling infant mortality, more children going to school, treatment for people with HIV/AIDS and malaria.[11]

There is a great deal of truth in this of course. Remittances sent home by migrant workers far exceed foreign aid levels. And countries such as Uganda and Tanzania, as they grow their economies, will depend less and less on outside help.

Paul Collier estimates that over the past thirty years aid has added about one percentage point to the economic growth rate of the bottom billion – those condemned to live in 'impoverished and stagnant countries' as he puts it.

> This does not sound like a whole lot, but then the growth rate of the bottom billion over this period has been much less than 1 percent per year – in fact it has been zero. So adding 1 percent has made the difference between stagnation and severe cumulative decline. Without aid, cumulatively the countries of the bottom billion would have become much poorer than they are today. Aid has been a holding operation preventing things from falling apart.[12]

Collier also demonstrates the ways in which even the best intended aid can fall short of its objectives or even make matters worse, for example by enabling recipient governments to free up other incomes for spending on arms, or by retarding the growth of labour-intensive export activities. He concludes:

> Aid does have serious problems, and more especially serious limitations. Alone it will not be sufficient to turn the societies of the bottom billion around. But it is part of the solution rather than part of the problem. The challenge is to complement it with other actions.[13]

He goes on to list a series of measures which he feels are equally important, based on the other instruments he sees as essential – security, laws and charters, and trade.

Roger Riddell's book is the most incisive study I have read of the complex issues around development. His depiction of the motives and actions of the various participants – from donor governments to NGOs to civil society to partner governments – rings true to me. He paints a picture of radical changes already taking place which will recast aid relationships and which aid practitioners will have to adapt to.

One of the points Riddell makes is the lack of reliable data on the impact of aid:

> . . . has *most* official development aid worked, or failed? The honest answer is that we still don't know – not for lack of trying, but due to the inherent difficulties of tracing its contribution. After more than five decades of aid-giving, the bulk of the most reliable and accessible information on impact relates to discrete projects, supplemented in the last decade by some assessments of the contribution made by individual donors in particular countries. Cross-country studies seeking to find the answer to the question 'Does aid work?' do not provide a reliable guide on the overall and explicit contribution of aid to development and poverty reduction. They never will.

> It has only been in the last five to ten years that donors have seriously acknowledged the need to begin to work more closely together, by coordinating and harmonising their individual aid efforts, and aligning their support with aid-recipient strategies and their institutional development needs. It will be some years before more rigorous, long-term, time-series data will be available to assess the overall impact of these continuing, discrete aid interventions and the aid which donors have pooled en bloc.[14]

The most effective response to the sceptics is to point out the advances being recorded in developing countries in recent years. The 2010 Summit on the Millennium Development Goals reviewed the record to date on achieving these goals and was able to report remarkable progress in many areas:

- The number of people living in extreme poverty fell from 1.8 billion in 1990 to 1.4 billion in 2005 and is expected to fall further to 900 million by 2015.

- In Africa, enrolment in primary education has risen from 46 per cent in 1960 to 95 per cent in 2006. Millions more children are emerging from school today having acquired at least basic literacy and numeracy skills.

- Significant improvements have been made in increasing the number of girls accessing primary education although there is a long way to go before the MDG goal of gender equality is realised.

- There has been progress in reducing child mortality. For the first time in documented history, annual childhood deaths have dropped below 9 million, from 12.5 million in 1990 to 8.8 million in 2008.

- Access to treatment for those living with the HIV/AIDS virus has improved dramatically – 5.2 million people in low and middle income countries now have access to HIV treatment, up from almost none in 2000.

- From 1990 to 2006 1.1 billion people in the developing world gained access to toilets, latrines and other forms of improved sanitation. The target of halving the number of people without safe drinking water is well on the way to being achieved.[15]

Much of the literature on aid's future is, as I have said, better at highlighting aid's shortcomings than at making realistic proposals for how to improve it. So I will end by suggesting a number of actions, which I think could help.

Donors should determine to do aid better, accepting that mistakes have been made and that there is no sure way to achieve the best results

All sorts of forces come into play in delivering aid: domestic pressures and especially political pressures, clinging to an approach after it has proved to be unproductive, fear of being seen as having taken the wrong direction, becoming too removed from the realities on the ground. Accepting that mistakes have been made is not easy for donors, nor is a recognition that there is no guarantee that a particular way of delivering aid will work. There is a lot of pressure to claim something is working when it is only partly successful or isn't working at all. This is true both of official donors who have to demonstrate value for money to the taxpayer, and for NGOs who need to persuade their supporters to continue giving them cash.

I believe that donors should be modest about the likely impact of what they are doing and open-minded and flexible about their approach. They should bear in mind Jeffrey Sachs' warning: 'One of the weaknesses of development thinking is the relentless drive for a magic bullet, the one decisive investment that will turn the tide.'[16] If anything has been learned over the past sixty years it is that there is no such thing as one magic bullet.

We should listen to partners

Fairly obvious you would think. But it is still far from being the universal practice. There is a catalogue of projects which failed utterly because they did not suit the conditions in the partner country or they were imposed without regard to the realities on the ground. And, needless to say, it should not be a case of going through the motions – listening and then ignoring – but full involvement of the beneficiaries who are usually far better placed than any donor to know what will or won't work for their country.

I think it is no accident that in my research Irish Aid's partners singled out Irish people's capacity to listen closely to what they have to stay. This quality has been a hallmark of the Irish approach.

Others may not have the same DNA as the Irish but listening is vital and is something we all can do, as the most effective donors – the Scandinavians, the UK, Luxembourg and the Netherlands – know.

Have a mix of aid modalities

Why is this important and will it not lead to a scatter fire approach? The first reason is that it makes sense to try different approaches. As Riddell and others have pointed out, there is no firm information yet as to which aid modalities work and which don't. Until there is more certainty, it is a sensible precaution not to put all your eggs in one basket.

The second, related, reason is the danger of a politically correct orthodoxy deciding what is the best way to deliver aid. Approaches have changed radically over the years. Once a new approach becomes popular there is an almost religious zeal among development practitioners to show that the new way is right. They tend to forget that, in their day, individual projects were seen as the way to do aid, and then district and area-based programmes. Integrated rural development was another favoured modality.

Today, budget and sector support are seen by many in the development field, not only as worthwhile, but as the *only* way to do aid. But I was struck by the number of my interviewees who expressed reservations about budget support. Even the most staunch advocate of budget support would acknowledge the problems and risks attached to channelling large amounts of money through governments. Clearly, it should only be used where the necessary conditions exist – good governance, sound financial systems, pro-poor policies and a commitment to fight corruption.

And, whatever aid modality is pursued, every donor needs to stay in close contact with ordinary people in the partner countries.

Hold Governments to account

Relations between donors and partner governments are highly sensitive. All sorts of issues arise: on the one hand, there is a risk of donors intruding in a sovereign country's affairs; on the other hand, there is the risk that donor funds could be diverted or misspent. The development community has wrestled with the challenge of balancing the two sides' interests for years. In the 1990s the debate centred around the idea of conditionality; aid, it was argued, should be made conditional on good governance and accountability in the receiving state. Conditionality then lost favour; indeed, it came to be regarded as an example of the patronising attitude of donors who are in the driving seat.

Whatever name is put on it, donors have to be sure that money transferred does not go astray. It is a great advantage if a country has a strong democratic track record – as Tanzania has and as Liberia has under the leadership of President Johnson Sirleaf. But corruption and misrule in Africa are too prevalent to ignore. In Irish Aid's programme countries alone there have been some noteworthy instances – Zambia under Frederick Chiluba for example, and in Zimbabwe, a country which Ireland would like to have assisted.

Jeffrey Sachs sounds a warning note about western countries pontificating on corruption:

> The outside world has pat answers concerning Africa's prolonged crisis. It comes back again and again to corruption and misrule. Western officials, including the countless 'missions' of the IMF and World Bank to African countries, argue that Africa simply needs to behave itself better, to allow market forces to operate without interference by corrupt leaders . . .

> Africa gets a bad rap as the 'corrupt continent'. . . . Many African governments are desperately trying to do the right thing but they face enormous obstacles of poverty, disease, ecological crisis and geopolitical neglect or worse.[17]

Nevertheless, there has to be accountability for donors' funds, even if that offends some. And donors must be prepared, as a last resort, to pull funding. If the public in donor countries concludes that funds are being wasted they will stop supporting the aid project.

The best thing donors can do is to assist the forces in the partner countries to hold their own governments to account. There are plenty of courageous people in Africa whose aim is to fight corruption and ensure that governments use public funds properly. When the Irish Public Accounts Committee met their Zambian counterparts it was clear from the discussion that the parliamentarians in Zambia were struggling with the same issues. And I was impressed by the work of the Auditor General's Office in Kampala where Mrs. Keto Kayemba told me about her office's efforts to ensure accountability for public spending.[18]

Robust evaluation

One of the biggest drawbacks in development, in my view, has been the unwillingness to exit a project or programme which is not producing the required results. I was surprised when looking back at Irish Aid's history how interventions which were clearly not performing lingered on well past their sell-by date. For example, as early as 1992 it was clear that we could not continue with our work at Wad Medeni in central Sudan and I remember the Minister, Dick Spring, agreeing to my recommendation that we withdraw from Sudan. Yet funding continued: it was 1998 before funding stopped.

There are understandable reasons: the time and effort invested at home and in the field, expectations raised among the recipients, an unwillingness to accept failure. But the result can be that a programme is continued when it should be closed down.

A lot comes down to the role of the evaluator. To be effective, a consultant must not pull their punches and must be prepared to tell the truth as they see it. Irish Aid has been blessed by some excellent consultants whose work has shaped the programme and improved the quality greatly. But, like all donors, it has had its share of poor evaluations as well.

Back at headquarters there must be the will and determination to implement the evaluator's recommendations. If exiting is the answer, so be it.

Strengthening the private sector

I have always resisted the idea of placing one sector over another or dedicating a fixed percentage of the budget to this or that sector. But sometimes it is necessary to point to areas where the effort is less than it ought to be. One such area, in my view, is support for the private sector. I think that this merits greater emphasis in aid programmes.

There has been some improvement – at least today aid practitioners talk about the private sector. I remember when it was a dirty word in aid circles, seen as an intrusion into the purer work of building up education and health services. Today there is more recognition of the central role that entrepreneurship plays in economic growth and hence in emergence from poverty.

In Kampala I met Andrew Mwenda, publisher of the *Independent* magazine and an outspoken critic of many aspects of aid.[19] I expected him to condemn all forms of aid and he certainly had no time for budget support for Uganda. But he did feel that the private sector merits donors' support. He argued that the approach of many of the people working in development is based on liberal, leftwing thinking and that they are suspicious of the private sector. If donors really want to help, he argued, they should foster innovation and productivity. I think that there is something in what Mwenda says and food for thought for people who work in development.

Support for the role of the private sector was echoed by someone from a very different background, Patrick Bitature, a highly successful Ugandan businessman who owns one of the best hotels in the capital.[20] He has great confidence in Uganda's economic prospects and feels that that would be the best use of donor money (interestingly, he also supported Irish Aid's work on strengthening the rule of law and described corruption as 'a cancer'). It is hard not to see a country benefiting from the energy and optimism of a representative of the private sector such as Patrick Bitature.

Support reform of the multilateral agencies

Most national aid budgets are dwarfed by those of the multilateral agencies such as the World Bank and the UN bodies, especially the United Nations Development Programme. Yet there have been many controversies and criticisms of these bodies' approaches over the years. Scepticism about the fate of funds channelled through multilateral organisations may be justified, but in the end they are key players and the focus has to be on making them as effective as possible.

In fairness, some, such as the World Bank under James Wolfen-sohn and the UNDP under Mark Malloch Brown, have done major soul searching and have changed course when approaches were seen to have failed. This is less true of some of the UN bodies or of the overall UN effort, despite numerous attempts by some member states to effect reform.

Probably the most important recent initiative was the attempt to have a single UN approach in the partner countries. The 'One UN' model was launched in 2007 and had as its aim to reduce the organisation's costs and render its actions more efficient by having one programme framework in each partner country, one budget and one overall person in charge of all the agencies. Eight pilot countries were identified to see if this approach would work but it has run into predictable 'turf' battles. But it is worth donors perse-vering with. In Angola I remember waiting to meet the UNDP Res-ident Representative and seeing the names of 11 different UN organ-isations listed on the wall. There must be a better way of doing this.[21]

I asked my interviewees for this book whether they felt that Ireland should continue to give aid to poor countries. The answer – from aid practitioners, diplomats, politicians of all parties, from people in all walks of life in our partner countries – was overwhelmingly 'Yes'.

I heard all sorts of views about how best to deliver aid and how it should not be seen as a permanent feature but should have an end point. But almost without exception those I spoke to felt that helping the poorest people in the world was the right thing to do and that we should go on doing it.

I would like to see more public discussion about development. Too much of the debate has concentrated on two topics: corruption and the size of the budget. Important though these topics are, they are far from being the only ones. They have diverted attention from issues such as the effectiveness of different approaches to aid, whether we are getting value for money, the role of the NGOs, how Ireland can influence bigger donors and especially the multilateral institutions, coherence between development and other policies such as trade and agriculture.

It is also important, I believe, to expand the discussion out beyond the development community. So often, at meetings on aid, the participants are 'the usual suspects'. This is understandable but it is not healthy as it reinforces the notion that aid is the sole preserve of development experts.

How to broaden the discussion out? That is a challenge, as we found when holding meetings around the country to prepare the White Paper. The Oireachtas Committee on Foreign Affairs holds interesting sessions but again they mainly involve the initiated. Maybe there is scope, as Vinnie O'Neill has suggested, for a summer school on development.[22] Whatever way it is done, the public should be more involved and have their say.

Delivering aid is an imperfect science and the way it is done has its faults. But I still feel that it is well worth doing.

I take my line from the missionary who, after telling me that all the work he and his order had done in Africa was just a pinprick compared to the scale of the problems, added, 'But what would it be like if nothing was done?'[23]

Endnotes

1. Frank Sheridan pointed out that the postcolonial boundaries of many African countries were arbitrary and did not reflect the historical and tribal divisions. It inevitably weakens loyalty to a State if it is seen as an artificial entity.

2. See, for example, *The White Man's Burden,* William Easterly, Oxford University Press, 2006; *The Trouble with Africa: Why Foreign Aid Isn't Working,* Robert Calderisis, Yale University Press, 2006; *Dead Aid: Why Aid is not working and how there is another way for Africa,* Dambisa Moyo, Penguin Books, 2009. Other writers who take a critical view of aid include Carol Lancaster, Michaela Wrong and Linda Polman. Further back were the critiques of Rene Dumont and Graham Hancock.

3. Simon Heffer, *Daily Telegraph,* 30/7/10.

4. Easterly, pp. 127, 138, interventionism, p. 293.

5.   Calderisi, p. 209.

6.   Moyo conflicts, pp. 59-60, fosters, p. 60, destiny, p. 66.

7.   Moyo Chapter 'A Capital Solution' pp 8off; 'the Chinese are our Friends' pp 98ff.

8.   Calderisi chapter, 'Ten Ways of Changing Africa', pp. 209-10.

9.   Sachs, p. 208.

10.   Paul Collier *The Bottom Billion: Why the poorest countries are failing and what can be done about it*, Oxford University Press, 2008. Roger Riddell, *Does Foreign Aid Really Work?*, Oxford University Press, 2007.

11.   Philip O'Brien interview.

12.   Collier, p. 100.

13.   Collier, p. 254.

14.   Riddell, p. 254.

15.   Figures from *Irish Aid: Report on the Millennium Development Goals*, DFA publication, 2010.

16.   Sachs, pp. 188-9.

17.   Sachs, p. 255.

18.   Mrs. Keto Keyemba and colleagues from the Ugandan Auditor General's office, interview.

19.   Andrew Mwenda interview.

20.   Patrick Bitature interview.

21.   Irish Aid has been a strong supporter of the One UN model both with funding and on the ground in countries such as Vietnam.

22.   Vinnie O'Neill interview.

23.   Fr. Joe Whelan, interview.

FURTHER READING

The literature on development is enormous. The publications mentioned in the Notes and References are just a fraction of many dealing with development aid generally and Irish Aid in particular. The following is a selection of material likely to be of interest to those interested in pursuing the topic in greater depth.

Basic Documents

Development Cooperation: Ireland's Bilateral Programme, Published by the Department of Foreign Affairs in 1979, this was the first booklet to set out the programme's objectives.

Irish Aid: Consolidation and Growth, A Strategy Plan. The Department of Foreign Affair's 1993 publication.

White Paper on Foreign Policy: Challenges and Opportunities, Government Publications Dublin 1996.

White Paper on Irish Aid, DFA publication, 2006.

Other Irish Aid Publications

The Irish Aid and Department of Foreign Affairs websites contain a wealth of material on all aspects of the programme including policy papers, strategies for individual countries and sectors as well as press releases and updates on recent developments.

Irish Aid's Annual Reports

Published by the Department of Foreign Affairs, these have been appearing since 1981 and they are a great source of information on the programme. They describe the main aspects of the work done each year and also contain thematic articles. Of particular interest are the detailed statistical annexes. Two which stand out as especially important are the 1983 and 1998 Annual Reports which contain reviews of Irish Aid on its tenth and twenty-fifth anniversaries respectively.

Archives

The National Archive in Bishop's Street, Dublin houses files over 30 years old for Foreign Affairs and other Government Departments. The number of files relating to development aid already runs into the hundreds and will be in the thousands as more are released.

DAC Peer Reviews

There have been six Peer Reviews of Ireland's ODA performance by the Development Assistance Committee of the OECD: 1986, 1988, 1994, 1999, 2003 and 2009. These reports provided a detailed picture of the stages of the programme's performance.

Professor Helen O'Neill

Professor O'Neill carries out an annual review of the programme which is published in *Irish Studies in International Affairs*. See, for example, 'Ireland's Foreign Aid in 2009' in Volume 20 of the ISIIA, pp. 253-84.

Selected Critical Studies

Report of the Advisory Council on Development Cooperation. *Ireland and the Third World: An Official Overview of ODA*, 1991.

Report of the Ireland Aid Review Committee, DFA, 2002.

Farrell Grant Sparks *Management Review of Irish Aid*, 2009.

Trocaire and Irish Commission for Justice and Peace publications from the 1970s and 80s such as *Irish Government Aid to the Third World – Review and Assessment*, Mary Sutton, 1977, provide important critiques of the programme in its early days.

Brendan Lyons *Threads in the Cloth of Ireland's Bilateral Development Aid*, MPA Thesis, UCD, 1975.

Garret FitzGerald, 'Ireland's Development Policy: Aid and Trade', *Studies*, Autumn 1988.

Margaret Hennessy *Efforts to Build a Quality Overseas Aid Programme*, TCD dissertation, 2000.

Kevin O'Sullivan, 'Biafra: The Evolution of Irish Government Policy on Official Development Assistance 1969-75' *Irish Studies in International Affairs*, Vol. 18, pp. 91-107.

Specific Aspects

In the notes to the text reference is made to books on individual aspects which I have found useful. On missionaries, for example, I found Daniel Murphy's book very helpful. Others telling the missionaries' story are Richard Quinn, *The Missionary Factor in Irish Aid Overseas*, Dublin, 1980, and Irene Christina Lynch *Beyond Faith and Adventure: Irish Missionaries in Nigeria tell their Extraordinary Story*, ICDL, Wicklow, 2006. Tom Arnold kindly drew my attention to the Daniel Murphy book and sent me two papers he has written on aspects of the missionary experience.

A good description of the factors influencing Europe's approach to development is contained in Chapter 4 of Mirjam van Reisen's *Window of Opportunity: EU Development Cooperation after the End of the Cold War*, Africa World Press, 2009. Also of interest is Chapter 1 of *EU Development Policy in a Changing World*, Andrew Mold ed, Amsterdam University Press, 2007.

The European Commission's own website contains much information on the EU's approach, including on such issues as budget support.

Finally, for publications on best practice and documents an all aspects of development, the OECD.org website is a mine of information.

Appendix

Table 1: Comparison of Irish Official Development Assistance with Gross National Product, 1974–2010

	Total ODA (£ million)	Percentage of GNP
1974	1.5	0.05
1975	3.0	0.08
1976	4.6	0.10
1977	6.4	0.12
1978	8.4	0.13
1979	13.3	0.18
1980	14.7	0.17
1981	18.8	0.18
1982	24.6	0.21
1983	30.0	0.22
1984	33.0	0.25
1985	39.0	0.25
1986	40.5	0.25
1987	39.1	0.22
1988	32.4	0.18
1989	34.5	0.17
1990	34.6	0.16
1991	45.0	0.19
1992	40.7	0.16

1993	53.2	0.20
1994	75.2	0.24
1995	96.8	0.28
1996	112.0	0.30
1997	124.1	0.31
1998	139.6	0.30
1999	181.4	0.31
2000	200.7	0.30
	Total ODA (€ million)	
2001	320.1	0.33
2002	422.1	0.41
2003	445.7	0.40
2004	488.9	0.40
2005	578.5	0.43
2006	814.0	0.54
2007	870.9	0.54
2008	920.7	0.59
2009	722.2	0.55
2010	675.8	0.53

Table 2: Net Official Development Assistance in 2010

Country	ODA (US$ million)	ODA.GNI %
Australia	3,849	0.32
Austria	1,199	0.32
Belgium	3,000	0.64
Canada	5,132	0.33
Denmark	2,867	0.90
Finland	1,335	0.55
France	12,916	0.50
Germany	12,723	0.38
Greece	500	0.17
Ireland	895	0.53
Italy	3,111	0.15
Japan	11,045	0.20
Korea	1,168	0.12
Luxembourg	399	1.09
Netherlands	6,351	0.81
New Zealand	353	0.26
Norway	4,582	1.10
Portugal	648	0.29
Spain	5,917	0.43
Sweden	4,527	0.97

Switzerland	2,295	0.41
United Kingdom	13,763	0.56
United States	30,154	0.21
Total DAC	128,728	0.32
Average Country Effort		0.49

Table 3: Comparison of Irish GNP Growth and ODA Growth

	GNP Growth (%)	ODA Growth (£ million)
1994	6.5	75.3
1995	8.0	96.8
1996	7.2	112.0
1997	9.0	124.1
1998	8.1	139.6
		(€ million)
2004	4.5	488.9
2005	6.0	578.5
2006	6.5	814.0
2007	4.5	870.9

INDEX